THEOLOGY AS REVISIONARY METAPHYSICS

Theology as Revisionary
METAPHYSICS

Essays on God and Creation

Robert W. Jenson

EDITED BY
Stephen John Wright

 CASCADE *Books* • Eugene, Oregon

THEOLOGY AS REVISIONARY METAPHYSICS
Essays on God and Creation

Cascade Books
An Imprint of Wipf and Stock Publishers
199 W. 8th Ave., Suite 3
Eugene, OR 97401

www.wipfandstock.com

ISBN 13: 978-1-62032-634-3

Cataloging-in-Publication data:

Jenson, Robert W.

Theology as revisionary metaphysics : essays on God and creation / Robert W. Jenson ; edited with an introduction by Stephen John Wright.

xviii + p.; 23 cm—Includes bibliographical references and index.

ISBN 13: 978-1-62032-634-3

1. Trinity. 2. Philosophical theology. I. Wright, Stephen John. II. Title.

BT111.3 .J46 2014

Manufactured in the USA.

Contents

CULTURE

Preface

by Robert W. Jenson

I will leave introducing these essays to Steve Wright, and instead begin by thanking—and indeed praising—him. One day an Aussie appeared—by email, in a blog emanating from Sydney, where I had thought there were only hedonistic secularists, and later in person at our door in Princeton—who knew my thought at least as well as I do, and had a well-conceived project to edit a collection of my essays. Beside my gratitude for his concern with my work, I am delighted to have come along the way to know so talented a theologian. And let me generalize a bit. Those who weep real or crocodile tears over a supposed dearth of constructive theology are looking in the old tired places, and miss an international and productive next generation of theologians, like Wright.

One semi-interpretive point I will make. An early essay is titled "Proclamation without Metaphysics." For a time I shared the German supposition that the tradition culminating with Hegel was identical with metaphysics as such, and that we were past all that. This was an error on my part, of which I hereby publicly repent. The question "What is it to be?" has not gone away, though it is now often discussed in egregiously jejune fashion. And readers will see for themselves that the essay is itself a piece of metaphysics, just materially different from what Germans expected under the label, and that the piece therefore belongs in this collection.

The third thing I should do in this preface is give some account of predecessors who have been exemplars for my attempt to continue Western theology's work of revising inherited pagan Greek metaphysics to fit the gospel. I do not mean that I have taken much from every one of them, but rather that I have been inspired by their example. I will name them in order of encountering them.

In college I heard of Thomas Aquinas' teaching that "What is this" is one question and "Is there this something?" another, and that with creatures the answer to the first provides no answer to the second, and that with God

it does, and said "That has to be right." It was one of the events that turned
me on to philosophy. I did not, to be sure, then quite grasp what a decisive
revision of Aristotle's doctrine of being Thomas' teaching was. But it made
me aware of a revision done at the instance of Christian doctrine, in this
case the doctrine of creation.

Then came certain Lutherans, starting with Johannes Brenz, who, to
make sense of their uncompromising doctrine of sacramental real presence,
redid the whole structure of ontology around the tradition-defying maxim
finitum capax infiniti ("the finite can accomodate the infinite"). Next and
crucial for my resolve was a byproduct of my dissertation-labors on Karl
Barth, the realization that the whole *Church Dogmatics* was a massive christological metaphysics.

There followed the Cappadocian fathers, who turned the Platonic mediation of being and salvation, vertically to time, on its side—so to speak—
to make an eschatological narrative. Finally came a late preoccupation with
Jonathan Edwards, who turned the constructions of the great lights of Enlightenment, Newton and Locke, inside out in service of a vision of Trinity.

For the rest, read Wright and then—I hope—the essays.

Introduction

by Stephen John Wright

"This Jesus hath God raised up, whereof we all are witnesses." –ACTS 2:32

"How much we have written about so few words." –AUGUSTINE

ROBERT JENSON ONCE SUGGESTED that his most venturesome thinking takes place in the form of essays.[1] In this genre only succinct arguments succeed. The essay grants an author a unique measure of liberty to explore uncharted lines of thought. In the way of the French *essai*—"attempt" or "trial"— the theological essay experiments with ideas and arguments impossible through the usual scholarly procedure. Theology is a hedge maze with many entrances and exits. The article and the essay are two ways of navigating the maze; the article charts a path through the maze, deliberating over each turn, avoiding dead ends and false paths—while the essay is not averse to tilting a ladder against the wall. This volume is a collection of such ladders.

The organizing theme of these essays is revisionary metaphysics. A minefield of modern scholarly opinion surrounds any discussion of metaphysics. Metaphysics, in some theology, is irrelevant at best, if not violent. Other theologies argue for the necessity for metaphysics and an ontology of participation.[2] Any stance taken on the usefulness of metaphysics is a theological move. To take one instance of the critique of metaphysics, Heidegger argues that "beings" cloud the philosopher's view and preclude inquiry into "Being as such." Metaphysics, in Heidegger's sense, is like staring at the spines of books in order to understand what a library is—without ever actually getting around to looking at the structure that places books before our eyes: the shelves, the catalogue, the ordering of the books. Such a critique

---

1. Jenson, "Christological Objectivity of History," 62.
2. See Pabst, *Metaphysics.*

of metaphysics is thick with theological implications.[3] Translating from the Heideggerian language of "Being as such" and "beings as such" to the more biblical language of "Creator" and "creatures" we find that the same critique holds. We cannot reason to an understanding of the Creator from creatures. This is the heart of the critique of natural theology so perfectly evoked by Barth: "We can say 'man' in the loudest voice. We can ground our statements about man on the most profound metaphysical premises. But this does not mean that we say 'God.'"[4] Metaphysics, in this sense, is the epistemological priority of creatures or creaturely notions over the revelation of God. However, rejecting this epistemological priority does not dissolve the possibility of an ontology. As Bruce McCormack notes, "to speak of Barth as 'anti-metaphysical' refers to his attitude towards a particular *way* of knowing (the path taken); it does not entail the bracketing-off of particular regions of discourse from discussion in an a priori fashion."[5] Barth responded to metaphysics by grounding ontology in the life of Jesus Christ. Taking revelation as his epistemology, Barth set out to engage the questions that occupied his metaphysically minded antecedents. Barth's particular christological ontology was "non-metaphysical" in that it did not move from knowledge of creatures to knowledge of God. Rather, knowledge of God comes through an act of divine freedom in the event of revelation. Metaphysical theology thinks that we must discover God; non-metaphysical theology believes that this method will only result in the construction of idols. Any deity that lies at the end of the metaphysical path will be nothing more than our own projection of the god we set out to find.

Jenson had encounters with both Barth and Heidegger in his early years. The impact of the former on Jenson is the most pronounced and long lasting, but Jenson's engagement with Heidegger is also important for his work. When studying in Germany for his doctorate, he found himself at the feet of Heidegger for the famous Black Forest seminar: "I listened awestruck, if also Anglo-Saxon skeptical."[6] However, Jenson discerned—with some horror—that Heidegger's involvement in Nazism was in no way accidental to his philosophy; death was a central fascination for Heidegger. Motivated in contrast by the concerns of Christian theology, Jenson developed

---

3. As Kevin Hector notes, "Heidegger's account of metaphysics parallels Karl Barth's account of natural theology in crucial aspects, as well as Rudolf Bultmann's account of 'objectification.'" Hector, *Theology without Metaphysics*, 3n2.

4. Barth, *CD* II/1, 269.

5. McCormack, *Karl Barth's Critically Realistic Dialectical Theology*, 246.

6. Jenson, "Theological Autobiography, to Date," 48. The skepticism is possibly most pronounced in Jenson's dismissal of Heidegger's *Sein zum Tode*: "his fascination is not a good thing to be long exposed to." Jenson, *On Thinking the Human*, 9.

the idea that Christ's "being-unto-death-and-resurrection" is central, rather
than Heidegger's "being-unto-death."[7] Yet there is still some small remnant
of Heidegger in Jenson.[8] Jenson frequently makes use of Heidegger's return to the question of Leibniz: "Why is there anything at all rather than
nothing?" The question, in Jenson's view, is inescapable and irreducibly
metaphysical.

Jenson for a time considered metaphysics to be incommensurate with
the gospel. In his view, the gospel is simply "the story about Jesus, told
as a promise."[9] As the orienting narrative of Christian faith and thought,
the gospel is meant to be *told*, not sublated under meta-categories. In the
1960s Jenson discovered the value of making central to theology the most
basic claims of the Christian faith—claims like "Jesus is Lord" and "Jesus
is risen": "I have tried to hammer them against the metaphysical structure
of traditional theology, until they make more systematic difference than
heretofore."[10] During this early period, however, he was operating with a
very narrow definition of "metaphysics." In his 1963 *Alpha and Omega*,
derived from his doctoral dissertation, Jenson could still identify metaphysics with Feuerbachian projections.[11] However, anticipating McCormack's
interpretation noted above, he saw Barth's solution to metaphysics as the
construction of a new christological ontology: "What is it to be? Barth answers: It is to have a part to play in Jesus' life story."[12] It was not until later
that Jenson came to see that this new ontology was itself a metaphysics,
albeit in a slightly different sense. The transition in his thought is clearest
in his 1969 book, *God after God*. Here Jenson admits that the doctrine of
the Trinity was "born of the meeting between Greek metaphysics and the
Gospel," as is often claimed by the doctrine's critics. However, this does not
mark the dominance of alien metaphysics over Christian thought, but "rep-
resents the redefining of what Greek metaphysical religion had meant by
'God,' in the light of faith's apprehension of its object."[13] At the heart of the
Christian gospel is a critique that attacks all our metaphysical projections.
This critique opens anew the questions of being that enabled us to construct
our metaphysics in the first place. But the answer to the question is now

---

7. Jenson, *God after God*, 150.

8. In a recent letter to *First Things*, Jenson observed that he still takes *Einführung in
die Metaphysik* with him when he travels.

9. Jenson, "Theological Autobiography," 48.

10. Jenson, "About Dialog," 41.

11. Jenson, *Alpha and Omega*, 170.

12. Ibid.

13. Jenson, *God after God*, 47.

provided by the revelation of Jesus; the content of a Christian metaphysics is populated in advance by the life and history of Jesus of Nazareth.

Jenson's earlier ideas about metaphysics were folded into his critique of religion. This critique, rather than shutting down metaphysical discourse, enables new and revised metaphysics. What Jenson once called "metaphysics" is now an item of what he calls "religion."[14] Jenson derives his concept of religion from its celebrated discrediting in the second edition of Barth's *Römerbrief*. Religion, in Jenson's thought, is the human quest for the "metaphysical" deity. It is the attempt to bring God under control by stretching across the perceived space between God and creation with human concepts. Religion is the human project to "wield" God in order to take control of our own futures.[15]

Jenson once described his theology as, in large part, "revisionary metaphysics."[16] It is the type of theology one finds when the central claims of the Christian faith are loosed upon one's metaphysical presuppositions. Jenson is certainly not its only practitioner. Despite the common reading of Barth as a "non-metaphysical" theologian, I believe Barth can be claimed for this kind of project. Barth and Jenson both attempt to answer the deep questions of being and meaning with their gaze fixed on the mystery of Christ. Jenson claims that one of his greatest lessons from his time with Barth was that "theology is willy-nilly metaphysics, to be engaged on a level field with such as Aristotle or Hegel."[17] In another way, Jenson is a "non-metaphysical" thinker, in that the critique of religion in his thought functions much as the critique of metaphysics does in Barth's. Both are concerned to ward off a crude natural theology.

If we are to decide against metaphysics, we must quickly explain *which* metaphysics we are opposing. It is possible for a theology to avoid a negative kind of metaphysics while still addressing the questions of being.[18] Understanding theology as this kind of revisionary metaphysics has animated Jenson throughout his career, as the essays of this volume demonstrate. His theology, viewed from one angle, appears to get along fine without metaphysics, but seen from another angle it is nothing but metaphysics under the

---

14. So in his *Systematic Theology* Jenson argues that "neo-Feuerbachian theory" reveals religion "as a struggle for metaphysical power." Jenson, *ST*, 1:53.

15. See Jenson, *A Religion Against Itself*, and *ST*, passim.

16. Jenson, "Response to Watson and Hunsinger," 230.

17. Jenson, "Theological Autobiography," 50.

18. Hector allows that his own proposal for "theology without metaphysics" may be read by some as advocating a "revisionist metaphysics." Hector, *Theology without Metaphysics*, 3.

rule of the proclamation that the God of Israel has raised Jesus of Nazareth from the dead.

It has been a great pleasure to edit this book. I am deeply grateful to Jens and Blanche for their hospitality and encouragement. I offer special thanks to my wife, Heidi, who helped with the preparation of the manuscript. Thanks also to Ben Myers, whose unique dedication to books and writing meant that he was always enthusiastic to discuss the conceptualization of this volume. My thanks to Brad East, whose excellent bibliography of Jenson's essays published after 1999 helped me track down a number of essays that I otherwise might have overlooked. I also remember with thanks conversations about the book with Peter Kline, Bruce McCormack, Ian Packer, Janice Rees, Ry Siggelkow, and Matthew Wilcoxen.

Acknowledgments

THE ESSAYS IN THIS volume first appeared as follows. All essays are reprinted here with permission.

"A Reply." *Scottish Journal of Theology* 52:1 (1999) 132. © Cambridge University Press, 1999.

"Proclamation without Metaphysics." *dialog* 1 (1962) 22–29. © Wiley Periodicals.

"On Hegemonic Discourse." *First Things* 45 (1994) 13–15. © First Things.

"What if It Were True?" *Neue Zeitschrift für Systematische Theologie und Religionsphilosophie* 43:1 (2001) 3–16. © Walter de Gruyter.

"Second Thoughts about Theologies of Hope." *Evangelical Quarterly* 72 (2000) 335–46. Printed by Paternoster Press.

"How the World Lost Its Story." *First Things* 36 (1993) 19–24. © First Things.

"Can We Have a Story?" *First Things* 101 (2000) 16–17. © First Things.

"The Hidden and Triune God." *International Journal of Systematic Theology* 2:1 (2000) 5–12. © Blackwell Publishing.

"Identity, Jesus, and Exegesis." In *Seeking the Identity of Jesus: A Pilgrimage*, edited by Beverly Roberts Gaventa and Richard B. Hays, 43–59. Grand Rapids: Eerdmans, 2008.

"*Ipse Pater non est impassibilis.*" In *Divine Impassibility and the Mystery of Human Suffering*, edited by James F. Keating and Thomas Joseph White, 117–26. Grand Rapids: Eerdmans, 2009.

"Can Holiness Be a *nota ecclesiae*?" *Bijdragen* 67:3 (2006) 245–52.

"You Wonder Where the Spirit Went." *Pro Ecclesia* 2:3 (1993) 296–304. Published by Rowman & Littlefield.

"Once More on the *logos asarkos*." *International Journal of Systematic Theology* 13:2 (2011) 130–33. © Blackwell Publishing.

"On the Doctrine of the Atonement." *Princeton Seminary Bulletin* 27:2 (2006) 100–108.

"Evil as Person." *Lutheran Theological Seminary Bulletin* 69:1 (1989) 33–42.

"The Strange New World of the Bible." In *Sharper than a Two-Edged Sword: Preaching, Teaching, and Living the Bible*, edited by Michael Root and James J. Buckley, 22–31. Grand Rapids: Eerdmans, 2008. © Wm. B. Eerdmans Publishing.

"Creator and Creature." *International Journal of Systematic Theology* 4:2 (2002) 216–21. © Blackwell Publishers.

"An Ontology of Freedom in the *De servo arbitrio* of Luther." *Modern Theology* 10:3 (1994) 247–52. © Blackwell Publishing.

"Christ-Dogma and Christ-Image." *dialog* 2 (1963) 146–51. © Wiley Periodicals.

"Christ as Culture 1: Christ as Polity." *International Journal of Systematic Theology* 5:3 (2003) 323–29. © Blackwell Publishing.

"Christ as Culture 2: Christ as Art." *International Journal of Systematic Theology* 6:1 (2004) 69–76. © Blackwell Publishing.

"Christ as Culture 3: Christ as Drama." *International Journal of Systematic Theology* 6:2 (2004) 194–201. © Blackwell Publishing.

Abbreviations

The following abbreviations will be used for frequently cited titles:

WORKS BY ROBERT W. JENSON:

ST   *Systematic Theology*. 2 vols. Oxford: Oxford University Press, 1997–99.

WORKS BY KARL BARTH:

CD   *Church Dogmatics*. Edited by G. W. Bromiley and T. F. Torrance. 4 vols. in 14 parts. Edinburgh: T. & T. Clark, 1936–77.

KD   *Die kirkliche Dogmatik*. 4 vols. in 14 parts. Zollikon: Verlag der Evangelischen Buchhandlung, 1932–70.

WORKS BY MARTIN LUTHER:

WA   *D. Martin Luthers Werke: kritische Gesammtausgabe*. 120 vols. Weirmar: Hermann Böhlau, 1883–2009.

Story

1

A Reply *(1999)*

Some thinkers find themselves compelled to what has been called "revision-ary metaphysics," urging changes not merely in affirmations made within a particular discipline, but in the conceptual ways commonly followed by all disciplines within an historical culture. Christian theologians are especially liable to this urge, on account of the gospel's contrariness to human procliv-ity; indeed the history of Christian theology within any culture can always be read as a sustained effort to dislocate that culture's "common sense."

An occasional response to such revisionary efforts is sheer inability to entertain the proposals made, even as experiment. Thus my systematic theology urges that the metaphysics that construes being as perdurance, and contingency as an ontological deficit, is antithetical to the gospel. If a reader takes this metaphysics as unchallengeable, and assumes that the writer also must at bottom depend on it, he will, of course, discover the most horrid consequences and absurdities. But to the elucidation of the book or to cri-tique of its claims, these discoveries will be neither here nor there. Particu-larly, critique will be simply an exercise in *petitio principii.*

2

Proclamation without Metaphysics *(1962)*

"The gospel" is the telling of Jesus' story—*as* the decisive event in the life-stories of teller and hearers. The gospel tells of Jesus' death and reputed resurrection—and claims therein to recount the crisis and resolution of the story *I* am now living. Therefore the telling of the Church's story requires two kinds of words. It requires ordinary words with which we narrate matters of fact: "born," "preached," "died." And it requires, as a story which determines the lives of its hearers, the special words with which man seeks to grasp, indeed to create, the meaning of his life: the words of myth, ritual, metaphysics, existential analysis. It requires words like "sin," "history," "eternal," or "god." We confess: "Jesus is Lord"; "Jesus" names a human story; "Lord" is a mythic title.

The first sort of words is a relatively constant vocabulary throughout man's history. In all times men are born, suffer and die; they preach and eat bread and drink wine and have friends. And all generations have words for these events. But the vocabulary of man's search for the point of his life is not constant. Indeed, the search itself changes—the words *are* the means of man's grasp on himself. It is precisely this changeability of man's understanding of his own meaning which constitutes him an historical being. Some men "sin," others "err," and others live "*sub specie aeternitatis.*" Some men have "souls" and some are made of "matter." The birth and death of such words is the true content of history.

Therefore the proclamation of the gospel, which involves these meaning-creating, "existential" words, never can or should be pinned to any established set of them. Like the mankind to which it is addressed the gospel has a history, the history of the ever-new incarnations of its claim on its

4

hearers: "This Jesus whom you crucified God has made *Lord* and *Messiah*." "He is of *one substance* with the *Father*."

New incarnations of the gospel's claims are demanded whenever the gospel must be spoken to a new human self-understanding. Sometimes the gospel enters a new territory; sometimes the words which grasp men's hearts die and new ones are born. The hellenization of the gospel, the entry of Christianity into the Latin world and the breakdown of the medieval synthesis have all been such turning points in the history of the human reality addressed by the gospel. I believe that such a decisively historical event has again happened in the history of the West and that the Western Church has not yet mastered it.

The Gods and Their Fall

The fundamental faith of man has been that reality sanctions and supports his goals and dreams, that what is constitutes a guarantee for what ought to be. This faith has been shaken.

Man's life is a continual venture into the future. We plan, we prepare, we anticipate. At the most decisive points, we choose, we venture, we leap. And always we move on. Always we abandon what we have and are in favor of what is not yet. A man marries—and in the promise that he speaks abandons the structure of his life to project a new. He posits a new definition of himself. Tomorrow you may be a lover, or a friend of someone you have not met—or a believer in a now strange god. In the moment of faith, we say man is "a new creature."

Man receives himself from the future. He is the creature of his goals, of what is not but must be, of the "end." Therefore he is the seeker of meaning, the quester after the goal, the one who asks what the point might be. He must know where he is going, for only there can he find himself and only in his grasp on his goal does he himself exist.[1]

But the future is always dark. We do not know what will come of our plans and hopes. Therefore human life is possible only by faith, by the conviction that there is after all something out there, that the road does have a goal. Only in this conviction can life be meaningful (and so human); only in this conviction does our planning and working have a point (so as to be "planning" and "working" at all). We live by the words—"god," "man," "justice"—which reach into the darkness to posit a goal beyond the one-thing-after-another of time.

---

1. Despite everything, the fundamental discussion of this is Heidegger's *Sein und zeit*.

But man has found a wholly strange and uncontrollable future intolerable. What comes from the future is death and he has been unable to bear this without some evasion. Only by positing a future tied to the present has he been able to bear the call to receive his life from it. Therefore the words he has used to grasp the future have been words which seek to encompass what is and what is not yet; they seek to derive fact and value, what is and what ought to be, from each other. They have been words which will to abolish the ultimacy of time, to break the line between present and future and posit an eternal reality from which both derive.[2] Man has populated the darkness with eternal projections of all he has found best in past and present, with "goodness," "beauty," and "truth." Thus "humanity" names the unattained and unattainable future—yet is supposed now to subsist as law of my immanent growth. It is an eternally actual idea, future, yet a present possession.

Against such a background every event of life is meaningful. Each can be measured against this super-world, each choice against "justice," each shape against "beauty." And whether it be found adequate or wanting each is given a transcendent reference—an anchorage beyond the flux. When we view life's restless becoming against such a background we find it possible to believe that it moves toward a real goal.

Here is the world of the gods—Aphrodite, Democracy, the Church, Diana. Here is, in the one vast eternity of the good, the beautiful, and the true, the "Being" which is the content of every metaphysical system. Here is the faith whose failing fills our age.

Since the seventeenth century we have known a truth about what is which can be given no relation to what ought to be, which affords no support to our journey into the future. By definition a scientific statement is one which is open to change at any time. Therefore *eternity*-positing words find no link to science's description of what is and so can no more bridge the gap between what is and what ought to be.[3]

As scientific description annexes one area of reality after another the gods flee and metaphysics become ever more implausible. Bertrand Russell has described the end result:

> Purposeless . . . void of meaning, is the world which Science presents for our belief. Amid such a world, if anywhere, our ideals henceforth must find a home. That Man is the product of causes which had no prevision of the end they were achieving; that his . . . hopes and fears, his loves and his beliefs, are but the outcome of accidental collocations of atoms . . . [is] . . . so

2. Cf. Eliade, *Cosmos and History.*
3. Cf. Jenson, "A Dead Issue Revisited."

nearly certain, that no philosophy which rejects them can hope to stand.[4]

Since Kierkegaard and Nietzsche we have known a mode of apprehending the future which attempts to face its total strangeness without flinching.[5] The absolute man of the existentialists admits, even exults, that his movement into the future is a leap over a bottomless gap, a venture without guarantees. He dispenses with the eternity-positing words which seek to cover that gap and lives instead by words which would wrest the goal of life from the very uncertainty that there is one. He erects "anguish" into a value and puts "nothingness" where "being" used to be. If life has no meaning, so much the better, for then he is free to create one. If his leap has no given destination he will live by the leaping.

This secularized version of justification by faith (for "works" are what I now am and have in my power, and "faith" is a turning from what I am to dependence on what I am not yet, to what I absolutely do not control) is the secret of contemporary creative culture. It is the secret of the painter's attack upon reality—as he no longer seeks to find the meaning already present in reality but to create the meaning which it lacks. It is the secret of the novels without plot, which describe life with no place to go yet as acts of language remain affirmative acts of creation which, where there is nothing to be said, are defiantly not silent.

Camus has described us in his tale of a man condemned—on irrelevant evidence—for a murder he in fact committed—by accident.

> I'd passed my life in a certain way, and I might have passed it in a different way, if I'd felt like it. I'd acted thus, and I hadn't acted otherwise. . . . And what did that mean? . . . Nothing, nothing had the least importance, and I knew quite well why. . . . All alike would be condemned to die one day. . . . It was as if that great rush of anger had washed me clean, emptied me of hope, and gazing up at the dark sky spangled with its signs and stars, for the first time, the first, I laid my heart open to the benign indifference of the universe.[6]

The eternal world is no more. The metaphysical words have died. The new man born in this event is the hearer to whom we now have to tell the story. In this spiritual context the Church must learn to make the gospel's claim without assuming a set of beliefs which in fact have vanished, without

4. Russell, *Free Man's Worship*, 6–7.

5. Cf. Jaspers, *Nietzsche and Christianity*.

6. Camus, *The Stranger*.

seeking to grasp men's hearts with words which have lost their power to do so. The great threat now as always (for always there has just been *some* revolution in man) is proclamation to an audience no longer there.

The Demons

But there is more to be said before we shall have understood what has happened. Where the gods flee the demons enter. To live in the very teeth of nothingness, as Russell demands, is too much for man.[7] At best, a few Zarathustras can achieve it. When the gods are gone we will create idols—and if metaphysics are unbelievable we will believe ideologies. We will cling to Nazism or religious fundamentalism or "liberalism."

An ideology resembles a faith to a hair. All the sounds are the same: "divine," "eternal laws," "salvation." They are uttered with all evangelistic fervor: "Americanism is a faith," says J. Edgar Hoover. But ideology is only the husk of metaphysics.

A living metaphysic embodies a genuine grasp on life's goal. Words which seek to cancel time and mitigate the strangeness of the future are indeed a timid move forward and so a distorting hold on life's meaning. But in that distortion they do hold it.[8] An ideology is—and this is its defining characteristic—a screen of words created to conceal the lack of a meaning in life. A living belief in "God and the soul" or in "being" or in "matter" grows out of and shapes the daily decisions and hopes of the believer; an ideology has always a spectral air of forced relevance. Ideologies are invented, difficult, and must constantly be propped up. Thus, for example, "spirit" is a living conception when people use it to live their lives with, when they use it to think with and so do not need to possess proofs of its importance. For the one who must constantly polemicize against "un-American materialists" it is an ideologumenon.

A living metaphysic is a hesitant leap into the future, dared only on the premise that the future will be like the present since both are contained in eternity. But it is a leap. An ideology is an excuse to cling to the past, an excuse for not living. It is a screen thrown up to hide again that totally unpredictable future which the modern experience has unveiled.

Nazism is the textbook example of an ideology.[9] Here, quite cynically and deliberately, a system of values centered on the word "blood" was in-

---

7. Cf. Heidegger, *Einführung in die Metaphysik.* See esp. 14ff.

8. A classic example of this whole development is Macleish's last-minute failure of nerve at the very end of *J.B.*

9. This is the paradigm case for Helmut Thielicke's excellent analysis of what I have

vented—and seized upon by a people terrified by the disappearance of the gods, by history's first clear look into the abyss.

But we need not look so far away. On one side, religious "evangelicalism" is not theology, that is, thought about the gospel. Nor is it even living supernaturalist metaphysics. It is the perversion of the gospel into an ideological weapon against the future. It is one particular historically given theology drained of its content and left as a set of dead words, and so of course eternally unchangeable. These words are then used to hide from the changing world. On the other side, the vaguely liberal discussions in the average nothing-in-particular church differ only in the choice of which theology to ideologize. Religious words which God may once have used to imprint Christ's story on men's hearts now remain for their own sake, to be used as superficial palliatives. The ideological nature of this white-collar religion explains the often documented paradox that suburbia fills the Churches with ceaseless religious activity—as the activity of the most secularized segment of secularized society.[10] This religion functions precisely as the screen of untruth which allows us to evade facing our secularity honestly or creatively.

Man bereft of his metaphysics and strongly tempted to fall victim to a lie as a substitute, this is the man on whom the gospel's claim must now be made. There is a rich variety of ways for the Church to fail to tell its story as the story for this hearer.

Oblivious Theology

The gospel may be proclaimed in a metaphysical version which simply does not touch the place where the hearer lives, no matter how many of the words used he may think he believes in. We may speak to a vanished audience.

Let us put the various forms of this error into one outline: Of course there is a God. How else explain the universe? This God wishes us to live up to the eternal standards of justice. But we fail daily to measure up; billions are spent on liquor every year. Our souls would be lost if God had not sent his Son to pay the penalty. But he has and so, if we believe in him and let him into our hearts, our souls will live eternally in heaven. We know all this is so because the Bible affirms it, and the Bible is inspired.

It is not claimed, of course, that every use of these phrases is misdirected, but that the pattern within which they usually derive their meaning is. Point by point:

---

called "ideology." See Thielicke, *Nihilism*.

10. E.g., Marty, *The New Shape of American Religion*.

This form of proclamation assumes that the hearer lives a life oriented around objective, determinable moral realities. It assumes that there is for him such a thing as "justice" and that he measures his own life according to it. It assumes that if he fails it is not because of any obscurity about goals and purposes. These are dangerous assumptions to make about modern man.

By this I do not mean to say that modern man lives without imperatives; the law is written in his heart also. But they are the imperatives of man set in a seemingly meaningless world, imperatives of freedom, of independence, of self-choice.[11] The law for him is the command to make the leap into strangeness. Where this is not grasped, the theologian cannot see the imperatives which can be law for his hearer and is compelled to attempt to impose on him the mores and values of a past culture. And so he tithes beer, stewardship and the PTA, to the neglect of the relevant matters of the law.

The gospel itself is here proclaimed in terms of a series of metaphysical entities, which are assumed familiar to the hearers. The Father of Jesus Christ is introduced as a particular version of the First Cause. This God has a "Son" (no further explanation). And the point of it all is to get our "souls" into "heaven." The way in which this all leaves the gospel unconnected to our real lives is most dramatically clear with the last terms. No doubt most of our people believe in a "soul," but precisely as an unknown inside them quite distinct from their everyday life and person, indeed quite irrelevant to their everyday person. The salvation of this soul can thus be attended to while the person lives his actual life in utterly different categories. No doubt our people would like to be saved themselves—but since no provision has apparently been made for this they will settle for saving their "souls."

The hearers' lack of a worldview and so of a basis of proof for such metaphysical statements is vaguely felt by this theology. And so a substitute is provided by the attempt to impose the Scriptures as authoritative in abstraction from Christ, and their pronouncements on science, history, etc., as an *ersatz* worldview.

Rear-Guard Theology

The uneasiness last mentioned may grow into a dominant motif of theology and preaching, leading to an additional and complementary misdirection. We may become aware that we are not getting through and seek to remedy this by a preliminary apologetic and polemic aimed at persuading men to return to those words of their fathers which we insist on using.

11. Cf. Gogarten, *Der Mensch zwischen Gott und Welt*. See esp. 207ff.

This attempt is doubly disastrous. In the first place, it is doomed to failure, so that this preliminary step stretches out forever and we never get to the gospel. (It seems likely that this in part explains the remarkable phenomenon that just the most "conservative" preachers so often spend themselves in thoroughly "liberal" exhortations to "values" and "spiritual things.")

But more deadly yet is the confusion between fighting for a metaphysic and fighting for the faith. The traditional metaphysics of the West were the handmaid of the gospel; they were shaped as the instrument of the gospel's grasp on men. And so long as the words by which men lived were the eternity positing words of metaphysics, this was the only possible way. But one result of the long alliance is the practical difficulty in remembering that, however complicated the relationships may be, the traditional metaphysical beliefs are not the same as, or necessary to, the Christian faith. But to forget this and fight, as Christians, a rear-guard action against the disappearance of the old order is to pervert the gospel by turning it against itself. *For it is precisely the preaching of the gospel which has killed the gods of the West,* which has broken its metaphysical words even as it used them.

That science in the modern sense could have been born only in a culture long hammered by the gospel is a platitude.[12] To no one unexposed to the thoroughly singular Christian doctrines of creation and incarnation could it have occurred that the things of the world were a suitable place to search for truth. The science which has crowded out our big words is a cultural byproduct of the gospel's long assault on Western man.

The existentialist shrug, in which man casts off his crutches and tries to face an unknown future for what it is, is simply an attempt to perform the movement of faith, without God: "Leaving what is behind I press on to the high calling—of myself." The attempt may be foredoomed. But it again is a movement which could only be attempted in a culture long called to faith. One cannot imitate what one does not know.

For the gospel is a two-edged sword. Where it is proclaimed and heard, and not believed, it is a savor of death. It destroys the words by which men seek to make their leap into darkness tolerable. If what it gives in their place is rejected, man has nothing. Western civilization is the civilization which has heard and not believed—and now faces nothingness.

The gospel has been our great debunker.[13] The early Christians were not, after all, persecuted for being too religious but for being anti-religious, enemies of the beliefs which hold society together, atheists. He who says that

12. Cf. e.g., Whitehead, *Science in the Modern World*, ch. 1.

13. The very first chapter of the Bible is a vast debunking operation. Cf. Rad, *Das erste Buch Mose.*

God has happened in time and space ends all attempts to give life meaning on the basis of the timeless. The feeling of the ancient guardians of culture that Christianity was a menace was entirely accurate. Christians do not, in bitter fact, believe in the gods.

We weep for the emptiness which man finds when he hears the gospel but denies it. We are called to bind the wounds. But we are not called to build up again what we have torn down—lest we nullify the grace of God.

Emptied Theology

Now there have long been those who have marked that the heaven-storming old words no longer seemed to bite. Theologies have long been dominant in many quarters which were manfully determined to speak to the real needs and strivings of the hearers and to avoid "antiquated dogmatizing."

But too often this has been accomplished by simply abandoning altogether the attempt to tell of Christ as the meaning of life, by throwing out transcendence with metaphysics. Instead of "Jesus saves souls," we get "Jesus will cheer you up when depressed," or even eliminating the last shred of reference to anything outside of the hearers' immediate experience, "Believing is good for healthy living." Those who bowdlerize Dewey instead of James contribute: "Social progress needs religious values."

Here we do not tell of Christ as the goal of life but only as a beneficial factor within life. The only future we know is the spurious future of empirical prediction. Therefore we indeed need no mythic or metaphysical words to make our point. But this is only because we have no point to make. This preaching is even more irrelevant to contemporary life than others we have discussed in that it has nothing to say that our marvelous scientific practitioners do not say much better.

And it falls into alliance with the most dangerous of the ideologies, those which hide the abyss of the future with a fog of words drawn from empirical description of life. "Satisfaction," "adjustment," "full experience"— these are all pseudo-values. They are sentimentalized versions of notions quite legitimate in empirical description. If we repeat them long enough, we persuade ourselves that we have a "truly meaningful" life. The Church ought not abet this masquerade.

A Proposal of Words

What then shall we say? Let us try to answer this not by formal, third-person description, but by trying to say it, at one key point.

All the various ways in which the gospel has traditionally made itself effective as the final decision about its hearers are united in the word "God." "Jesus is God"—here is the all-encompassing confession of classical theology. "Lord," "Savior," "Judge," "being," "good," and a hundred other words are all united in the one word "God." In the ancient Church theology was identical with the attempt to elucidate the precise meaning of this sentence.

But now—do not all tell us that "God" is dead? Could not this (had it not become a cliché before its time) have been the title of this paper? The analyses of those philosophers who find that the word "God," whatever else it may be good for, can carry no more cognitive freight, has no literal sense, may or may not be conclusive *per se*, but as descriptions they are indubitably accurate.[14] Those who reject the gospel now usually do so not because they find it necessary to disbelieve in God, but simply because the whole matter seems insignificant. Indeed, there is the suspicion that many who say they believe find this possible just because it makes so little difference anyway. The word "God" is empty for us, that is, it is dead.

Why then can we not leave it alone? Why could not the logical positivists desist from reiterating how meaningless this meaningless word was? Why will this empty sound not disappear? Is it because by its very emptiness it serves to express a loss? Could it be imposed on us, almost as a fate, by the absence of something? Something we cannot do without? Is "God" the name for the darkness of that future which calls us? The name for what we wish were there to receive us?

"God is not." On analysis, this is just as factually meaningless as "God is." Let us admit this—and seek its non-factual meaning for us, its meaning as an utterance at the point of our leap into life. "God is," "God is not"—both factually meaningless. Very well, what does this meaninglessness do in our lives?

"God is not." This could be a simple statement of fact, and that would end the matter. But it is not a factual statement at all. What then can it be? It is a lament we cannot cease from. It is a fate imposed on us. Therefore to fully understand we must expand it: "God is not—but ought to be." "God is not—yet." Is this not the true content of our bereavement?

The one who is not yet, the future as post-metaphysical man faces it in its blankness and terror—this absence is real enough. We name it "God." We too have our—wholly negative—natural theology. Perhaps some day it too will be gone and men will simply live wholly in the present, content in

14. For a classical popularized statement, see Ayer, *Language, Truth and Logic*, ch. 6. Despite premature rejoicing by some theologians and religiously inclined philosophers, the newer and more flexible analysis holds the same basic position at this point.

the sciences and common sense. Then they will no longer be men. But the Apocalypse tells us that God will intervene before then.

"Jesus is God." Clearly, if we are to say this, the word "God" must mean something prior to our application of it to Jesus. Theology indeed depends on natural theology. We too possess one. But with our word "God" we bring to Jesus no rich fund of prior knowledge, no fine list of attributes and honors, as did our fathers. We bring an absence and a lack, a denial and a judgement. We bring an empty place of hope.

This is quite a different natural theology than that which we used to carry when we named Jesus God. But surely it is no less adapted to our need to speak of Christ than the most glorious evocation of Goodness, Beauty, and Truth? For all our words, if he truly is, are absolutely inadequate. Indeed, it is possible that precisely in its negativity it is a more honest confession of what God wills us to know of himself prior to Christ. ". . . the *wrath* of God is revealed from heaven . . ."[15]

Our word "God," just because it is mere lack, provides the empty space for Christ to fill. Whenever the Church has thought it knew all about "God" anyway and merely recognized him in Christ, it has been on the way to paganism. A truly Christian doctrine of God is a description of Jesus Christ. It says that this man shall come and every knee shall bow. It says that he is the one who has hidden behind the mask of the absent "God."

"Jesus is—the future happening, the absolute darkness become our true goal." Is not this the confession we must make? When Jesus meets our natural theology?

"Jesus is God." On our lips "God" may be a leftover metaphysical word—a falsehood. But perhaps we mean: "The absolutely last thing has happened, in the events of Jesus' existence. Suddenly our lives have a conclusion, a goal. Suddenly the ungraspable and 'wholly other' future, without ceasing to be ungraspable and strange, has become *our* future, a future for which we can live. We can narrate this conclusion of our lives—and the narrative begins, 'And it came to pass in those days . . .' We go to *meet* someone." Perhaps this is what we should mean. We mean: "There is one who comes, and his name is Jesus."

What shall we say? Let us say: "*God has happened!* He is coming, and has defined himself through a death and a resurrection." The doctrine of God and the doctrine of salvation will perhaps not be so distinct in a proclamation to the men whose eternal words have died. For them, "God exists" is a whole gospel. And their predicates for God are "the dead and risen one."[16]

15. Rom 1:18–23. Radical empiricism is perhaps merely a modern translation of this text.

16. The glory of Karl Barth's *Kirchliche Dogmatik* is its doctrine of God (II/1, II/2)

At the beginning we distinguished between two kinds of words: empirical narration of Jesus' story and the enforcement of this story's claim on us. There is one word we left out, a word which fits in neither classification, or rather, unites both. This is "resurrection." "And on the third day he rose again from the dead." Clearly this intends to recount a stretch of Jesus' story; it is told in no other tone than "suffered under Pontius Pilate." Yet what it points to is something quite beyond the possibility of historical knowledge. This bit of narration is already a demand for submission. To say "He is risen," and to say "He is Lord," are the same.

"He is risen" is the point in the story where it becomes gift and demand. It is the union of narrative and proclamation, of tradition and kerygma.[17] It is the "is" in "Jesus is Lord," the unity of the two kinds of words, empirical and existential, which are the gospel. With this word the gospel proclaims the unity of Jesus and the one who comes as judge. And so it too creates a union of present and future, of what is and the meaning of what is, of fact and value. But "risen" is a radically different union of present and future than that which man has sought to create by his metaphysical words. It does not name a static unity which we may rest upon, but an event. It is a bridge between us and our future, but one built wholly from the other side. It does not blur the strangeness and fearsomeness of true futurity, but gives us that awesome future as a gift.

The resurrection is the basis of our confession that God, the one who is coming, has happened. It is the resurrection that overcomes the rift between our lives and their goal; it makes God's future part of our present and makes an event in our history the coming End. It is the resurrection that gives our lives meaning, without the distortion of our attempt to do it ourselves.

A truly contemporary theology will be one which rejoices in being liberated from the dead works of metaphysics. Therefore it will be one in which the word "risen" is the logical hinge of every sentence, which proclaims: "Jesus Christ is our future."

. . . And of Aid

The Church is called to preach the gospel and to bind up the wounds of the broken. Therefore the Western Church has one more special task for this century.

---

in which this program is already realized.

17. ". . . Jesus rose in the kerygma." Bultmann, *Das Verhältnis der urchristlichen Christusbotschaft zum historischen Jesus*, 27.

It is a hard calling which God has given the West at this climax of its story—the calling to live without illusions. It is a hard calling, to have no gods to share the blame, to live knowing that life's meaningfulness has no guarantees other than the hidden God. Apart from God's miracle of grace it is impossible truly to fulfill this calling.

By ourselves we will always shrink from so naked a confrontation with truth into some degree of illusion. But absolute fidelity is not needed in the world. And "civil righteousness" is possible, a sanity and clarity sufficient for the daily tasks.

The great danger is that our century will recoil completely from the world it has created, and so fall into total ideology. Our governments may become divinely ordained. Our arts may cease their shocking creativity and become illustrators of values. Our science may become "socialist science" or "democratic science." The Church's service to the world is to help prevent this.

The Church must be a place where there are those who, because they know God and therefore can face living without gods, are free to tackle problems of life with that illusionless rationality which is the only proper response to a world without metaphysics, and who because they know God can be illusionless without being disillusioned, rational and yet warm. The Church must nurture humanity, for the sake of a society constantly threatening to become inhuman. It must give society people capable of rational reflection, of free experimentation, of warm interest. Only a few such breaks through to the "springs of true humanity"[18] may well suffice for a whole civilization to muddle through.

And the Church must be the total and implacable foe of all ideology, especially the "Christian." Only the eye of faith will be able to track down the winding subtleties of ideological evasion. This is our job on behalf of our brothers. And when ideology is clearly discovered, any compromise on the part of believers is a compact with the demons.

The world is capable only of a civil righteousness. This holds also for the peculiar righteousness demanded of our time. The world will not attain that full escape from illusion which is by faith alone. But it can attain pragmatism in politics, a plurality of schools in the arts, at least the pursuit of objectivity in science and tolerable reciprocity in personal life. We may not attain even these, but let it not be because the believers have missed their calling or refused their service.

18. Peter Brunner. To this whole subject, see his "Luther and the World of the Twentieth Century."

Summary

The words with which it is possible to grasp the hearts of contemporary man are the words of time, event, history. They are words like "future" and "purpose," as these are given specific weight in life by analysis of the conditions of man's existence, as they function as "dark future" or "sought-out purpose."

We are those who ask, "Why?" "So what?" "What for?" It is when we tell Jesus' story as the answer to these questions that it will be the story of and for our brothers and ourselves.

This is not a proposal to return to "Hebrew thought-patterns" from the Greek concepts of classical theology. There would be nothing canonical about Hebrew ideas even if they were the only ones used in Scripture. And we are not Hebrews. But neither are we Greeks. We are post-Greeks. We are Greeks in whom the Greek faith in the timeless has been toppled. The words that we must use are the inverted and broken metaphysical words that such men will cling to.

Nor is this a call to "make the gospel relevant." That is the Spirit's business. It is simply a call to preach it, in the only way possible for us.

Likewise, the service we have to do for the world is the same service of love as always—that clarity in hearing what God commands and which faith brings. This article proposes no new policy. It only hopes that the men we serve may be those now alive and the demons we fight those that really menace.

3

On Hegemonic Discourse *(1994)*

I

It is currently a favorite complaint and/or explanation: a "hegemonic discourse" is repressing someone. Thus, for instance, it is said that "patriarchal" societies practice a hegemonic masculinist discourse, and that this is why when gender-feminists try to say their truth they are driven to such linguistic enormities. Or again, Christians who actually believe the gospel are said to bind the religious impulses of their fellow denominationalists with dogmatically grammared language, which is why when the latter try to express the depths within them these come out seeming so paltry. *Et cetera.*

A hegemonic discourse, we are told, makes things that ought to be said unsayable; therefore those who nevertheless try to say them find themselves uttering nonsense though they know they have sense to say. The phrase "hegemonic discourse" is well established (in a hegemonic discourse?), and is equally beloved of charlatans and genuine thinkers; in view of the latter, there must be something to it.

But what is a hegemonic discourse? So soon as the question is allowed, its answer is—embarrassingly?—apparent: it is the way those talk who at any given time and place happen to be doing the talking. Perhaps they have come to be or remain in this position by shutting others up, by manipulating them, or by doing something else reprehensible. But it is not apparent that this must always be so. Maybe others just like to hear them.

There is of course the possibility that everyone could be doing the talking, that there would be no outsiders at all. The realization of this possibility is awaited by Jewish or Christian faith as the Kingdom of Heaven.

It is important to notice: nothing would necessarily be different about discourse in itself merely because it had no outsiders. It is just that nobody would complain of hegemony. Even in the Kingdom of Heaven there could still be governing linguistic rules of which someone could complain if, impossibly, there were anyone who wanted to.

If some of us at a time and place short of the Kingdom are not among those doing the talking and are unwillingly in that position, we have two recourses. We can join the going conversation, learning to talk its way. Or we can try to replace the way of the going conversation with the way we would talk if we were doing the talking; such an attempt is known as a revolution. By neither move can we create a discourse that is not hegemonic. Until the Kingdom comes somebody will still be doing the talking and somebody else will still not be doing the talking. Unless, of course, nobody at all is talking anymore.

II

All discourse is enabled by grammar, by implicit rules that let us, for example, put "horse" and "fast"/"slow" together but not "horse" and "vaporous"/"condensed." Grammar is primarily learned and enforced not by direct study—recalling junior high, that would be a lost cause indeed—but by apprenticed practice. Some people know not to say "My horse is condensed," and those who do not, learn it by trying to talk to them. Listen to a clever child with a new word try it out in endless combinations, alert to every response showing which work and which do not—and mourn the irremediable suffering of the child with no practiced talkers to talk to.

Thus a hegemonic discourse is finally just the way those talk from whom we learn to talk at all. Absent a hegemonic discourse and short of the Kingdom, there could only be silence. This could be the pre-linguistic silence of mystic experience. Or it could be the post-linguistic silence of fascist cacophony, in which speech has ceased to be discourse and has become simply one way in which we try to cause one another to behave as we want.

This does not mean that hegemonic discourses are not in fact oppressive, that we can never legitimately complain of a going hegemony and should attempt no revolutions. It is the human condition after the fall: what enables us is also what oppresses us. There are several such complaints I have been myself making for decades. To choose an example that is materially almost irrelevant to this article, I have urged the metaphysically revolutionary proposition, "God has plenty of time. It is we who want to be timeless." And I am indeed oppressed by the fact that folk adamantly presume a semantic rule of the very discourse I am assaulting, that for them the word "God" is assumed beyond question to be equivalent to "timeless entity," so that they "hear me saying" the nonsense, "The timeless one has plenty of time."

So if I can cry, "Down with the hegemony of Hellenic theological discourse, which hinders my saying what must be said," why should not others cry, "Down with the hegemony of patriarchal discourse"? Or "capitalist discourse." Or whatever. And of course there is no reason why not. Those who disapprove of such revolutions can then oppose them.

There is, however, one current cry that transfers to another genus. "Down with the hegemony of hegemonic discourse" is on its face only an especially inept pleonasm. But its actual force is desperate: it must be a demand either for silence or for the Kingdom of Heaven. The Kingdom not being in our achieving, and the silence of real mysticism being not commonly wanted, the demand works out as a plea for fascism's substitution of causation for discourse, for the replacement of politics by verbal manipulation.

III

Two questions present themselves. In what discourse do we complain of or defend a hegemonic discourse? And what would a non-hegemonic discourse be like? I will take up the second first.

If and when a non-hegemonic discourse comes to pass, perhaps it will prove different simply as discourse, in ways now unspecifiable. Perhaps it will have an altogether new kind of grammar. But this need not happen for there to be a non-hegemonic discourse. The necessary and sufficient condition is simply that those doing the talking do not merely by so doing come to fill the role we now call hegemonic. That is, a non-hegemonic discourse will come to pass when nobody any longer must be taught to talk. In other words, it will come to pass when history is no longer constituted by a succession of generations. A non-hegemonic discourse could therefore only be the discourse of the biblical Eschaton. Karl Marx noted this point, and repackaged it as the doctrine of ideology.

Marx's hypothesis that the biblical expectation of the Kingdom could be separated from biblical faith in God has—lamentably—been tested in a massive historical experiment and has been falsified. We may therefore assert with fully public confidence: there will be a non-hegemonic discourse only if there is the Bible's God and only if and when he achieves his final Kingdom and its discourse. This is of course a bitter pill for most who now complain of hegemonic discourse: there can be non-hegemonic discourse only if there is what they most dread, a real Hegemon. Those who first marshalled the noun on which the adjective depends were fathers of the Church, who used it for God, or an apostle or angel as a guide to God, or the deepest part of the soul as the place where God rules.

Discourse that was not oppressive would be a discourse with two characteristics. It would be the way people talked who were all those who wanted to talk. And all its actual sentences would be true, so that it repelled no other truth there was to say. As St. Thomas observed, such a doctrine could only be that of God and his perfected saints. Do we in this world want to cultivate a less oppressive—though still, of course, hegemonic—discourse? Then we must work at approximating the discourse of the saints in heaven. According to the Bible there is a way to do that: belong to one community with the saints and talk with them, join the people of the Lord (which is English for Adonai which is Hebrew for Hegemon).

And now we can turn also to the first question. How can it be that a hegemonic discourse only hinders what cannot be said within it? How can it be that, in however strangulated a fashion, we do sometimes manage to say what cannot be said in the going conversation? In what discourse do we protest a hegemonic discourse? Or oppose such a protest?

Evidently there must be a meta-hegemonic discourse (take that, fellow neologists!), a discourse that enables both any given ruling discourse and language beyond the latter's sway. If there is God, and if he talks to us and lets us answer, there is just such a discourse. Indeed, vice versa: if there is a transcending discourse, the one sustaining it must simply thereby be God. Precisely the possibility of protesting a human linguistic hegemony, whether wisely or foolishly, is an evidence of God. Those who want no Hegemon must, and regularly do, finally deny the possibility of transcending the going human conversation and despairingly acquiesce in its hegemony.

The reason we are not fully enslaved to the fellow humans from whom we learn to talk is that finally it is not they but God who so talks as to enable talking. There can be rebellion against, or defense of, any given discourse if and only if there is a Word before all human conversation that is the latter's possibility and beginning.

According to the heart of Christian interpretation—the doctrine that God is triune—there is indeed a meta-hegemonic discourse, a Conversation in progress before all created conversations. (This heart of Christian doctrine, one should note, is not so foreign to Judaism as might be supposed.) According to Genesis, in and as the beginning, God says, "Let there be" and whatever is, is. According to John's version of Genesis, in the beginning God's Word is with God so utterly as to be God, and all things come to be by being mentioned in this Word. God speaks his Word, which so completely is his truth as to be like him a person, who then must respond. This conversation, prototypically for any good conversation, has a Spirit that is of one being with the conversants. Thus God is a Conversation.

It is by being called into this Discourse that all who ever talk learn to talk. Creatures talk because God has decided to make room in himself for others to join in the Conversation he himself is. God creates all things by calling them in the third person: "Let there be." But some he not only speaks about but speaks to and asks for response. Just thereby, those creatures themselves come to speak, and so are human.

IV

The one meta-hegemonic Discourse is thus not itself a monologue; no one lays down the first and last grammar, since God himself is not merely one. The meta-hegemonic Discourse is antecedently in itself a true conversation. And moreover it is, in the contingency of the divine choice, a conversation that includes us. Therefore we live, move, and have our being in and over against a discourse that is liberating rather than oppressive. There will be a great discourse—indeed, à la the book of Revelation, a great liturgy—in which all join with perfect freedom. And insofar as we can hope already to speak freely, it is by anticipatory joining in that liturgy.

Therefore the penultimate enterprise of seeking less oppressive linguistic polities is not hopeless. We must only be aware of what a tremendous thing we are then attempting, and of the true possibilities and limits of human enterprise on such lines. My suspicion is that if we achieve such awareness, we will stop worrying about "hegemonic discourse."

4

What if It Were True? *(2001)*

The Christian gospel makes a good many statements that present themselves as would-be statements of fact, as what it was once common to call truth-claims. Some of these are epistemically or ontologically surprising, but that does not change how they present themselves. So the gospel's messengers have said there was a man named Jesus who prophesied, taught, healed, was executed for his pains, and was so rescued from death as to live with death now behind him; that the national God of Israel sent him on that mission and performed that rescue; that this same God is responsible for the existence of the universe; etc.

Much of modern theology has labored to interpret some or all of the faith's apparent truth-claims as indeed apparent truth-claims only, and as discovering their true import only when translated into some other mode of discourse. What they "really" are—we have been told—is value-judgments or expressions of religious experience or grammatical rules or *Vorstellungen* in need of conceptualization if they are to *become* truth-claims or myth in need of existential interpretation to show that they are not truth claims but something much better—but you see what I mean.

I do not mean to denigrate the theological enterprises of which these caricatures will remind you; they have all contributed indispensably, or anyway to me. To say what I am about to say, I have no need to deny that such a statement as "The Lord raised Jesus from the dead" does play such roles. Indeed, in a perhaps more commonsensical way than intended by any one of the great neo-Protestant projects themselves, most Christian propositions play many such roles at once: "The Lord raised Jesus from the dead" makes a judgment of value and expresses religious experience and functions as a grammatical rule and it indeed calls for a bit of conceptual working up and down. But what if it and propositions like it were also and antecedently *true*? That is, true in the dumb sense, the sense with which we all use the word when behaving normally, and which just therefore I cannot and do not need to analyze further, true in the sense that folk are likely to demand when they hear academic theologians and their academically trained pastors begin to talk about "deeper" meanings and the spiritual experience that so and so was trying to express and the religious tradition carried by the text, and so on.

What, indeed, if even some less primal and more controversial theologoumena were true in the ordinary way? What, for example, if Cyril of Alexandria's christology were true in that way? And were not only—to use language I often use—a conceptual "move" that I like to make but that others again prefer to avoid, etc.? That is my question for this essay.

Something heavy is, of course, presupposed by our normal way of saying that certain statements are true: it is presupposed that the word "true" has some constant meaning, if only, like most adjectives, in the way of Wittgenstein's rope; in the language of earlier philosophy, it is presumed that truth is at least analogically one. When we are behaving normally, we use "true" as an adjective which attributes a presumed common characteristic—or anyway Wittgensteinian rope of characteristics—to certain beliefs, assertions, etc; and we proceed so even if we are unable to analyze that characteristic further. In this paper I will assume this presumption is justified, and will not attempt to establish that it is. But I will pause just long enough to note that late modern failure of confidence in truth's unity is doubtless one cause of our skittishness about saying flat-out that some propositions are true, particularly big-ticket propositions like those made and implied by the gospel.

Many analysts have pointed to a shift at the beginning of modernity, in what is taken as the ground for confidence in truth's unity. The unity of truth was once conceived as a corollary of the simplicity and uniqueness of God, but in modernity it came to be conceived as a corollary of the unifying action of the human intellect. This shift is doubtless part of the reason for modern theology's uneasiness with ordinary truth claims, for the unity of the human intellect is pretty obviously too fragile to bear much weight—and postmodern thinkers' explicit pointing to this fact is doubtless a salutary purgation.

Yet I think there is another reason for our skittishness with the gospel's truth claims, that is probably more important and is moreover perennial. So soon as we pose the question, "What indeed if it were true?" about any ordinary proposition of the faith, consequences begin to show themselves that go beyond anything we dare to believe, that upset our whole basket of assured convictions, and we are frightened of that. The most Sunday-school-platitudinous of Christian claims—say, "Jesus loves me"—contains cognitive explosives we fear will indeed blow our minds; it commits us to what have been called revisionary metaphysics, and on a massive scale. *That*, I think, is the main reason we prefer not to start, and have preferred it especially in the period of modernity. For Western modernity's defining passion has been for the use of knowledge to control, and that is the very point where the knowledge of faith threatens us.

Let me give a prolegomenal instance. We sometimes join our daughter's family for the main Sunday Eucharist at New York's Cathedral of St. John the Divine. Besides seeing our family, we go there because what happens on a Sunday morning often makes an occasion within which we can credit biblical stuff that stumps us in other contexts. For our honoree's sake I will not mention clouds of incense or splendid processions, and will stick to what the cathedral's organist, the amazing Dorothy Pappadokos, does. While her French-style improvisations are shaking the stones of the building, and my stony heart, when climax upon climax each improbably eclipses its predecessor, I am able to sustain the notion that all God's various holy ones are gathered there with us, that in fact we are praising God, as the liturgy of my church has it, "with angels and archangels and all the company of heaven," that if only we could see what is actually there, we would see the mighty thrones and dominions and Mary and Paul and Olaf and my father-in-law and so forth around us in the cavernous spaces. But sitting in front of my computer to write for publication, in what the world decrees is comprehensible fashion, I chicken out, and begin looking for ways to pare down the proposition to what fits the antecedent opinion-stock of someone like myself, an academic of recently professional family and more or less liberal education. To be sure, theological reflection has always found it necessary to demythologize "six-winged seraphim" and such a bit, at least with respect to the wings, but *are* there distinct entities to which the biblical evocations refer? Or are there not? Normally inquiring minds would want to know, but insofar as we are limited by modernity's prejudices we hold back because of what a Yes would do to our vision of the world and what a No would do to our reading of the Bible. And of course it is a mind-bending exercize to consider in what ontological mode dead believers make one living company with living ones, but do they or don't they? Is Papa Rockne there for our Eucharist or is he not? If we say he is, the mind-bending exercize must be undertaken.

So much for introduction. The body of this essay will be a set of three cases. They are selected one for each article of a standard creed. And each belongs to a systematically different theological discourse. So there will be three mini-papers, which do somehow, I think, make a whole.

The first case. The Bible says that the world is created by God, specifically by the God of Israel. If there is a flat-out dogma in the Bible, this is it. Moreover, the Bible provides a fairly comprehensive unpacking of what it means by "creating." I will here adduce but one item thereof. To create, in Scripture, is not to make a *thing*, not even a big and beautiful and wonderful thing like a cosmos. It is rather to initiate, sustain and fulfill a *history*. Thus, as the fathers understood, even the beginning of the creation is not accomplished except as history, of the seven days. And what is posited at the beginning is not a container or platform for a history that may then commence, but simply the first and enabling event of a history that then continues. What God creates is *narrated* from beginning to end of Scripture.

Now let us consider some consequences. If it is true that what the Creator does is the history told by Scripture, and that what the Creator does is all there is besides him, then the beginning told by Scripture is the beginning of everything but God, the fulfillment prophesied by Scripture is the goal and conclusion of everything, including in some sense of God, and what is narrated in between is the actuality of everything. But then Scripture's story is the meta-narrative to end all meta-narratives, the necessary epistemic context of all true statements whatsoever. Then history is the defining mode of being, and precisely the history of salvation is the encompassing history.

If the doctrine of creation is true in the dumb sense, then—and this is the offense—any and all accounts of reality other than the biblical story are abstractions from the full account of what we actually inhabit, that is, they are abstractions from the story of God with his creatures. Some such abstractive accounts, as it turns out, are true within their range of abstraction, and some of the true ones are marvellously revelatory and practically powerful. Nevertheless, the moment we take such accounts for more than abstractions, they will lead us away from reality. Indeed, it is a necessary condition of their truth that we can, to some perhaps slight extent, describe their place within the biblical history of God with his people. An account of reality for which no place can be found within that history must be either false or empty. Now try maintaining all that in the modern university—and yet one must, if the biblical proposition that God created and creates all things but himself is true.

Modernity has been particularly deformed, spiritually, politically, and even in its sheer materiality, by one error on these lines, the ideology of mechanism, a metaphorical transcription of Newtonian physics that Enlightenments' second-stringers have proclaimed to the bourgeois world as science's discovery about what things really are. Now of course there are machines; people build thousands of them every day. And since the same laws govern the operation of these machines and the operation of, e.g., the solar system, there are indeed contexts in which metaphoric talk of mechanism can help to understand also that bulk of reality that people do not make. But even such modest metaphorical use is a risky business, for already the observable behavior of the solar system stretches any actual analogy with machines quite far. To jump to the universe and the ideology, is the universe anything like a big machine? If the doctrine of creation is true, not even remotely.

Those who know about creation, Jews and Christians, must be prepared to say that to whatever extent someone thinks about the universe as if it were a machine, or of the cosmic or political sub-universes in that way, to that extent they are alienated from what is actually out there, and must indeed become progressively unfamiliar with fact. And Christians must be prepared to say that any attempt to inhabit the cosmic or human world as if it were a machine will come into conflict with reality, that is, must eventually lead to disaster of one or another sort. It is worth noting that at the beginning of the mechanist nightmare at least one more courageous Christian theologian, Jonathan Edwards, did make the latter prediction, particularly in political context, and that it seems to be fulfilled around us.

Knowledge of the universe, that is, knowledge of everything other than God, is nothing like information about the workings of a machine. Indeed, it is not knowledge about any fixed context of change, not even of a stage on which history is then played—as I have myself misleadingly put it. It is simply knowledge of comprehensive history itself taken as a whole.

It is therefore an advance toward *concreteness* that the accounts given by the modern sciences increasingly take explicitly narrative form, or, more precisely, tend to devolve into narrative and sheer mathematics. And it should not surprise believers, that ideological attempts to obscure this, by positing that there just *must* be mechanisms underlying or controlling the great dynamic processes, now become increasingly desperate.

The more fundamental point, however, is this. The narratives with which we rightly are so impressed—the grand narratives of cosmological physics and evolutionary biology, and modernity's social and political narrative of initial state, contract, and liberty—particularly insofar as they continue to abstract from teleology, that is, from using propositions about what things are *for* as warrants of discovery and demonstration, and that is, so long as they continue to abstract from God, abstract from what is actually around us. Now there is nothing the matter with abstraction, it is at the heart of our intellectual gift. But there is one thing narrative made by such drastic abstraction from reality cannot do: it cannot be a comprehensive true account of what is, or make a part of one. Most particularly it cannot be a metanarrative within which the narrative of God's history with his creation could be located. The reverse has to be the case.

Modernity was in large part constituted by awe before the tactics and achievements of the new sciences, and this awe was well earned. It was doubtless historically inevitable that the culture, in the grip of this awe, supposed that those accounts of reality which could be labelled "scientific" must be parts and sketches of a universal account in process of construction, and indeed surely nearly complete. And it may even have been inevitable that Christian theology for a time made the same assumption, and thought it was the task of theology to find a niche for its talk about Israel and Jesus and God within a secular metanarrative supposedly in construction. But whether or not this abnegation was appropriate for a time, the time is in any case over. It is not over because the achievements of the sciences have become any less impressive but because theology has played out that line, and—more importantly—because the life of the Church, insofar as it has responded to the theology in question, has played out that line.

It may be that the sciences should continue to abstract from the teleology displayed by the actual world, though of course no one knows what possibilities of theory or experimental opportunities might accrue from eschewing this particular abstraction. But theology, anyway, can and should construe cosmological and evolutionary and social-political narrative as *meaningful* narrative, and that is to say, should construe cosmological and evolutionary and social-political narrative as partial narrative within the story of God's purpose to bring all things into himself.

It makes a difference which way we interpret our world as we inhabit it, and it is a public difference. Insofar as the sciences are human practices, not only the uses to which their results are put, but the directions in which inquiry is pushed, and perhaps even the paradigms by which results are accorded the status of results, are determined by the culture of the scientists—and one does not need to be a deconstructing perpetrator of "science studies" to say this. In fact the sciences as actual practices have been decisively determined by the culture's erection of them into a universal framework of interpretation, that is autonomous and forbids attributing purpose to events construed within it.

It is now a commonplace that acceptance of scientific accounts as a comprehensive meta-narrative, and as a meta-narrative which attributes no meaning other than succession to the events within it, especially when this works in combination with the machine-metaphor, lies behind the modern West's treatment of the world as a vast heap of raw materials, and so behind the ecological disasters we provoke. Nor, despite all activism and all warnings, do we desist from our plunderings. It may indeed be doubted that we can desist, so long as the culture's whole understanding of its own story is not changed.

There is a rule of the modern West's behavior, that if it can be done it will be done. Many years ago my *Doktorvater*, Peter Brunner, convinced me that this dynamism must finally destroy those whose behavior it determines. There are things that can be done that must not be done. But this will be seen only if some other narrative than any suggested by the sciences themselves provides the framework of their interpretation. Humans must not be cloned. Fetal stem cells must not be turned into immortal and impersonal cultures. The bomb should not have been built, even to counter a Nazi bomb. And this is a question not of deontological ethics but of truth: Peter Brunner's proposition is a fact about the universe. Those who do whatever they can do will come into conflict with reality, and if they persist will be broken on it.

It is time for my second instance, this time related to the second creedal article. It is of a very different sort: a specific and controverted theologoumenon. In 451 the Council of Chalcedon set out to establish Cyril of Alexandria's teaching, in the less alarming of its forms, as the norm of teaching about the person of Christ. It was Cyril's great concern that everything the Gospels say about their protagonist is to be taken as true of one and the same concrete subject, that whether the Gospels say Jesus told a parable or forgave sins, whether he wept for Lazarus or raised Lazarus, we are talking about the same personal protagonist. So the council, starting off on Cyril's line, laid it down as its primal doctrine that "one and the same" is the subject of the whole gospel-narrative. Particularly, in the council's polemic context, it is one and the same one who is born of Mary in Bethlehem and born eternally, begotten of the Father. And we can very straightforwardly continue with Cyril: it is one and the same who has the divine attributes displayed in the Gospels and who has the human attributes therein displayed, one and the same who forgives sin and who is tempted, one and the same who prays in anguish and rules all history, one and the same—though it took a few more councils to say it out loud—who is crucified and who orders the galaxies, one and the same who—as Luther loved to say—lies mewling and puking in his mother's arms and the while restrains Satan.

Chalcedon begins with the "one and the same," and so far, one may say, so very good. But when the fathers at Chalcedon moved on to the necessary work of setting boundaries for the contending schools of theology, outlawing the errors that each side feared the other must really be thinking, they did not quite dare carry on from their beginning. The formulas they produced have been memorized by centuries of theological students and have frustrated all of them, by their surface profundity and material elusiveness. Notoriously, the council stipulated that Christ has two "natures," one divine and one human, which while remaining unmixed, unadulerated, etc., are united in "one hypostasis." The trouble is, that they refrained from unpacking the notion of "one hypostasis," which one would have thought was more or less the whole point. Chalcedon's formulas fulfill some ecumenical and occasionally disciplinary functions, but conceptually they are close to being empty. Then finally the council appended the famous letter of Pope Leo as an authorized interpretation of the whole, which at least on its face says something rather different than the face value of the council's primal teaching. According to Leo, one entity, "the divine nature" does the glory bits and another entity, "the human nature," does the suffering bits, each "with" the other.

Ever since, at least in the West, we have found great relief in the notion that each of Christ's natures does its own thing. We have been relieved to think that while of course it is the one hypostasis of Christ who died on the cross, he did it in such fashion "according to his human nature" that we do not need to think that the God the Son himself was ontically affected. We have been relieved to think that while of course it is the one hypostasis of Christ who rules the universe, this is in *such* fashion "according to his divine nature" that Jesus qua human participates in this rule only by way of special but nevertheless creaturely human endowments. Christology, we have supposed, is a matter of discerning the relation between two entities, Christ's "divine nature" and his "human nature," and we have exploited that way of thinking to shy away from Cyril's blunt faithfulness to the narrative unity of the Gospels.

But what if Cyril's teaching, and the teaching with which the council began its decree, were true in the dumb sense? What if, given the Incarnation, there were not two entities for christology to relate to each other, but just the one person for christology to describe? Perhaps indeed with such analytical terms as "divine" or "human" or "nature"? What if talk of distinct human and divine "natures" of Christ were therefore only a sometimes useful, or even necessary, abstraction from what is actually given? What if it were the unadulterated fact of the matter, that this particular human individual with all his peculiarities, the executed Palestinian Jew, the prophet and rabbi from Nazareth, *is* the second identity of God? Getting down to the level I want to probe: that *he* is the being who appears in Scripture and theology as the *Logos* of God and God the Son?

For this essay, I will consider consequences of only the first of those two propositions: that Jesus of Nazareth is the *Logos* of God. God, we are taught by Scripture and dogma, has a *Logos*. That is, in part, he makes sense to himself, and so makes sense to us, if he wills there to be any us. In the long tradition stemming from the great Origen, it is taught that God has a self as which he knows and intends himself, knows and intends what sort of being he is, which includes knowing and intending what he can do and what he will not do, what is true for him and so for everyone else and what is false for him and so for anyone else, which includes knowing and willing, at the highest level of conceptual concentration, what it is to be.

Now accompanying that tradition there has always been the temptation to conceive this *Logos* not as in contingent but simple fact "one and the same" as the man whom Mary bore, but as a metaphysical extra entity of Ockham's worst fears, as a sort of immaterial mirror floating in empty ontological space, for God to see himself in, a mirror reflecting a "divine nature" in the abstract. The temptation is understandable, for indeed one must be alarmed by what comes of staying with christology's starting point and saying simply that Jesus, the Palestinian rabbi and prophet, Mary's child and Pilate's victim, is the *Logos* of God. For what comes of thinking such things is the contradiction of most antecedent religious wisdom.

God, it follows from thinking such things, does not know and intend himself as a divine essence, but as a particular, a specific someone, and indeed as someone whom we also know, and indeed as the man of the Gospels and the prophets, the man of sorrows acquainted with grief, the proclaimer of the Kingdom in which the last will be first and the first last, the friend of publicans and sinners, the enemy and participant of human suffering, Mary's boy and the man on the cross.

We can to a limited extent abstract the conception of a divine essence, of divinity as such, and this conception will be comprised of such predicates as "impassible," "omnipotent," "omniscient" and the rest of them. But God does not, if Jesus is the *Logos*, first know himself as an essence. Also for God, insofar as he knows himself this way, such knowing is a secondary abstraction.

It was doubtless, for example, proper that in the name of divine "impassibility" the ancient Church condemned "patripassionism," the doctrine that on the cross not only the Son but also the Father as such suffers. But this again is an abstraction. When I tripped on one of the mesas of which Princeton sidewalks are composed, came crashing down and for a moment knew myself as a bundle of pain signals, I could of course distinguish myself from this pain-constituted object, I could identify myself as the subject who knows this thing, and as that subject assure myself that this too will pass, that if when I get home I groan loudly enough I will even get some delightful sympathy, and so forth. When we say that the Father distinguishes himself from the suffering Son in whom he knows himself, this is doubtless true, in an analogous way—and profoundly uninteresting. To call God "impassible" or by any such adjectives is true and in some contexts a necessary abstraction, but God does not first know himself that way, he knows himself in the concrete history of the Israelite, Jesus.

We obviously will fear God best, and speak to him in prayer most appropriately, and be most likely to live in a way pleasing to him, when we comport our knowledge of him to his knowledge of himself. That is, when we direct our acquaintance with him not by divine attributes but by what the Gospels say about Mary's child and the prophet from Nazareth and the man on the cross.

Or look at it this way: when at the end, or now in worship or other religious experience, we are taken into the eternal life of God, no matter how far we are taken we will never get past the Jewish prophet and sufferer, the friend of sinners and radicalizer of Moses. I doubt one would understand that from the preaching and catechesis and liturgy in many churches, and I have no doubt that this is a chief reason why the Church's preaching and catechesis are mostly so dull. To the way in which the Western Church most often talks about God, the fact of the Incarnation has made far too little difference; most of what we say could equally well be said if God's *Logos* *were* that immaterial mirror and Jesus simply a great prophet or rabbi—or beach-boy guru. And that God and that Jesus are indeed fundamentally uninteresting.

Writing this paper, I here turned to a favorite target of mine, and had just started to write that since God knows and intends himself as a someone knowable by us, God is not after all "mysterious" as we usually understand mystery, that there is no abyss of God above or beyond or behind the Christ whom we know. But then I thought about a previous paper in the series for which I was then writing, David Tracy's lecture on "The Hidden and Incomprehensible God," and was reminded that some things I was about to elide cannot be elided. Luther, Tracy reminded me, was right: precisely Jews or Christians who know that God is love must often experience also the hiding of that love, must sometimes experience God's history with us as menacing rather than loving, indeed as horrific. And the other tradition that speaks of the incomprehensibility of God and cultivates apophatic theology, the evocation of what God is not, includes too many saints and lovers of Scripture to be ignored. What I must say instead of what I almost said, is that even God's most threatening gestures, and the incomprehensible depths of his being, are the hiddenness and mystery that belong—not to a featureless infinity but—to being a someone, even a human someone, indeed a knowable someone.

The analogy, once noticed, is obvious. The more profound another person is, and the better we get to know her or him, the more he or she will astonish us, not always in ways that please or affirm us, and the more we will glimpse depths we have not plumbed. The more I know that Blanche Jenson loves me, the more terrified I am by her occasional silences, the silences that belong of course precisely to her reality as someone other than me and of course only therefore able to love me.

So what I have to say instead of what I first thought of saying, is that indeed we will not at any height or depth of God get past Jesus of Nazareth. But that does not mean that now or in all eternity we will capture or control God, *because* we will not in all eternity capture or control this man. There is indeed an abyss in God and since he is God this abyss is infinite. But the abyss is that of Jesus' particular humanity.

Taking one more step on Cyril's line, God knows what it means for him to be. And so, since he is God, he knows what it means to be at all. And it is this man whom God knows as what it means to be. To be at all means to be this someone, Jesus of Nazareth, or to be someone or something involved with him. Thus "being" is not refuge from the commerce of someones, to be is rather to be caught up in a specific such commerce. To be is to be involved in a drama; the universal dramatic narrative that Scripture tells.

It makes a difference. What do we think we inhabit? A system of some sort? Even if not particularly machine-like? If so, we are victims of an illusion. What we really inhabit is rather a drama, the drama of Israel's Lord Jesus. To understand anything at all, is to trace its relation to the events so named.

It makes a difference. I do not know if our culture can be rescued from the superstition that recognizes only subpersonal forces as finally real, and insists it must construe all drama as epiphenomenal. If it cannot be rescued from that illusion, we will, for but one matter, continue so to present reality to students in the schools as to persuade them of their own meaninglessness and of the inconsequence of all their actions, except perhaps those most like cosmic collisions or natural selections, that is, the most brutal ones.

I acknowledge that left to myself, I would despair of the late-modern West's ability to recover any sort of dramatic self-understanding, for the society or for its victims. But since we are not left to ourselves, who knows? The Church, anyway, must fight in all the ways she can against the realization of the Clockwork Orange—also in her own life.

It makes a difference if Cyril was or was not right, and for those caught by the fascination of theology, the difference is wonderful in itself. But let us consider one more matter, of immediate religious practice and experience, prayer. If God knows his own being as an essence or force or ousia or hyperousia, it makes little sense to talk to him, and particularly it makes no sense to try to persuade him of something. But if God is also for himself a someone, it must of course make sense to *talk* to him. And if he is also for himself a someone among us other someones, then we are present in his own self-understanding, then he is *for himself* your fellow and my fellow. Then his mere deity, his omnipresence and omniscience and all the rest of it, cannot intervene between us. Then our cries for help are not alien to his absolute freedom but rather constitutive of it, just as my freedom is constituted by your addresses to me, and yours by mine. Then my telling him of my situation is not alien to his omniscience; rather this conversation between us is constitutive of his omniscience. Then his presence where two or three are gathered is not an instance of his general everywhereness but just the other way around. Then precisely humble petitionary prayer is the greatest honor we may show him. Simple proclamation that God the Son and Jesus of Nazareth are not two persons but one, as the truth about God, might make some considerable difference to our churches, that have become so very diffident with our prayers.

And so to the third mini-paper, on a Christian truth-claim located in yet a different sort of discourse. The Niceno-Constantinopolitan creed takes up the matter of spirit, which, with much of the religious world, it regards as lordly and life-giving. Then it identifies which spirit is these things: it is the one who proceeds from the Father of Jesus the Son, whose worship is simultaneous with their worship, and who spoke by Israel's prophets.

There are, as Paul reminded his churches, many spirits around. But according to the creed, only one of them is fully and authentically what a spirit should be, transcendent and animating, and that is the one identified as we have just rehearsed. Now what if that creedal claim were true, in the dumb sense?

Let us consider first ". . . who spoke by the prophets." If the spirit who did that is the one and only Spirit, then any dynamism that lifts us out of ourselves either lifts us into what it lifted those prophets into, or this elevation is not true transcendence but only projection, then its dynamism is not life but the death-spasm, however fulfilling we may find our transports to be. Am I truly lifted beyond myself in my experiences and disciplines? Am I coming alive in them? There is a way to tell: I can read Isaiah or Jeremiah or Amos, and see if I swing with them. Does this spirit within me make me long for justice to roll down like waters, and righteousness like an ever flowing stream? Does it free me *for* the community, or from it? Does it animate my rights and choices, or my duties and loves? Does it fulfill what I anyway envision as human flourishing, or does it give me a new vision?

The prophets were, after all, prophets: that is, they were engaged with the future. And at prophecy's penultimate fulfillment, that future was discovered to be a future beyond the possibilities of this world, not describable within the limits set by the way things now go. A new heaven and a new earth are envisaged, where the death-shroud is removed, and those who are now first are last and those now last are first, and the nations are pacified in the worship of the Lord. Is the spirit that moves me a spirit of impatience for that day? Or is it a spirit of calm and reconciliation to the way things are? If it is the latter, it is a fraud or a demon, if indeed the creed is true.

We may next consider, ". . . who proceeds from the Father of the Son." A spirit always proceeds from someone; for a spirit is just someone's own liveliness as that life transcends its own boundaries to animate others. So what a spirit is, is determined by from whom it proceeds. According to the creed, the only lordly and life-giving spirit is the one proceeding from the Father, which of course means the Father of the Son.

If this be true, believers have again been insufficiently triumphalist in our expectations. It is not just that the *Logos* of all things is the man Jesus. Also the dynamism of all things is the dynamism of the life lived between the Father and this man. The metaphysics of dynamic processes are very different than custom assumes.

How do we face the future? Modernity has oscillated between experiencing the dynamism of temporal succession as determinism and experiencing it as chaos. Most of the time we still suppose at the back of our minds, even if we have banished the supposition from the front, that if we knew the past history of every item of the universe we could predict its future in every detail. This is false of course; among other points, it is now well understood that the carriers of change are events which themselves have to be understood as either free or random. If we can force ourselves actually to think them as random, a yet more chilling vision must open. But how are we to think temporal succession as *free*?

It is at this point that not only Christian reflection invokes the notion of spirit. In this late- or post-modern West, the culture has not the strength to think of the *universe's* history as moved by freeing spirit, but hopes to find sanctuary from the Nietzschean horror in various little spirits of individuals or groups, each hoping to sustain a "spirituality," a feeling of freedom within its little shelter in the chaos. For freeing spirit is always someone's, and if you and I and others are the only someones around, there can only be little patches of spirit in the dispirited universe.

It will not help simply to say that there is some God or other, and that time is moved by it, or that there is spirit, and that this is the universal dynamism. That the world is blown onward by *something*, countervenes neither determinism nor the apprehension of chaos. Only if the world is animated by *someone*, and by someone who knows himself, who has a *Logos*, is the world encompassed and moved by a freedom.

With the first two cases, I instanced matters both of general interpretation and of believing existence. There remains only to do the latter with this case also. It is by no accident that the "forgiveness of sins" appears in the Spirit's creedal article, or that when in John's Gospel the risen Christ gives his disciples the Spirit, the actuality of this is the power to forgive sin. For in Scripture, forgiveness is a gift of life; in Jesus' mission healing and forgiving are two sides of the same thing. And so of course forgiveness is a work of the "Giver of life.'

There is and can be no greater offense to the way all of us now manage our lives, than the forgiveness of sins. Also the Church has much difficulty with it. On the one hand, if we are all ok in any case, there is nothing to forgive; "acceptance" is not the same as "forgiveness." "Accept yourself as you are" is not the same as "I forgive you," and assuredly not as "In the name of the Father and of the Son and of the Holy Spirit, I absolve you of your sin." In the mainline churches, and it seems increasingly in the evangelical churches, forgiveness is taken for a matter of course; but then it is not forgiveness. Voltaire's God cannot in fact forgive at all.

On the other hand, the more we deride "guilt trips" the more we send one another on them. When you add one group to another, a sizeable part of the American people regard themselves as my victims. But were I to accept this burden, there would be no way to get absolution, none of my victims will grant it, since we mutually define ourselves by our status as victims. For professed antinomians, we show a remarkable inability to get over past sin.

There is a reason for this deadlock. The only spirit who actually exists to deal with sin is the one who proceeds from the Father of the Son. "Acceptance" and guilt-tripping cannot work, neither can be life; because the only real life-giving Spirit is given by the crucified and risen one, and proceeds from that Father who sees his own character in him. There is therefore no way past sin except death, that is, here, repentance; and there is no new life possible but absolution. But that way is in fact open. The life-giving Spirit, who enables forgiveness, is the Lord.

That is three mini-essays. Perhaps they do, despite their difference, make a whole. Let me state its two theses, which are more general than my method of instances can strictly support. First: the encompassing reality called forth by the Father is a history, whose plot is determined in the life of Jesus the Son and whose dynamism is the Spirit that liberates these two for each other. Second: that this is so, instead of what we all want to be so, makes all the ontic and epistemic difference, which could make all the public difference.

5

Second Thoughts about
Theologies of Hope *(2000)*

For a systematic theologian, a conference on "theology of hope," even with an adjective, must have something of a retrospective character, the call to a conference on the matter must mandate something of a second look. The movement of the 1960s and 1970s has now its place in theological history, for better or worse; its themes and questions are standard items of ecumenical theological discourse. What do we now think of them? What are we now to do with them? The situation will inevitably lend a certain historical cast to my paper—even once or twice an autobiographical cast.

To take this partly backward look, and simultaneously to avoid a mere antiquarian exercise, I will explicitly structure the paper by the questions posed in the announcement of the conference, which do in fact show the character of second thoughts about a known phenomenon. And it may in any case be the task of the systematic theologian on the roster to address the conference questions head on. I will try to build one of the questions upon another, to make a more or less coherent discourse.

Two of the questions can, it seems to me, be answered with dispatch— even flippantly—but the answers have nevertheless considerable methodological import. So I will put them at the beginning, to make a sort of prolegomena.

Can eschatological hope survive Marxist and ecological, and other such criticism?

The quick and flippant answer to this question is, Certainly it can; the real question is, Can Marxist and other such projections survive criticism from an *authentically* eschatological viewpoint? But now see what that smart-aleck answer displays, a turnaround of whose critique trumps whose.

The gospel by its missionary nature lives always in conversation with the antecedent religion and religious wisdom of each time and place where the Church finds herself, a conversation that is always at once constructive and mutually critical. In the strain of Christian history that leads to such things as theologies of hope, the great interlocutors have, of course, been the theologians of Olympian-Parmenidean revelation, the famous "Greeks," Plato, Aristotle, and their epigones. The exchange has been notably fruit-ful, also and in some aspects especially during the period of modernity just behind us.

But insofar as this conversation is mutually critical it is, of course, always discomfitted by the question, Which critique trumps, if it comes to that? Who settles the question about truth, Socrates or Isaiah? Despite rhetoric about "openness" and the like, we have to choose and always do choose, especially when we claim not to. For we cannot float above the con-versation as if we were the Olympian-Parmenidean deity itself—or perhaps G. F. W. Hegel—though those who make each move regularly accuse those who make the other of trying to.

The choice was perhaps especially urgent in modernity, and for the most part Christian theology in the period chose the one alternative. For the most part, modernity's theology was "mediating" that is, it accepted that Western modernity's wisdom finally trumps. It took modernity's religious and metaphysical prejudices for foundational truth, and it therefore cut its understanding of the gospel to fit them. Despite my pejorative description of this move, I do not mean to say it was unproductive. A century earlier, I suppose I would myself have been a mediating theologian. Moreover, the West's standard religious and metaphysical assumptions, that is, our par-ticular derivatives of Socrates' theology, are themselves not conceivable apart from the gospel's long history in the West, which introduces a nice complication, much explored by historians of thought. Nevertheless, I do indeed think modernity's dominant theology made a wrong step.

Which brings me to the point of all this for now. Some of us who have spoken much of promise and hope have in part been moved by a contrar-ian methodological intention: to plant a stake in territory irretrievably dis-playing the gospel's *offense* to Western modernity's received wisdoms. It is arguable that the Enlightenment has found precisely the gospel's promises especially indigestible; the bourgeoisie being dedicated to stability relieved by bouts of random revolt. Just so we set out to make assertion of the gospel's promises a conscious criterion of our thinking, in my case not the only criterion, but a decisive criterion.

What then of specifically Marxist critique? Is the Kingdom of God pie in the sky by and by? That depends, surely, on whether the promise of the Kingdom is *true* or not, a question Marx did not entertain. Marxist ideology-doctrine maintains that all metanarratives—as we are now likely to call them—are founded on interest, so that the question of truth does not arise. Except of course for the ideology cast by—or rather for—the proletariat. We need not, I think, be much bothered by this latter claim, it being an only feebly disguised *petitio principii*: the reason the proletarian meta-narrative is supposed to be in good faith when others are not, is that it is the final one. Which, since the narrative is eschatological, is the same as to say, because it is the true one.

The situation between Marxist eschatology and Christian eschatology is thus quite simple: we have two sets of eschatological promises, both of which claim to be true and at least one of which must be false. So why would we think the gospel-promise is a true one? Because Christ is in fact risen, and must therefore make good his claim to be Lord.

An aspect of what is sometimes called "post-modern" thought is willingness to accept the irreducibility of one's own starting point or points. If we are Christian, it is willingness to take the fact of the Resurrection as a warrant also in discourse with those who do not think there is such a fact, *and* not to suppose that this necessarily terminates mutual intelligibility or persuasion or even resultant change of conviction. The will to unabashed assertion of biblical promises surely partakes of this mood; there is some affinity between at least my sort of "theology of hope" and certain aspects of post-modern intuition.

As to "ecological" critique of biblical eschatology, I do not know what that would be, but there is indeed a *cosmological* critique, which has so triumphed in the cultural mind that it is scarcely recognized as critique of something. The universe, current cosmological speculations propose, is doomed either to fall back from the big bang into a concluding big crunch and singularity, or to thin out indefinitely into what would be a sort of field but hardly anything like a universe. Or, as theorists who cannot quite stand either scenario dream, perhaps our universe may be so doomed, but never mind, there are many parallel universes and new ones can bubble up in the quantum field at any time. In none of these scenarios is there room for events fulfilling the gospel's promises.

And here I cannot but be flippant; but were I to undertake a serious discussion, it would take all this paper and several more. A continuing group sponsored by the Center of Theological Inquiry, where I now work, is just finishing a four-year study of this very problem, led by John Polkinghorne and Michael Welker, and a volume of essays will be published. What I myself have to offer is now available in the second volume of my *Systematic Theology*, and I will not rehearse it here.

For now, let me simply say that in my judgment Christian theology must in this matter venture a very drastic reversal of critiques. Who, after all, has decreed that the narrative spun by current cosmology is the encompassing story of reality, within which room must be found, or not found, for other narratives? We must, I think, follow the lead of Enlightenment's most constructive and robustly trinitarian Christian theologian, Jonathan Edwards, who by a non-mechanistic construal of Newton and Locke found room for *their* narrative within the *triune* narrative.

We come to the second announced question that I will use prolegomenally.

What is the proper place of eschatology in Christian theology at the beginning of the new millennium?

To this question too there is a quick and impertinent answer: the same place as in the old millennia. Which is more soberly to say, the systematic place of eschatology in Christian theology is not a variable. A theology that did not examine why and for what Christians may and must hope, and make the results of that examination normative for the resolution of other questions, would not be Christian theology at all. Therefore there is a way in which the designation "theology of hope" is superfluous, there being no other kind.

But of course, what in one time and place may need no explication may in another become very puzzling, indeed something essential to Christian theology may at a theological time and place nevertheless be quite innocently suppressed, even inevitably suppressed, only at another theological time and place to be grasped as new opportunity. During modernity, the gospel's eschatological character was suppressed so far as possible or, if it broke out, tended to take rather bizarre forms.

Thus Friedrich Schleiermacher, the great inspiration of neo-Protestant theology and now of much European and American Roman Catholic theology, reported "the Church teaching" about the return of Christ, the resurrection of the flesh, the last judgment, and the eternal Kingdom, accurately and with considerable acuteness, and then as his own teaching had only a warning about Church teaching, that it cannot "yield knowledge."[1] It cannot yield knowledge, because knowledge about the course of the universe is the province of the sciences, which were thought to present a universe impervious to change of such magnitude and character as Church teaching predicts.

And for an example of what a. more biblically stubborn mediating theologian could be driven to, we may think of Richard Rothe, who, bound to the standard mechanistic construal of material reality and to the idealist metaphysics often correlated to it, yet hoping to salvage something of biblical hope, seized on the idea of "organism" as something at once spiritual and natural, so that one could think of a spiritual-natural organism. Then to accommodate the biblical hope of resurrection and such, he posited a "*Holy*-Spiritual natural organism," which in the life of faith "ripens" under "the material garment"; the resurrection is then that this organism, now ripened, casts off the old garment.[2]

Insofar, then, as I would now be willing to speak of "theology of hope" as a specific phenomenon, and to confess myself to it, it was and is methodologically a reaction. Theology of hope is a biblical theology in the sense that, against the practice of modern theology, it does not think the deliverances of Enlightened religion or of ideological interpretations of scientific procedures or results must always trump, that it does not suppose that truth taught by Aristotle or Newton is more foundational or comprehensive or natural than truth taught by Isaiah or John. And it chooses eschatology as a specific ground to hold in part because this locus was a chief victim of mediation in the period just behind us.

So I come to the question with which I will begin more material discussion.

How is the End related to the Beginning?

The first course of lectures I attended as what Americans call a graduate student was one of the first given by Wolfhart Pannenberg as a *Privatdozent*. I was there not because he was famous, which he was not yet, but because he was lecturing on the history of nineteenth-century German theology, and as an American in Germany I was aware of my shortcomings. It was a brilliant course, even though, as it turned out, it did not get much beyond Schleiermacher, Schelling, and Hegel. It is something Pannenberg said about Hegel that provokes this reminiscence. If only, Pannenberg said, Hegel had not finally held history within the iron bracket of Spirit as timeless rationality,

---

1. Schleiermacher, *Der Christliche Glaube*, 2:433–40.
2. Rothe, *Dogmatik*, 3:103–4.

the *Phänomenologie des Geistes* would indeed have marvelously conceptualized an essential feature of Christianity, that is, its appropriate construal and
ontological placement of history. But as it is, when you get to the end of
the *Phänomenologie*, you discover there is nothing in the End that was not
there in the beginning. Spirit's venture into its opposite and recovery of itself
therein turns out to have been repristination rather than creation. After all
the heavy dialectical lifting, history after all turns out only to illustrate essentially timeless truth.

But even in his error, I want to go on to say, Hegel is revelatory. For his
bracketing of history by timeless reason does conceptualize something in
Western theology, namely a pervading error. Our theology has regularly, if
sometimes subliminally, construed the End as a repristination of the beginning, and Hegel's great error was that he only too faithfully followed tradition. To put the bluntest possible point on it, we have seen God's history
with us, in Israel and Christ, as a repair job. It is surely the understanding of
what in my country we call Sunday-school, *and* of most elite theology when
you get down to it: God made a world and it was good; but then something
went wrong, and God undertook restorative measures.

Whether Sunday-school or Hegel—or Schleiermacher or Rothe—
what is at work here is the understanding of eternity and time which has
attracted and confused Christian theology ever since those Greeks became
its interlocutors: the posit of eternity as the sheer negation of time, and so
of eternal being as constituted above all by "impassability," by immunity to
the threats and possibilities that time brings. Note also the language one
must use to characterize this sort of eternity: it is, of course, the *future* which
can *bring* something, and so the future to which eternal being so construed
must be immune. The theology of Olympus and the Goddess' revelation
to Parmenides was moved by passion to keep deceitful hope in its box, for
the truth, they thought they knew, is that the future devours its children.
Remember only the final line to which all the mighty tale of the *Iliad* brings
us: "And so that is how they held the funeral for Hector, tamer of horses."
Eternity as the Greeks construed it is salvific precisely as it is supposed to be
the guarantee that time's hastings have no other end than their beginning,
that whatever happens on the fields of Troy where time and its hopes are
disappointed, the gods remain unchanged—and because, perhaps, if we can
join with them, we can share some of their immutability.

But it would be a very uninteresting *story* about which the maxim
could be true, that in my beginning is my end, and no story at all that
wholly neutralized the future's possibilities in advance. Aristotle observed
this about stories, which is why he wanted no story-telling about reality—he

would have agreed with the Chinese that "May you live in interesting times" is a curse.

All of which is, just by itself, a sufficient argument that the eternity revealed to Homer and Parmenides will not do for Christian theology. For the story the Bible tells *is* interesting, and for better or worse it does let hope out of the box. And then it claims to be about the real world, indeed, first to constitute the real world for our habitation.

Readers will after all this anticipate my answer to the present question. If the gospel is true, the End is *dramatically* related to the beginning, or what is the same thing, historically related. God does not create a cosmos, which thereupon is shocked into movement so as to have a history. God creates precisely a history, which is a universe, an intelligible whole, because it has an intended end. God creates a temporal sequence, which is a whole because it has a plot, because it has a beginning and an end and between them a reconciliation.

It is often supposed that the Bible contains no metaphysics, no provision or suggestion of concepts for a general interpretation of what can be real. But this is supposed only because it is antecedently supposed that the Greeks' material metaphysics are the only possible one, which surely they are not. If we take the notion of metaphysics formally, it is plain that the Bible provides and supports a rich and coherent description of what is and can be real.

And that brings us back to Hegel. I have agreed with Pannenberg that Hegel would indeed have brilliantly conceptualized the understanding of time demanded by the gospel, if only he had not at the last moment capitulated to Parmenides (as for him represented by Aristotle). One reason for giving Hegel the benefit of this doubt, is Hegel's acute discernment of the *sort* of sense history makes, in Scripture and indeed in experience, and his refusal—up to the last moment—to subordinate this logic to some other. The logic of thesis, antithesis, and synthesis, if it is not employed to constrain what is possible but is grasped rather as possibility's own pattern, is surely indeed the logic of specifically historical being. Thesis and antithesis are the conflicts definitive of temporality, whether in the life of an individual, a civilization, or all creation. And the notion that thesis and antithesis are sublated by and into a new future, is precisely the biblical point. Moreover, if what God creates is a history, then history's sort of logic defines being, as Hegel almost said.

Indeed, whatever *could* be an end of history? If we got to history's end, what might we discover? That time and discourse had simply stopped? Why would anyone want to get to that point? And is the notion even intelligible?

Since what God creates is a history, the one conceivable end of history must be again a sublation, now into the only thing left to be taken into, God. An end of history, if not a sheer nothing, can only be temporal history's sublation into the infinite history that Father, Son, and Holy Spirit are between them. Whether or not proofs of God work, that say the chains of causation have to start with something uncaused, it is, I suggest, plain that the chains of historical sublation do not make a whole history unless they eventuate in a sublation that is not himself sublated. Thus the doctrine of *theosis*, the doctrine that our end is inclusion in God's life, is not simply the brand of eschatology preferred by the Eastern churches; it names the only *possible* "end" of a *creation*, the only possible end of being that is history and drama.

This can be said, of course, only of a God who indeed is himself a history, only of the God who is the archetype of thesis, antithesis and synthesis, only of the triune God. We can be taken into the life of only such a God as has a life to be taken into.

The problem with Hegel was not that he thought of history's final sublation into an infinite living sublation, the triune God, but that he misconceived this God, that his doctrine of Trinity was bad. And here again his error is but the conceptualization of pervasive theological error. We have at bottom supposed that the Father fulfills the definition of God in such fashion that, so far as concepts can carry us, he could have been God on his own. And this supposition has a kickback: it compels a construal of deity that an isolated "Father" could indeed instantiate, that is, a construal of deity by the beginning rather than the end, by perdurance rather than freedom, by timeless reason rather than history's reason. The problem with Hegel is that, despite his grandiloquent talk of *Geist*, he like most Western theology did not make the biblical Spirit's role decisive for his construal of deity. His God, despite all his rhetoric and the insight behind it, is timeless reason, it lacks life, and therefore the sublation of history into his God is after all a return to the beginning and very much like death.

But that we can fix—not in Hegel to be sure but in our own theology. The tradition has described the Spirit as the bond of love between the Father and the Son, and for the most part has done so as if this bond were not itself a someone, as if the Father and the Son loved each other in any case, and "the Spirit" was a subsequent name for that love. But the Spirit unites the Father and the Son in love only in that he is an active agent who *intrudes* to reconcile them, only in that he is the third party who gives himself to both, just and only so freeing them for each other.

So how is the End related to the Beginning? Neither as its restoration nor yet as its development. Neither mechanist nor organicist ideologies will help us here. Indeed, we will understand how the End is related to the

Beginning only in the context determined by them, only as the Spirit gives himself to us as he does to the Father and the Son, so that in the Church we become able to understand freedom and love. With God, and therefore with his creation, the beginning occurs only as it is freed for the end beyond it, and the end occurs only as love for all that already is.

So—

Does a theology of hope diminish the living presence of God?

We all, of course, have the worry behind this question. Its root is the feeling that emerges in such expressions as "Well—we can only hope . . . ," the feeling that hope is somehow a weaker relation to the future than some other. But what would that other relation be? Control, perhaps? By which we try to deprive the future of its futurity? By which, in the case of God, we try to restrain his *living* presence? To make it indeed his dead presence? Our distrust of hope is an illusion, cast by our fear.

In the triune God, whose life is constituted by the futurity of the Spirit, there occurs the archetype of all that we call hope. And since this God is the Creator, what can only be grasped by hope is just so the most surely real, the most availably present. It does not usually seem so to us, but our perceptions are not the measure of reality, if there is God.

I have been trespassing my next question:

How does one name the God of hope?

I am trying to build these questions one upon the other; therefore you will again not be surprised at my answer. We name the God of hope "Father, Son, and Holy Spirit." It is not, of course, that we first conceive a God of hope, and then look around for ways to name it. It is rather that the biblical God is uniquely identified as Father, Son, and Spirit and that as we come to know this specific God we find that he can appropriately be described as a God of hope. How does this work out?

Father, Son, and Spirit are biblical names for the *dramatis dei personae* that in fact appear in the Bible's telling of God's history with us. And the "trinitarian relations" by which in classical trinitarian doctrine the identities of the three are constituted—that the Father begets the Son and the Son is begotten, that the Father breathes the Spirit and the Spirit is breathed—are slogans for plot lines of this story. If we ask what may be the being of this God, as one God, we can therefore only answer that he is the life, the history, that occurs between these *personae* and that has this plot. He is not a something or even a someone who has a history; no one has this history except the three. This God simply *is* the life lived between Jesus and the one he called Father, in the Spirit who liberates them for each other. And of course there is no life or history without hope, without the future's opening of possibility and the courage to meet that future without fear.

The foregoing is about God, not yet about us. The triune God is not first the triune God as a God of *our* hope; he does not need us to be the God of hope. The pattern of argument is ancient in theology: we identify true divine attributes by inquiring how "justice" or "love" or some similar predicate may be conceived as real in God without supposing the existence of creatures. If we keep the triunity of God firmly in mind, we find that the argument works excellently for "full of hope." Indeed, if we amplify the tradition as earlier demanded, and give the Spirit his biblical due, we may find that "full of hope" is the great illuminating attribute of God. Christian hope, therefore, is nothing other than a certain participation in the life of God—which would be another way to approach the previous question.

"Who do we name the God of hope?" The interrogatory sentence could of course mean something quite different than the question just discussed. It could mean: "How is it possible to do this at all, to attach language to such a God? And if it is possible, by what exertions do we manage it?"

The great insight here is that there is no problem. The God who can be full of hope, the triune God, is the Father, Son, and Spirit of the story that Scripture tells; that is, to our present point, he lives his own life as that same history into which he takes us. Thus we come to know him in the way in which we come to know each other, as we live together. And since this common life embraces a far wider span than our little three score and a few, we rely on documents as we do in any such situation.

I do not, of course, deny that God is mystery, only that there is a problem about knowing the mystery. I have lived with my wife for forty-five years, and she becomes more mysterious daily; but there is no problem about how I know her and her mystery. And I have lived with God at least since my baptism sixty-eight years ago; it is no trope to say I know him, and what I know is the mystery of the hope that he is for himself and for me.

So we do in fact address God, and name him to each other, every day in the Church. "Our Father in heaven . . ." we say, simply because by baptism and in Eucharist we are one with his Son Jesus so that we do in fact live with this Father. If we think there is a problem—and we do of course—it is because we are subliminal unitarians. A monadic God, whose otherness from us can not include us, could indeed only be known by laboriously obtained glimpses and named by projections and metaphors pressed from such experience. And should we construe our relation to such a God as hope, that would indeed much impede the cognitive effort. For with such a God, to say we can only hope in him would be to say he was simply not yet available to us. Were I a unitarian, or even fashionably an Arian, I would indeed fear to construe God by hope.

We are already talking about alternatives, and so I come to the last of the questions I take from the announcement:

What are the alternatives to God being a God of hope?

It must be put as plainly as possible: the only alternative to faith in a God who can decisively be so named is, at least for us modern Westerners, sheer *lack* of hope, that is, nihilism. Every theology is an apologetic theology, it is molded to a diagnosis of its time and place. If we ask again, and now plumbing for rock bottom, "Why did theologians suddenly start making so much of hope?" The answer, I think, is that we began to lose hope, began to fear that Nietzsche was right. Every historical time and place is characterized—precisely if the theology of hope is right—by waiting for some advent. The advent looming on *our* horizon is the advent of nothingness, the hour of Nietzsche's last man. It took a while for the century's catastrophes to make us see that, but finally post-war prosperity turned the trick.

The question has occupied me from the first time I wrote a paper for a more or less scholarly society: What happens to a culture whose self-understanding was once enabled by the gospel, when it turns against that gospel? I do not think my preoccupation with this question betrays overmuch nostalgia or romanticism; I do not suppose that there was some period when folk were more Christian or faithful than they are now. Humans, I imagine, are about as faithful and unfaithful to communally acknowledged goods and virtues at one time as they are at another. I refer only to the much-researched multiplicity of ways in which the West's acknowledged goods and virtues were those proposed by Scripture and actual in its narrative. That they have always been honored mostly in the breach is beside my present point.

We have been taught by Scripture to construe history by its End, in accord with a final sublation into an infinite history. What when those so taught no longer believe there is such history to be taken into? Then we will of course see precisely nothing for us and our world finally to be taken into, and all the little sublations that make up our temporal existence will confront us with that void.

In other terms: we bourgeois have wanted a world to live in that is palpable, reliable, coherent and adapted—as it is currently fashionable to say—to our flourishing. *And* we have each individually wanted to be the autonomous definers of what constitutes coherence and flourishing. That we cannot have it both ways is in itself apparent; but only after staring long into the emptiness that opens between them have we taken fright.

Whether actual nihilism is possible is arguable. But life under the shadow of its threatening advent must be possible, since we are living it. This shadow is the apologetic context of at least my sort of "theology of hope."

It was perhaps more by its title than by its material positions that Jürgen Moltmann's book once reminded Christian theology of one of its own necessary tasks: to construe God as the God of hope and so foster hope in the lives of its believers. We have been reminded. I doubt that books like Moltmann's—or Gerhard Sauter's *Zukunft und Verheissung* or Carl Braaten's and my joint volume *The Futurist Option*—will again be written. But it is to be hoped [!] that we have not only been reminded of an essential aspect of the theological task, but will remember it and carry on with it.

6

How the World Lost Its Story *(1993)*

I

It is the whole mission of the Church to speak the gospel. As to what sort of thing "the gospel" may be, too many years ago I tried to explain that in a book with the title *Story and Promise,* and I still regard these two concepts as the best analytical characterization of the Church's message. It is the Church's constitutive task to tell the biblical narrative to the world in proclamation and to God in worship, and to do so in a fashion appropriate to the content of that narrative; that is, as a promise claimed from God and proclaimed to the world. It is the Church's mission to tell all who will listen, God included, that the God of Israel has raised his servant Jesus from the dead, and to unpack the soteriological and doxological import of that fact.

That book, however, was directed to the *modern* world, a world in which it was presumed that stories and promises make sense. What if these presumptions are losing hold? I will in this essay follow the fashion of referring to the present historical moment as the advent of a "postmodern" world, because, as I am increasingly persuaded, the slogan does point to something real, a world that has no story and so cannot entertain promises. Two preliminary clarifications are, however, needed.

The first of these is that while the Western world is now "post"-modern in the sense that modernity is dying around us, it is not "post"-modern in the sense that any new thing is yet replacing it. Most of those who talk of postmodernism are belated disciples of Friedrich Nietzsche. And to understand ourselves, we must indeed study Nietzsche. Specifically, we must learn from Nietzsche about *nihilism,* about an historical reality defined purely by negations. But only half of Nietzsche's prophecy shows any sign of being fulfilled. In Nietzsche's vision, the nihilism in which Western civilization ends was to be at once a collapse into decadence and the fulfillment of an absolute freedom. There would at once appear the hollow "last man" and the glorious "superman." The "last man" is plainly on the scene, but superman is so far missing. In my use of "postmodern," "post-" has purely apophatic force.

The second clarification is terminological. When general or theological historians refer to the "modern world" or "modernity," they mean the Western era dominated by the strategies and organizations of instrumental and critical reason. Whether they then date the beginning of modernity with the first appearances of the Enlightenment or earlier depends on their interpretation of Reformation and Renaissance.

But the term "postmodernism" became current outside this general discourse, within artistic and literary criticism, and in this other, more specialized discourse, the "modernism" to which "post-" was prefixed has meant the sensibility that emerged in the arts around the turn of the present century, in deliberate *rejection* of the world shaped by Enlightenment and Romanticism, that is, of the world otherwise called "modern." "Postmodernism" in its original use merely named a variant of that "modernist" sensibility itself, insofar as the avant-garde was perceived to have somehow survived itself.

When participants in and historians of the more general intellectual and spiritual culture outside the arts have subsequently come to speak of "postmodernism" in larger application, the "modern" to which something is said to be "post-" is modernity in its more general historical sense. Thus "postmodernism" in *this* use denotes the penetration into the wider spiritual and cultural life of that sensibility which appeared earlier in the arts and there was called precisely "modernism." That is, "postmodernism" *outside* the arts is the same thing as "modernism"—including "postmodernism" as there spoken of—*in* the arts. That a "postmodernist" turn is seen in the general culture all these years after modernism/postmodernism appeared in the arts simply marks the usual historical lag between developments in the arts and analogous developments in politics and philosophy and theology and daily life.

II

The modern world, the world that instrumental and critical reason built, is falling about us. Modernity, it now becomes evident, has been all along eroding its own foundations; its projects and comforts have depended on an inheritance to which it has itself been inimical. Walter Lippmann spoke of "the acids of modernity"; as it turns out, the stones attacked by this acid have been those on which the modern world was itself erected. Analysts from all relevant disciplines converge on one insight: Modernity has lived on a moral and intellectual capital that it has not renewed and indeed could not have renewed without denying itself. They moreover agree that this intellectual and moral capital was that built up by the Christian Church's long establishment in the West, even if they themselves do not share the Church's faith or even admire it.

Perhaps the fall of modernity will be complete in our lifetimes; perhaps it will occupy another century. However long it takes, any successor society is still too distant—or perhaps too precluded—to discern. It is the collapse itself amidst which the Church must for the foreseeable future live and speak the gospel; it is modernity's time of ending as such that constitutes the Western Church's postmodern mission field. As the Church once lived and conducted her mission in the precisely *post*-Hellenistic and *post*-Roman-imperial world, remembering what had vanished but not knowing what if anything could come next, so the Church must now live and conduct her mission in the precisely "post"-modern world.

The self-destruction of modernism can be described basically under two rubrics: story and promise. The question is what the Church is now required to do with respect to each. First, story.

III

The modern world's typical way of knowing human life was what Hans Frei has taught theologians to call "realistic narrative." The novels of Jane Austen and James Baldwin are "realistic narratives"; so are the histories of Gibbon or your local newspaper; so are soap operas. "Realistic narrative" is a particular way of telling a sequence of events that is distinguished from other possible forms by two characteristics.

First, the sequential events are understood jointly to make a certain kind of sense—a dramatic kind of sense. Aristotle provided the classic specification of dramatically coherent narrative. In a dramatically good story, he said, each decisive event is unpredictable until it happens, but immediately upon taking place is seen to be exactly what "had" to happen. So, to take the example of Aristotle's own favorite good story, we could not know in advance that Oedipus would blind himself but once he has done it instantly see that the whole story must lead to and flow from just this act.

Second, the sequential dramatic coherence is of a sort that could "really" happen, that is, happen in a presumed factual world "out there," external to the text. Thus Len Deighton's story of the Winter family did not in fact occupy time and space in pre-Nazi and Nazi Germany, but there is nothing in the story itself to say that it might not have. With this kind of narrative, the question of whether the story depicts something beyond itself, and if it does, how accurately, are therefore subsequent and independent questions.

But now notice two things supposed by this way of reporting our lives to ourselves. First and obviously, it is supposed that stories dramatically coherent à la Aristotle are the *appropriate* way to understand our human task and possibility. The modern West has supposed that living on the patterns of King Lear or Horatio Alger is appropriate to beings of the sort we are, and living on the patterns of a schizophrenic or Till Eulenspiegel is not. We have supposed that we somehow "ought" to be able to make dramatic sense of our lives. (We should note that humankind does not universally share the supposition: Not shamanist cultures nor Confucian or Taoist China nor the high Indian religions suppose any such thing.)

And it is further supposed that some stories dramatically coherent à la Aristotle are "realistic," that is, that they may be fitted to the "real" world, the world as it is in itself prior to our storytelling. The use of realistic narrative as the normal way of understanding human existence supposes that reality out there, "the world" itself, makes dramatic sense à la Aristotle, into which narrative the stories we tell about ourselves can and sometimes do fit. Put it this way: The way in which the modern West has talked about human life supposes that an omniscient historian could write a *universal* history, and that this is so because the universe with inclusion of our lives is in fact a story written by a sort of omnipotent novelist.

That is to say, modernity has supposed we inhabit what I will call a "narratable world." Modernity has supposed that the world "out there" is such that stories can be told that are true *to it*. And modernity has supposed that the reason narratives can be true to the world is that the world somehow "has" its own true story, antecedent to, and enabling of, the stories we tell about ourselves in it.

There is no mystery about how Western modernity came by this supposition. The supposition is straightforwardly a secularization of Jewish and Christian practice—as indeed these are the source of most key suppositions of Western intellectual and moral life. The archetypical body of realistic narrative is precisely the Bible, and the realistic narratives of Western modernity have every one been composed in, typically quite conscious, imitation of biblical narrative. Aristotle's definition found its future through a strange channel.

Postmodernism is characterized by the loss of this supposition in all of its aspects. We can see this most vividly in literature. The paradigmatic fictional works of the twentieth century either present accounts that make dramatic sense in themselves but tell of events or sequences that could not occur in the world outside the storytelling, or they meticulously describe events that could occur or perhaps actually have occurred in "the real world," but in such fashion as to display precisely their lack of dramatic coherence. Gunter Grass' *The Tin Drum* may serve as an example of the first mode, Sartre's *Nausea* as an example of the second, and Joyce's *Ulysses* of both at once.

The same modes appear in the visual arts. The classical visual art of the modern West was at once realistic and narrative; it portrayed the world beyond itself and constrained within itself some portion of a narrative possible in that world. Thus one of Valesquez's royal family portraits depicts both a set of actual and recognizable human individuals and relationships between them that can be described only by narrative.

Modernist/postmodernist art is in most of its modes defined precisely by a passion to avoid any such portrayal. Most usually this is done by elevating the formal or expressive aspects of the act or product of art to be themselves the subject matter of the work. I have long remembered the remark of a notable art critic—though I have forgotten which one—that many modernist paintings could be understood as *fragments* of classical painting blown up for their own sake, displaying the formal and technical elements by which painting is accomplished but eschewing the narrative depiction within which such patches of paint on canvas would earlier have had their place.

But there is also a meticulously realistic modernism that carefully reproduces pieces of the world out there, but in such fashion as either to tell a story that is impossible in the world, as in surrealism, or to alienate the depicted reality altogether from our quest for coherence. So every item in a painting by Magritte is an item of our accustomed world, and yet nothing hangs together in the way we expect; we cannot make out what story has been, or will be, going on with the persons and objects depicted. And precisely to induce this schizophrenic apprehension in us was the stated purpose for which Magritte and other surrealists and modernist realists have made their works.

If there is little mystery about where the West got its faith in a narratable world, neither is there much mystery about how the West has lost this faith. The entire project of the Enlightenment was to maintain realist faith while declaring disallegiance from the God who was that faith's object. The story the Bible tells is asserted to be the story of God with His creatures; that is, it is both assumed and explicitly asserted that there is a true story about the universe because there is a universal novelist/historian. Modernity was defined by the attempt to live in a universal story without a universal storyteller.

The experiment has failed. It is, after the fact, obvious that it had to: If there is no universal storyteller, then the universe can have no storyline. Neither you nor I nor all of us together can so shape the world that it can make narrative sense; if God does not invent the world's story, then it has none, then the world has no narrative that is its own. If there is no God, or indeed if there is some other God than the God of the Bible, there is no narratable world.

Moreover, if there is not the biblical God, then realistic narrative is not a plausible means for our human self-understanding. Human consciousness is too obscure a mystery to itself for us to script our own lives. Modernity has added a new genre of theater to the classic tragedy and comedy: the absurdist drama that displays precisely an absence of dramatic coherence. Sometimes such drama depicts a long sequence of events with no turning points or denouement; sometimes it displays the absence of any events at all. Samuel Beckett has, of course, written the arch-examples of both, with *Waiting for Godot* and *Krapp's Last Tape*. If we would be instructed in the postmodern world, we should seek out a performance of Beckett—the postmodern world is the world according to Beckett.

The arts are good for diagnosis, both because they offer a controlled experience and because they always anticipate what will come later in the general culture. But the general culture has now caught up with post-modernism, and for experience of the *fact,* we should turn from elite art to the streets of our cities and the classrooms of our suburbs, to our congregations and churchly institutions, and to the culture gaps that rend them.

There we will find folk who simply do not apprehend or inhabit a narratable world. Indeed, many do not know that anyone ever did. The reason so many now cannot "find their place" is that they are unaware of the possibility of a kind of world or society that could have such things as places, though they may recite, as a sort of mantra, memorized phrases about "getting my life together" and the like. There are now many who do not and cannot understand their lives as realistic narrative: John Cage or Frank Stella; one of my suburban Minnesota students whose reality is rock music, his penis, and at the very fringes some awareness that to support both of these medical school might be nice; a New York street dude; the pillar of her congregation who one day casually reveals that of course she *believes* none of it, that her Christianity is a relativistic game that could easily be replaced altogether by some other religion or yoga—all inhabit a world of which no stories can be true.

IV

So how, with respect to "story," must the Church's mission now be conducted? The prescription itself is obvious and simple, carrying it out hard and in some situations perhaps impossible.

Throughout modernity, the Church has presumed that its mission was directed to persons who *already* understood themselves as inhabitants of a narratable world. Moreover, since the God of a narratable world is the God of Scripture, the Church was also able to presume that the narrative sense people had antecedently tried to make of their lives had somehow to cohere with the particular story, "the gospel," that the Church had to communicate. Somebody who could read Rex Stout or the morning paper with pleasure and increase of self-understanding was for that very reason taken as already situated to grasp the Church's message (which did not of course mean that he or she would necessarily believe it). In effect, the Church could say to her hearers: "You know that story you think you must be living out in the real world? We are here to tell you about its turning point and outcome."

But this is precisely what the postmodern Church cannot presume. What then? The obvious answer is that if the Church does not *find* her hearers antecedently inhabiting a narratable world, then the Church must herself *be* that world.

The Church has in fact had great experience of just this role. One of many analogies between postmodernity and dying antiquity—in which the Church lived for her most creative period—is that the late antique world also insisted on being a meaningless chaos, and that the Church had to save her converts by offering herself as the narratable world within which life could be lived with dramatic coherence. Israel had been the nation that lived a realistic narrative amid nations that lived otherwise; the Church offered herself to the gentiles as their Israel. The Church so constituted herself in her *liturgy*.

For the ancient Church, the walls of the place of Eucharist, whether these were the walls of a basement or of Hagia Sophia or of an imaginary circle in the desert, enclosed a world. And the great drama of the Eucharist was the narrative life of that world. Nor was this a fictive world, for its drama is precisely the "real" presence of all reality's true author, elsewhere denied. The classic liturgical action of the Church was not about anything else at all; it was itself the reality about which truth could be told.

In the postmodern world, if a congregation or churchly agency wants to be "relevant," here is the first step: It must recover the classic liturgy of the Church, in all its dramatic density, sensual actuality, and brutal realism, and make this the one exclusive center of its life. In the postmodern world, all else must at best be decoration and more likely distraction.

Out there—and that is exactly how we must again begin to speak of the society in which the Church finds itself—there is no narratable world. But absent a narratable world, the Church's hearers cannot believe or even understand the gospel story—or any other momentous story. If the Church is not herself a real, substantial, living world to which the gospel can be true, faith is quite simply impossible.

Protestantism has been modernity's specific form of Christianity. Protestantism supposed that addressees of the gospel already inhabited the narratable world in which stories like the gospel could be believed, and that we therefore could dismantle the gospel's own liturgical world, which earlier times of the Church had created. Protestantism has from the beginning supposed that the real action is in the world, and that what happens "in church" can only be preparation to get back out into reality. This was always a wrong judgment—indeed a remarkable piece of naiveté—but the blunder is understandable and in the modern world Protestantism could, just barely, get away with it. In a post-modern world, those days are gone forever.

Of course ritual as such is not the point; the point is the Church's reality as herself a specific, real, narrated world. Which leads to a further matter.

To be a real world for her members, and not just a ritual illusion, the Church must pay the closest attention to the substance of her liturgical gatherings and to their constitutive language. If the Church's interior drama is not fiction, this is because the subject of that drama is a particular God, the Creator-God who authors all reality. If liturgy is not to be sickly pretense, if it is to be the real presence of reality's God, everything must enact the specific story Scripture actually tells about that particular God. Two polemical points here insist on hearing, and come together in a third.

Polemical point one: The story is not your story or my story or "history" or "her-story" or some neat story someone read or made up. The story of the sermon and of the hymns and of the processions and of the sacramental acts and of the readings is to be God's story, the story of the Bible. Preachers are the greatest sinners here: The text already is and belongs to the one true story; it does need to be helped out in this respect. What is said and enacted in the Church must be with the greatest exactitude and faithfulness and exclusivity the story of creation and redemption by the God of Israel and Father of the risen Christ. As we used to say: Period.

Polemical point two: Modern Christianity, that is, Protestantism, has regularly substituted slogans for narrative, both in teaching and in liturgy. It has supposed that hearers already knew they had a story and even already knew its basic plot, so that all that needed to be done was to point up certain features of the story—that it is "justifying," or "liberating," or whatever. The supposition was always misguided, but sometimes the Church got away with it. In the post-modern world, this sort of preaching and teaching and liturgical composition merely expresses the desperation of those who in their meaningless world can believe nothing but vaguely wish they could.

Now the synthetic polemical point: There *is* one slogan-like phrase that is precisely a maximally compressed version of the one God's particular story. This is the revealed name, "Father, Son, and Holy Spirit." It is thus no accident at all that in our postmodern situation, the struggle between realistic faith and religious wool-gathering settles into a struggle over this name. The triune name evokes God as the three actors of this one story and places the three in their actual narrative relation. Substitutes do not and cannot do this; "Creator, Redeemer, and Sanctifier," for example, neither narrates nor specifically names, for creating, redeeming, and sanctifying are timelessly actual aspects of the biblical God's activity and are moreover things that *all* putative gods somehow do. In the postmodern situation, we will easily recognize congregations and agencies that know what world they inhabit by their love and fidelity to the triune name, and we will recognize antiquated Protestantism by its uneasiness with the triune name.

V

So much for story. Now for *promise*. Here too modernity was constituted by secularization of an aspect of Christian faith. The gospel is ineradicably an eschatological message; it tells its story as the story of created time's end and fulfillment. Modernity's secularized version of eschatological faith was its notorious confidence in progress, and was constitutive for modernity's whole practice and self-understanding. In its liberal version, confidence in progress shaped Europe and founded the United States. In its Marxist and pre-Marxist versions, confidence in progress fueled the great modern revolutions.

In a world that was progressing, or thought it was, Protestantism supposed the Church's role was to provide motivation and direction for movement that was anyway occurring. In the most recent and already rather quaint version of this supposition, it was said to be the Church's role to look around the world to see where God was at work, and then jump in to help. This—again—was always a remarkable piece of naiveté, but occasionally someone got away with it.

The First World War terminated Western Europe's liberal faith in progress, and this disastrous experiment has now terminated the Marxist version. America escaped the worst devastations of the wars and has always been more exclusively shaped by modernity than other nations, and so held on a couple of generations longer; now America too seems slowly to be accepting the evidence.

Modernity's hope was in progress; the model of this hope was biblical hope in God as the Coming One, the *Eschatos*. Modernity cannot hope in the biblical God, founded as it is in a declaration of independence from him. Therefore, when hope in progress has been discredited, modernity has no resource either for renewing it or for acquiring any other sort of hope. The mere negation of faith in progress is sheer lack of hope; and hopelessness is the very definition of postmodernism.

Much modernist/postmodernist literature and art is directly and thematically either lamentation about, or defiant proclamation of, hopelessness: Promises, our artists tell us in drumbeat monotony, should not be made, because they cannot be kept. Promises, in the postmodern world, are inauthentic simply because they are promises, because they commit a future that is not ours to commit. Where the impossibility of promise appears less thematically and more formally, it runs together with the renunciation of plotted narrative instanced earlier: Promises can be made only if reality is getting someplace, that is, if it has a plotted story.

And again, while the arts are diagnostic, the condition they reveal is the condition of our streets and institutions. The impossibility of promises is there in our daily experience. And in this matter, we have a paradigm case, in which the whole situation is instantly manifest and which I need only name. There is a human promise that is the closest possible creaturely approach to unconditional divine promise and that is therefore throughout Scripture the chosen analog of divine promise: the marital promise of faithfulness unto death. Among us, that promise has become a near impossibility, socially, morally, and even legally.

VI

So again, how, in a world that entertains no promises, is the Church to speak her eschatological hope with any public plausibility? There is one line here that obviously must be followed: The Church must herself be a communal world in which promises are made and kept. But this line has already been pursued with enormous energy by Stanley Hauerwas, whose work deserves its own study. Let me take the question in a different direction.

It is the whole vision of an Eschaton that is now missing outside the Church. The assembly of believers must therefore itself be the event in which we may behold what is to come. Nor is this necessity new in the life of the Church. For what purpose, after all, do we think John the Seer recorded his visions?

If, in the postmodern world, a congregation or whatever wants to be "relevant," its assemblies must be unabashedly events of shared apocalyptic vision. "Going to church" must be a journey to the place where we will behold our destiny, where we will see what is to come of us. Modernity's version of Christianity—that is, Protestantism—has been shy of vision and apocalypse alike. Just so, its day is over. As before, I can see two aspects of the new mandate.

First and most obviously, preaching and teaching and hymns and prayers and processions and sacramental texts must no longer be shy about describing just what the gospel promises, what the Lord has in store. Will the City's streets be paved with gold? Modernity's preaching and teaching—and even its hymnody and sacramental texts—hastened to say, "Well, no, not really." And having said that, it had no more to say. In modern Christianity's discourse, the gospel's eschatology died the death of a few quick qualifications.

The truly necessary qualification is not that the City's streets will not be paved with real gold, but that gold as we know it is not real gold, such as the City will be paved with. What is the matter with gold anyway? Will goldsmiths who gain the Kingdom have nothing to do there? To stay with this one little piece of the vision, our discourse must learn again to revel in the beauty and flexibility and integrity of gold, of the City's true gold, and to say exactly why the world the risen Jesus will make must of course be golden, must be and will be beautiful and flexible and integral as is no earthly city. And so on and on.

Because Jesus lives to triumph, there will be the real Community, with its real Banquet in its real City amid its real Splendor, as no penultimate community or banquet or city or splendor is really just and loving or tasty or civilized or golden. The Church has to rehearse that sentence in all her assemblings, explicitly and in detail.

Second, the Church's assemblies must again become occasions of *see-ing*. We are told by Scripture that in the Kingdom this world's dimness of sight will be replaced by, as the old theology said it, "beatific vision." It is a right biblical insight that God first of all *speaks* and that our community with him and each other is first of all that we *hear* him and speak to him. It does not, however, follow, as Protestantism has made it follow, that to listen and speak we must blind ourselves. In this age, accurate hearing is paired with dimmed vision; it is precisely a promised chief mark of the Eschaton that accurate hearing will then be accompanied by glorious sight. And in this age, the Church must be the place where beatific vision is anticipated and trained.

Late antiquity suffered and lamented the same blindness with which postmodernity is afflicted, the same inability to see any Fulfillment up there before us. Gradually, as the Church worked out the theology, the Church made herself a place of such seeing.

She did this with the icons of the East and the windows and statues of the West. Protestantism supposed that folk in civil society already envisioned glorious Fulfillment, and needed no specific churchly envisioning, and therefore Protestantism for the most part eliminated the images and even where it retained them forgot how to use them. Protestantism's reliance on the world was here too an illusion, but here too an illusion it got away with for modernity's time. That time is over.

If we are in our time rightly to apprehend the eschatological reality of the gospel promise, we have to hear it with Christ the risen Lord visibly looming over our heads and with His living and dead saints visibly gathered around us. Above all, the Church must celebrate the Eucharist as the dramatic depiction, and as the succession of tableaux, that it intrinsically is. How can we point our lives to the Kingdom's great Banquet if its foretaste is spread before us with all the beauty of a McDonald's counter?

VII

A necessary afterword, lest all the above be misunderstood. It was modernity's great contribution to Christian history to have recognized the Church's mandated preferential options for the poor and oppressed with a clarity previously cultivated only in the monastic orders. It was perhaps the real substance of Protestantism that it demanded that all believers live with the attention to justice and charity which had for centuries been demanded only of those under special vows. We must maintain modernity's insight. The Church must indeed pursue God's action in the world.

But modernity's contribution will be lost if the Church fails to notice that modernity is dying and to face the new necessities mandated in that death. And *those* necessities—which I surely have not exhausted—are necessities of concretion and density and vision laid upon the life of the Church within herself.

7

Can We Have a Story? *(2000)*

Some time ago I published in this journal an essay on "How the World Lost Its Story" (October 1993). Modernity's project, I said with great unoriginality, was the attempt to maintain the Bible's grasp of reality while dispensing with the Bible's God. The long reading of Scripture in the West taught us— including those who did not notably obey Scripture—to perceive reality Scripture's way, as a history that makes a whole because it has a conclusion and so a plot. The modern West tried to inhabit this world while believing in no Teller of the story.

"Modernism" (if you are in the art-historical discourse) or "postmodernism" (if you are in the culture-diagnostic discourse) is merely the self-conscious collapse of modernity's project. It is the despairing or gleeful recognition that you cannot very well have a drama without a dramatist. The recognition should not, of course, have been quite so long in coming, but humanity has a notable capacity for persistence in self-deception. If God is not, or is of deist persuasion and entertains no histories, that leaves only two possibilities: either we are to make up the world's story, or the world just happens to have one. The latter possibility is remarkably implausible. As to the former, postmodernism proclaims the further unsurprising discovery that whatever universal stories we make up, whatever "metanarratives," must be oppressive.

Then, more recently, I reviewed here T. J. Clark's history of modernist painting (October 1999). Clark's diagnosis is very much like mine. Clark construes modernist painting—not modern painting, which begins much earlier—as prophecy of a world freed from the bourgeois passion for comprehensible wholes, a world whose actual advent turns out, alas, to make

62

no room for painting. The present moment is, he thinks, a "travesty" of the prophesied heaven, and hellish for art. Nevertheless, Clark wants to be hopeful: what we are in is not permanent hell but only "purgatory," Unfortunately, Clark can give no account of this hope that is in him.

With this pair of *First Things* pieces behind me, I thought I might revisit the subject at the journal's anniversary. So: can we have a story again?

It is not of course that there are no metanarratives still around. Modernity's social-political story—running from initial situation through contract, fictive, or actual, to the liberal society—retains its rule over our political self-understanding. And to very different effect, reality is forcing the hard sciences into story form. This would be a welcome development, if only popularizers did not make science's story itself another metanarrative.

The framework of the biological sciences has been narrative at least since Darwin. The implications of this have been disguised by the ideological insistence that below the narrative there must be deterministic mechanism. This ideology has no evidential basis, but is nevertheless taught in seventh grade as "what science tells us."

More remarkably, physics also assumes story form. The universe goes from big bang to big crunch/whimper; and at the other end of magnitude, we discover that an elementary particle just is its own history. Again ideologues among the scientists insist that a theory will yet be found that generates the cosmos and its story sheerly from timelessly underlying mathematics. Those not so desperate to avoid religion will be content to wait and see.

Moreover, postmodernist theories are themselves metanarratives. They are one and all stories about how it came to pass that we thought we had a story, and how we are now to be liberated from this delusion. (At an American Academy of Religion session a time or two ago, where the panelists were holding forth against oppressive hegemonic discourses, an elderly nonacademic finally interjected, "I wonder if you people know how you are oppressing me.") The form of these narratives is quite directly dependent on Scripture; they are narratives of fall and redemption.

Scientists generally believe their own narratives. Postmodernists are supposed not to. No one but John Rawls any longer believes modernity's social narrative, but we find none other to cling to. The joint effect is the problem. For the scientists' narratives do not seem to be about us, the political narrative no longer suffices, and the postmodernist narratives, which are obsessively about us, finally conjure spiraling contradiction. At the turn of the millennium, what awaits appears indeed to be an eschaton, Nietzsche's minus the superman—nihilism.

What is to be done within church and synagogue seems relatively plain. God's people must gather the courage to subordinate other narratives to their own, to proclaim and live within a metanarrative that is "meta" in superlative degree. If the story the Bible tells, running from creation to consummation and plotted by Exodus or Exodus-Resurrection, is *true*, it is not just our story but God's. If it is God's story, it is universal. And if it is the *triune* God's story, it cannot be oppressive.

Astrophysical cosmology and evolutionary narrative do not tell the encompassing story within which all others must be construed. For all this story's melodrama, it is an abstraction of reality, and believers must have the gall to say this, indeed to say that such abstraction touches reality only as it is construed within the story of God and His creation. Modernity's political narrative is not the comprehensive story within which the Church must be assigned its place. On the contrary, Augustine was right: the polities of this world are feeble imitations, for emergency conditions, of the divine polity.

If the coming period is to be any special period in the history of God's people, it will be the time when we are at once reduced to a sect and forced to claim universality with unprecedented boldness, when we must openly and intentionally be tellers of a particular story that is either a fairy tale or the comprehensive truth. If the turn of millennium indeed is anything special, it is the moment when God's people will have no choice but to summon such chutzpah and live by it.

Will we do it? Yes, because Hell's gates cannot prevail. Will any particular segment of God's people do it? Not necessarily; there is no promise that, for example, American Protestantism will not disappear or adopt for good and all the mask of Nietzsche's "last man."

Will the world itself have a story? God knows. Perhaps there is indeed to be a penultimate end of history, not an end of newspaper events but a global imposition of storyless procedural society, of Clark's "purgatory." In any case, church and synagogue, in charity for humankind, must pray against such a time of trial and meanwhile do what we can for our fellows.

We can but make the claim. We can note the post-modernist critique of metanarratives, and then offer a narrative that, because it is about God and us at once, is of a different species altogether. Will there be enough people in the world who entertain this obviously self-serving offer to make a difference? God knows. We can strengthen the voices of those in the scientific community who are considering the implications and possibilities of their disciplines' transformation into narrative; and we can actually produce such accounts of God's history with creation as show the truth and benefit of the sciences' stories. Will this suffice for the culture to acquire a new version of "what science says," a version that helps folk inhabit a coherent history rather than hinders it? God knows. We can not only expose the mythic character of modernity's social narrative—this is anyway almost universally admitted—but as synagogue and church display how there can be a polity shaped not only by measures to alleviate the love of domination, but also by love for the good. Will enough of the world look and emulate to make a difference? God knows.

God

8

The Hidden and Triune God *(2000)*

The following article is a first and perhaps still too programmatic attempt to respond to a friend's[1] urgent suggestion. I should, he said, think harder about the relation between the biblical God's triunity, of which I had written much, and his hiddenness, about which I had written little and in explicit context of his triunity even less.

Martin Luther is of course the master exponent of God's hiddenness, and will be a chief interlocutor. The theme, moreover, is especially dominant in the tract that of all his writing I have most read and reread, the *De servo arbitrio*. At each new reading or reflection I have said to myself, "This about God's impenetrable hiddenness is really great stuff! And moreover, it surely must somehow be true." But I have not known—or perhaps wanted to know—where to go from there.[2]

The problem about God, I have insofar long agreed with Luther, is not his metaphysical distance from us. After all, mere distance, however great and metaphysical, could not *hide* him but could only attenuate his visibility, and such a distancing of our view of God might very well only clarify the picture. Rather, God is hidden, and our problem with him is constituted precisely by the character and importunity of his *presence*.

In *De servo arbitrio*, God's hiding presence is instanced at two locations. The first[3] is his very present rule of his creation. If God were off in

1. David Tracy.

2. As I have with such other theologoumena as Luther's christological founding of sacrament—which, by way of response to the reviews in *International Journal of Systematic Theology* 1:1 (1999), my *Systematic Theology* does not attempt to rehabilitate but simply receives with rejoicing.

3. See esp. Luther, *WA*, 18:784–85.

the metaphysical spaces, we might in some moods complain of this, but the situation would have the advantage that we could construe buffering mediations between God and this world with its evils. But if God rules in his creation as its present Lord, the fact of even one tortured child must indeed mask his visage and that most horridly. Readers will recall Luther's famous dictum, that if we consider God's rule of his creation, and judge by any available standard, we must conclude "either that God is not or that he is wicked," *aut malum aut nullum esse Deum*.[4] I have always thought Ivan Karamazov a notable disciple of Luther, who simply chose the one horn of Luther's dilemma.

Another location[5] is christological. If the Antiochenes and many neo-Protestants were right about the relation between the person of Jesus and God the Son, if the Son were one subject and the Suffering Servant another, who works with the Son or points to him or is in whatever such prepositional relation to him, then Jesus' rejection and suffering on the cross—or Israel's rejection and suffering in Babylon and the ruins of Jerusalem— would not need to trouble our picture of divine power and bliss. But if in any straightforward sense of the copula the figure up there on the cross just *is* God the Son, or Israel in Exile just *is* the first-born whom the Lord called from Egypt, then the face without form or comeliness, from which we can but turn our own faces, is God's own.

A third location occurs in the *Commentary on Galatians*—not so great a favorite of mine but of course required reading. There Luther says that faith itself is a hiding of God in the soul.[6] Faith, he there says, is a very peculiar sort of perception, not so much a light in the heart as a darkness, within which Christ is present as was God in the darkness over Sinai. Faith is precisely the hidden indwelling of Christ; indeed it is God hiding himself from us by entering that most obscure of locations, our own hearts.

All this I have thought right from my first encounter with it. But I have not sufficiently tried to make it a systematic part of my own interpretation of God.

At most I have used Luther's insights therapeutically, to ward off a bowdlerized apophaticism which has recently been popular. That God is unknowable must not be construed to mean that he is but vaguely glimpsed through clouds of metaphysical distance, so that we are compelled—*and* at liberty—to devise namings and metaphors guided by our religious needs. It means on the contrary that we are stuck with the names and descriptions

4. Luther, *WA*, 18:784.

5. Luther, *WA*, 18:689.

6. Luther, *WA*, 1:28.

the biblical narrative contingently enforces, which seem designed always to offend somebody; it means that their *syntax* is hidden from us, so that we cannot identify synonyms or make translations. It means that we have no standpoint from which to relativize them and project more soothing visions.

Luther's famous "theology of the cross" has more or less the opposite force from that given it by many who recite the phrase: his point is that the vision of God-crucified crucifies us, and precisely in our religious needs and seekings at their most compelling and most innocent. I have used Luther's evocation of God's hiddenness to debunk pop-Feuerbach, and think the weapon good for the purpose; but using so powerful a theologoumenon only in this way is indeed shooting mosquitoes with an elephant gun.

So why have I not gone after bigger game? My thinking has been moved above all by the conviction that the doctrine of the Trinity is both the great *specificum* and the great task of Christian theology; and the attempt to integrate serious trinitarianism with Luther-style discourse about God's hiddenness opens a very daunting can of worms.

According to classic trinitarianism, Father, Son, and Spirit are distinct identities as and only as poles of the relations between them. The Father begets the Son and breathes the Spirit, and just and only so there is the Father; and just and only so there is the one God. So the classical doctrine. And I want to go on to say: the Spirit liberates the Father and the Son for each other, and just and only so there is the Spirit; and just and only so there is God. And, the Son reconciles the Father and the Spirit, and just and only so there is the Son; and just and only so there is God. Is hiding yet another such relation or web of relations? If it is, how does it fit with the others?

Or is hiddenness a simple predicate of the one God, like omnipotence or omniscience? To be sure, in my own development of doctrine, there *are* no "simple" predicates of the one God. Attributes supposed to be true of the one God are properly predicated of the life lived between Jesus the Son and the One he called Father, in the Spirit of their freedom, so that a divine predicate is properly construed only when the different role of each divine identity in this aspect of their mutual life is told. To speak of omniscience, the Father sees himself and his works in the Son, with the creative freedom of the Spirit, and so we can say that the one God is omniscient. If now we want hiddenness to be a predicate of God, does then the Son's hiddenness on the cross hide God the Father from himself? Or to speak of omnipotence, the Spirit frees the Father to originate from nothing by works he lays upon the Son. Do the evils in creation cloud the Father's intent or the Spirit's joy?

Or is hiddenness a divine reality in some other fashion altogether? Let me instance two major theological enterprises which do, each in a way unique to itself, integrate hiddenness and triunity.

A major stream of Orthodox theology, going back to Gregory Palamas,[7] adapts some language of the Cappadocians and distinguishes three modes of being in God: the triune identities or persons, the one life constituted in the perichoresis of their "energies," and God's "natural entity," his "ousia" or "physis." Systematically, this theology posits a third mode of deity, a "divine *ousia*," in order to say that while God takes us to share in the mutual life of the three, so fully that our participation can even be called "deification," there remains a depth in which God is non-participable, which is epistemically to say, unknowable even apophatically, which is finally to say, "hidden." Here the hiddenness of God is a depth in which he is inalienably closed to us.

For the very different other instance, Karl Barth notoriously made a dialectic of revealedness and hiddenness the very root of trinitarian doctrine. "We arrive," wrote Barth, "at the doctrine of the Trinity by no other way than by" a conceptual analysis of the revelation—that is to say unhiding—of God in Christ.[8] Barth then makes two runs at such analysis, the second the more serious.[9] This begins with the maxim that "revelation means in the Bible the self-unveiling to humanity of the God who essentially cannot be unveiled to humanity."[10] Nevertheless, unveiling happens, that is, God occurs as other than his inviolably hidden selfhood.

Since unveiling in fact happens, there must be in God the possibility that it happens, there must be in God a *Bedingung der Möglichkeit* of this reality of God as other than God; and so we know the distinction of the Son from the Father. Thus revealedness is both an event that happens with God *simpliciter*, and a character appropriated to the Son—in a way that works rather differently from the traditional doctrine of trinitarian appropriations.

And then the other side of the dialectic: God is unveiled *as himself*, and that is, as the one who cannot be unveiled. Just so, the unveiling begins as and remains the underivable and unconstruable act of the God who is unveiled; God remains hidden Lord of his own unhiding. And again, since this is so, there must be in God the possibility thereof; and so we know the distinction of the Father from the Son. Thus hiddenness both is a fact of God, and is appropriated to the Father, again in an untraditional way.

I owe very much to both of these theologies. But their proposals at precisely this point can for me only be examples of what not to do. To the

7. For my analysis in slightly fuller form and the references, see Jenson, *ST*, 1:152ff.

8. Barth, *KD* I/1, 32.

9. For my analysis in slightly greater detail and the citations, see Jenson, *God after God*, 97–102.

10. Barth, *KD* I/1, 332–33.

extent that Palamitic theology tends to identify the divine *ousia* as the one God, and does so in virtue of a hiddenness not characterizing the revealed and revealing life of the three persons, Palamitism is ironically afflicted by temptation to a subtle modalism: God himself is an entity elevated above and immune to the events of his triune life with us. And to the extent that Barth tends to appropriate to the Father uniquely the hiddenness by which God maintains his deity even while revealing it, his theology is ironically afflicted by a subtle subordinationism. I say "ironically" in both cases, because of course the Eastern temptation is generally thought to be subordinationism and the Western to be modalism.

So how would *I* do it? Let me start with the observation that the hiddenness of God as Luther construes it is an impenetrability of his *moral* agency and only so an epistemic limit. And with the further observation that therein Luther seems faithful to Scripture: when Paul cites Isaiah and Job that God's ways are "unsearchable," and asks "Who has known the mind of the Lord?"[11] it is the moral problematic of God's providence which resists our insight; and so it goes throughout Scripture. The scriptural hiddenness of God is not primally a matter of our epistemic weaknesses or God's ontological uniqueness.

The locus of God's hiddenness is his reality as a moral agent involved with other agents, his history with us. Thus the locus of God's hiddenness is the very substance of all trinitarian teaching. For fundamentally, the doctrine of Trinity is simply the insistence, against all objections from otherwise founded intuitions of deity, that God in himself is not other than he is in his history with us. "Father," "Son," and "Holy Spirit" are the biblical names for the *dramatis personae dei*, the dramatic agents whom Scripture in fact names as carriers of the one divine agency in God's saving history with us. And the "relations" by which in classical doctrine the three subsist in the first place are plot lines of the narrative constituted between them and with us, of the story Scripture in fact tells. If, then, God's history with us hides him, God is hidden precisely by his triunity, by the mutual life of Father, Son, and Holy Spirit.

We have therefore to consider God's hiddenness three times, starting each time from the particular role of one of the divine identities within their joint moral agency. I will start with the easy one.

As Orthodoxy, or some Orthodox theology, teaches us, the one ultimate fact is the mere Fatherhood of God the Father.[12] It is not even quite

---

11. Rom 11:28–36.

12. The great sponsor of this teaching in the West has been one book, Zizioulas, *Being as Communion*; most succinctly to the immediate point, 41.

right to say that the ultimate fact is God. There is not God, who then happens to love Israel. There is the One who raises Israel from Egypt; and the ultimacy of this election, to be demonstrated finally only when all nations flow to Zion, is the fact that there is God. There is not God, who then happens to be fatherly to the one Israelite Jesus; rather there is the Father of this Son, and the ultimacy of this Fatherhood is the fact that there is God. And that God is thus in God a source of God is the possibility of God being also the source of things other than himself, of creatures, and the impossibility of there being anything other than God that is not created by him.

Thus there is a Source of all being that neither we nor yet God himself can get behind, for reasons or other explanations; and that is the Father merely as Father. There is a German word for which I have been unable to devise a translation: *hinterfragen*. So I have to make my point in that language: *Man kann die Tatsache des Vaters Vaterseins nicht hinterfragen*. Clumsily in English: one cannot question one's way back behind the Father's Fatherhood.

And so we have a first aspect of God's hiddenness: because there is the Father, theodicy is finally impossible. When we seek sufficient reason for what is or occurs, we will if we keep going long enough be reduced to mere pointing at the fact of the Father. And the fact of the Father has no reason. Thus all propositions of the form, "God willed or allowed this thing because . . ." must, if pushed far enough, lose purchase on reality.

We may put it so: a God whose plotted actions *could* be, in Paul's phrase, "searched," would not be God in Paul's sense or in that of Scripture generally. In the divine life, it belongs to the Father to terminate such searching.

This does not mean that penultimate theodicies are not sometimes meaningful: that it does not in some contexts help to distinguish between what God wants and what he permits; or that it does not in other contexts help to say that some events have their place within a more comprehensive situation that is the best possible; or that created free wills are not accountable for events in a different way than God is. But it does mean that these and similar moves cannot finally get God off the hook. His ways will remain morally unsearchable, even as they are the very matrix of all righteousness.

We have not yet reckoned with the actuality of God's actions, only with their possibility. We have mentioned creation only in respect of its being created, and only incidentally in respect of its actual character. It was the first of the offenses that hid God for Luther, that the ways of the actual creation are very much in need not just of reasons but of justifications, and that God does not provide them. With the way in which the actuality of creation hides the goodness of God, we are brought to the one in, through, and for whom all things are created, the Son.

And when we come to the Son we come to the man on the cross. For we have no access to what would have been the case had the second identity of God been other than the crucified and risen Jesus. Presumably God could have been Father, Son, and Spirit otherwise than as the Father of Jesus, Jesus the Son, and the Spirit who frees them to love one another. But the fact of the Father, as just discussed prevents us—and perhaps even God—from assigning any content to that "otherwise"; we know no other *Logos* or Son, and this is not ignorance. The only *Logos* or Son we—or even the Father— may reckon with is the Suffering Servant, and him exiled and trampled and crucified.

What I called two locations of God's hiddenness in Luther's writing Luther never distinguishes that way, and now we must see why. The second triune identity is *Logos* and Son. The *Logos* that God speaks to command heaven and earth into being is no other Word than the Word of the cross, the Word the Father speaks by the mission, death, and resurrection of Israel and this Israelite. The Son in whom—according to the great patristic and mediaeval theologoumenon—the Father recognizes himself and understands what he wills to do, is not an abstraction, a pattern of could-bes and might-have-beens, but the actual people in the desert and the actual son of this people on the cross. Indeed the Father knows *himself* only in a people and man of sorrows, acquainted with grief.

And so we have a second hiddenness of God: the second commandment, the rejection of idolatry. For it is as we seek to evade the Exile and the cross that we create idols.

We do not want God to appear in our world as the Suffering Servant, whether Servant Israel or the One Israelite. We do not want to recognize him in weakness and rejection. And this is not a mere moral failing or adventitious flaw; it is not a feature of some religions or cultures only, but defines the human situation. Until we are swept into the perfect community of God, we are bound to seek each our own good, whether grandly or pitiably, whether as a master of the universe or as the most desperate refugee, and therein we are bound to practice religion as Karl Barth describes it, the recruitment of the absolute to our finite ends. If we pray, we have no choice but to pray for our needs, mystically or rhetorically sublime as we may. As we are likely these days to put it, our self-fulfillment is incomplete without some spirituality. We therefore demand divinity that somehow or other completes us, if only by its superior nothingness. And we do not want to be completed with more suffering and helplessness. But the real God, even primally for himself, has the face of the Suffering Servant; so if we want visages of immunity and serenity, we have to make them up for ourselves, whether we hew them like second Isaiah's God-carvers or deploy them in the sophisticated mind's eye or practice theology.[13]

Current research[14] suggests that Martin Luther's initiating problem was not in fact that of finding a gracious God to meet his need as sinner—which would, after all, have been a prime piece of idolatry. It was rather the traditional Augustinian problem of knowing whether he indeed worshipped the true God, defined as God you cannot use; it was the problem of avoiding idolatry. Does not every religious move I make turn me from the true God and erect an idol, by its inevitable inner self-seeking? His initial answer, not very Augustinian, was the theology of the cross found in the Heidelberg theses: God comes to us so exclusively in suffering and rejection that no one could possibly turn to him out of self-serving. Later, according to current findings, he turned to a very different sort of solution, but that need not diminish the interest of this first theologoumenon.

And finally, there is the Spirit, in his own entity very nearly *defined* as hiddenness: "The *pneuma* blows where it wills, and you hear the sound of it, but you do not know where it comes from or where it goes. So it is with everyone who is born of the Spirit."[15]

How does that work out in trinitarian teaching? The Spirit is God's freedom, in a recent slogan, his openness to the future. The Spirit is not, to be sure, freedom as a mere quality of the Father or the Son; the Spirit is freedom as yet an identity of God, that is, he is the third party whose self-giving frees the Father and the Son for each other, frees the Father to find himself in the other of the Suffering Servant and frees the Son to be the Father's Servant, cost what it may.

The Spirit is God as his own future. Since God is his own future, that future cannot be alien to him or beyond his will, as ours can. But, though it strains the capabilities of language to say it, somehow God the Spirit is truly a *future* for the Father and the Son, that is, surprising when it comes and present only in anticipation. The Spirit frees God to surprise himself. If I may stretch language on the rack by one last turn, there is in God something like a game of hide-and-seek. And it is of course that word "hide" I have been working to get in.

Here, I suggest, is the encompassing mode of God's hiddenness. God, after all, "*is* Spirit," the only such definition in Scripture. As we are creatures and children of the triune God, we are involved in the play of an infinite

---

13. All honor to Feuerbach *ipse*.

14. For an introduction, David S. Yeago, "The Catholic Luther."

15. John 3:8.

freedom. This is not the empty freedom of post-modern horror; it is the freedom of a good story, and the story is determinate as that enacted by the Servant and not someone else. But conversely, the story is drawn on by a freedom that is there even for the Father and the Son, and therefore is a story full of divinely drastic turnings and detours. As we live in that story, we may be sure of the character of its outcome, by which after all all its surprises are granted in the first place; but we do not know where God may be hiding around the next corner.

The Samaritan does not expect a beaten-up Jew in his way nor the Jew a Samaritan benefactor. According to a beautiful meditation on the passage by my sainted doctor-father, Peter Brunner,[16] the one hiding on the side to see what will happen is God. And what if the suggestion should be appropriate also, that the Samaritan is first of all the one who tells the story?[17] Then on the way to Jerusalem it was the Father's question as he waiting: will the Son also go by on the other side?

16. Brunner, *Erbarmen*.

17. I owe the suggestion in adducing this tradition here to Wallace Alston, Director of the Center of Theological Inquiry.

9

Identity, Jesus, and Exegesis *(2008)*

I

Faith and theology ask, "Who is Jesus?" because the primal proclamation of the gospel, "Jesus is risen," is a simple subject-predicate proposition, with the personal name "Jesus" as the subject. That the gospel is indeed gospel therefore depends on who Jesus is; the proposition "Stalin is risen" would not be good news for many. "The unconditional friend of publicans and sinners is risen" is good news to anyone willing to try those shoes on; "the chief keeper of the gulag is risen" would be good news to very few.

Thus, those who encounter the gospel and try to understand it must know who Jesus is. If they do not already know, they must ask, and the Church must respond. We will find that our hypothesized inquirer's demand turns out to involve several different but related requests for identification.

In what follows, we will briefly consider the general notion of identity. We will go on to sketch its role in the theological tradition; the survey will along the way encounter places where the tradition impacts the question before this group. We will then turn more directly to some of the different but related senses of "Who is Jesus?"

II

The notion of identity is hard to specify directly, which is not necessarily a deficiency. Proceeding in the oblique fashion often appropriate to fundamental notions, we may begin by noting that we successfully, and often interchangeably, make use of proper names[1] and what Bertrand Russell iso-

---

1. In the commonsensical sense, not in that of logical positivism.

78

lated as "uniquely identifying descriptions." We successfully say things like "Mary Jones [proper name] is happy," attributing happiness to one person and not necessarily to any other, that is, *identifying* her as the one of whom we wish to say this. And we successfully say, "The current president of the United States [identifying description] is a Republican," attributing being a Republican to one person and, so far as this sentence goes, to none other. What these sentences must first succeed in doing, in order to do what they set out to do, is to specify an identity, which it seems they indeed manage to do. This may be all we need to know about the notion of identity as such.

It does seem however, that the temporality of the things that might have or be such an identity requires further observation. Identities must surely be diachronic: an entity's identity is what allows it to be identified by the same proper name or identifying description on different occasions without equivocation. If I cannot meaningfully say, "Mary Jones is now happy but may not be tomorrow"—whether this is true or false—it does not seem that "Mary Jones" succeeds in its mission of identification. My identity is my identity *with* myself across time; and here we are getting into more problematic and metaphysical waters, for it is possible to lose faith in one's own diachronic self-identity, as did the protagonist of Sartre's *Nausée*.

Thus, "self" and "identity" are closely related notions and indeed are often used interchangeably. To lose myself or to lose my identity would be the same disaster. This leads to a further point: the most natural use of "identity" is not in discourse about pots and pans or galaxies but in discourse about persons. Doubtless this is because the diachronic self-identity of persons can become problematic, as that of cookware or galaxies does not.[2] Whether it can actually be lost is another question, to which I suspect the answer is no. Having an identity is something *persons* do—or want or hope to do, or even not to do.

Let us say that an identity, in recent usage, is what can be repeatedly specified by a proper name or an identifying description,[3] particularly with respect to what, again in more recent usage, may be called a person. There is doubtless more that could be said, but I think this is enough to be going on with.

III

In the theological tradition, much of the semantic field now covered by "identity" was covered by *hypostasis*, and its various—invariably

---

2. Though when we get to quantum behavior, things are not so clear.

3. Or perhaps by other of the devices linguistic analysts call "indexicals."

unsuccessful—translations.[4] The word was adapted, during the trinitarian and christological labors of the fourth and fifth centuries, from antecedent and philosophical use. There it had been used more or less interchangeably with *ousia*—which we sometimes translate "nature" and sometimes "substance"[5]—for "real something." For the purposes of their trinitarian proposals, the fourth-century "Cappadocian" fathers made an ontologically innovative distinction between *hypostasis* and *ousia*. They appropriated the former for one aspect of being a real something: that a real something is *distinguishable* from others that otherwise are the same, and just so is *countable*. The *hypostasis* of something is the distinguishable and so countable x that has/is some *ousia*—for example, "Peter" picks out an x that has/is the *ousia* "human," just as do "Paul" and "Andrew" and others. Thus, a fundamental piece of Cappadocian trinitarian analysis:[6] Father, Son, and Spirit are three *hypostaseis* who have/are one *ousia*, deity.[7] Of course, the Greek thinkers had known about persons being countable somethings that share humanity but would have regarded stipulating Father, Son, or Spirit—or indeed Peter, Paul, or Andrew—*by* such relations as an ontological put-down. In their view, it was *what* I am that is worthy of note, not *that* I am it or that *I* am it.

Thus, the creed of Nicaea-Constantinople affirms of the Son—who is Jesus—that he is *homoousios* (note the *ousi* between the prefix and suffix) with God the Father; we struggle to translate, and have most recently come up with "of one being." It was the Cappadocian analysis that the Father and the Son are nonetheless two, as being distinguishable *hypostaseis*, that enabled the affirmation.[8]

That the Son is *homoousios tō patri*, "of one being with the Father," is said without qualification of the Son of God and of the subject of the following creedal narrative; and so it is said simultaneously of one of the three who are God *and* of the second-Temple male Jew Jesus of Nazareth. This of course provoked a question about the relation between this one person's being God and his being a human. The Council of Chalcedon in 451 once

---

4. By and large, scholars have given up and now simply take the transliteration as a loanword.

5. Thereon hangs a tale of endless conceptual confusion.

6. Which won out at Constantinople and became the linguistic vehicle of ecumenical dogma.

7. This of course raises the question why Father, Son, and Spirit are not three gods, as Peter, Paul, and Andrew are three humans. The question was brilliantly answered, but pursuing that would be afield from our purpose.

8. At Constantinople. At Nicaea, folk had little idea what they were saying when they said the Son was *homoousios tō patri*; they just knew that Arius had once said he wasn't.

again recruited the term *hypostasis*,[9] now from its trinitarian use. There is in Jesus the Son, they said, but one *hypostasis* of two *ousiai*: there is but one identifiable and countable x to be whatever is to be said of the Son because he is God and whatever is to be said of the Son because he is human. The lively concern behind this rather lifeless formulation was the insistence by Cyril, the great fifth-century bishop of Alexandria, that there is but one protagonist of all that the Gospels narrate of the Christ, whether what he is said to do or suffer is a divine thing to do or suffer or a human thing to do or suffer.[10] God the Son was born of Mary[11] and hung on the cross;[12] and Jesus of Nazareth saves sinners and rules the universe from the Father's right hand.

Thus, it is ecumenical dogma,[13] now in more modern terms: you cannot accurately pick out Jesus of Nazareth without in fact simultaneously picking out the second person of the Trinity, and you cannot accurately pick out the second person of the Trinity without in fact simultaneously picking out Jesus of Nazareth. It seems to me that this is already a rather important result for our project. Unless we are willing to reject the historic teaching of the Church at its very heart, we must obey the rule: when we ask about the identity of Jesus, historical and systematic questions cannot be separated.

IV

We can come to the same result by another route, which leads more directly back into the question of Jesus' identification. The character of the predicate

9. By way of a compromise formula of Cyril of Alexandria.

10. To see what Cyril and, less decisively, the council opposed, one might read Theodore of Mopsuestia's commentary on John, which laboriously labels each deed or experience of the protagonist according to whether he does it as God or as man. Or, most unfortunately, one might consider Pope Leo the Great's *Tome*, affixed to Chalcedon by his legats' insistence, which in effect says that in Christ deity and humanity each does its thing. To be sure, since Leo was a great pope and the council did accept the *Tome*, we must in other contexts interpret his language *in bonam partem*.

11. Thus, affirmation of Mary as *Theotokos*, the Mother of God, became and has remained a chief test of orthodoxy and indeed of theological acuteness. *Sancta Maria, mater Dei . . .*

12. It later became dogma that *unus ex trinitate est pro nobis*, "one of the Trinity has suffered for us."

13. I am aware that "dogma" has acquired a variety of adventitious associations, most of them likely to put readers off. But there is no satisfactory other word to denote that small body of teaching that the church has formally determined is essential to the gospel. And it is a very small body of teaching indeed; it is certainly *not* the mass of what churches have mostly taught or "theologians" opined.

". . . is risen" imposes a sort of conceptual backflip, for ". . . is risen" is not only a concept predicated of Jesus' story; it is itself part of the story.[14]

Indeed, that Jesus is specifically *risen* is the precise point of identity (that word again!) between the various common names and concepts or titles that may be predicated of Jesus, and the particularity of this person. "Lord" or "Messiah" or "divine" or ". . . redeems" or ". . . saves" can—even if in some or all cases falsely—be predicated of anyone, for they are not themselves biographical items. But ". . . is risen" *at once* ascribes a universal significance to the one of whom it is predicated and is an item of that one's particular story. Thus, in the case of "Jesus is risen," the person determines the universal significance, and the universality is that of the individual person—which is, of course, the great offense of the gospel. "Is risen" is of a logical sort not contemplated by the Greek thinkers; it predicates universal significance of a particular person and is itself an identifying item of his biography.

When, then, we ask—and now, we should note, we find ourselves following the pattern of the Gospels—"Who is the one who was born of Mary and taught Torah as if he were the author and cast out the demons and . . . and was crucified *and rose*?" we are asking a question that is at once historical and dogmatic. That Jesus is, for example, "of one being with the Father"—or that he is not—is part of a possible answer. Note that this answer responds to the question about "the one who was born of Mary" and so on, so that *if* it is true, no narrative of "the historical Jesus" can be correct that conflicts with it.

And then there is another flip—the last such, I think. It is itself an item in the Gospels that the Crucified and the Risen are the same one person, that ". . . is risen" is not predicated of Jesus of Nazareth in any tricky sense; a chief locus is the story of "doubting Thomas." Also according to dogma, the two must be straightforwardly the same one embodied person; consider, for example, the confession required of Berengar,[15] that the body that was broken on the cross and the body broken on the eucharistic table are the

---

14. The principal error of Rudolf Bultmann's students was to deny this—the case of Bultmann himself is complicated by his denial that any story at all needs to be told. Neither Ebeling nor Fuchs denied that Jesus is risen. What they taught was that "Jesus is risen" is our necessary true *response to* the Gospel narrative, not *part of* the narrative itself. In this, they intended to carry on the tradition of Wilhelm Herrmann. They were in my judgment wrong, but if they are to be charged with error, the error must be properly located.

15. An eleventh-century advocate of an extreme Augustinian view of the sacrament, who recanted by signing a confession beginning, with splendid rhythm, *Ego Berengarius . . .*

same body.[16] Therefore, no item even of the narrative by which we can make that first identification, of who it is that is supposed to be risen, can be—historically!—true if it conflicts with dogma. (Of course, this rule holds only if he is indeed risen and if the Church's dogma rightly construes that.) Precisely for the sake of historical truth, we are bound to construe also the pre-resurrection story of Jesus by the christological and trinitarian dogmas.

V

A first sense of the question, "Who is Jesus?" is often referred to as a search for "the historical Jesus." The question in this case is, "Who is it of whom '... is risen' is predicated?" Already this question is theologically decisive. For disputes about "the historical Jesus" cannot, in cases where the identifying descriptions proposed are not mutually compatible, be disputes within the same religion. For example, what members of the "Jesus Seminar" say they believe in, and what those who think of Jesus as the final prophet of the kingdom and the final interpreter of the Torah believe in, are two different gospels. No one can simultaneously cling, for life and death, to "Jesus, the ultimate beach guru, is risen"[17] and, with the Gospels themselves, to "Jesus, the final prophet of Israel's kingdom, is risen."[18]

"The historical Jesus" is not, however, a reliably univocal term.[19] In scholarly jargon, it often refers to the figure reconstructed by historical-critical research. But in normal usage, "the historical Jesus" will less counterintuitively be taken to name someone who occupied time and space together with, for example, Tiberius Caesar and the reader of these pages,

16. They are, to be sure, that body in different ways. According to Paul, the risen body is a *sōma pneumatikon*, whereas the body that died is a *sōma psychikon*. In Paul's view, however, this does not mitigate either the bodiliness of the Risen One or the identity of his body as dead and risen (1 Cor 15:43–44). As to what "body" means in "Jesus' dead organic body and risen spiritual body are the same body," discussing that would take us far beyond the bounds of this volume. Here we must rest with the proposition itself.

17. This formulation of course gives the seminar too much credit; most of its members do not apparently suppose that anyone is risen.

18. Nor will a Fregean account of reference allow this, as was once suggested in our consultation. "The morning star" and "the evening star" can indeed refer to the same thing, even though they are different descriptions. But many sets of descriptions predicated of the same thing make contraries, that is, a set of propositions of which at least one must be false. "The ultimate beach guru" and "the final prophet of the kingdom," given any historically plausible account of "guru" and "prophet of the kingdom," make such a set.

19. For a longer account, see Jenson, *ST*, 1:171–78.

and who must be supposed to have done and suffered many things not now recoverable by research.

It does not detract from the necessity of historical-critical research—to which we will come—to note that simple identification of the historical Jesus with any critically obtainable reconstruction will not do for Christian theology. For such an identification depends on a radically idealist notion of "historical"—unless the historical-critical investigation in question is in the mind of God, or is one that humans could continue forever. In the following I will therefore mean by "the historical Jesus" what really happened with the person of that name, however we find (or do not find) out about it. For the class of historians' reconstructions I will use "the historians' Jesus."

Nor is identification of the historical Jesus with the historians' Jesus philosophically necessary. The Jesus who occupied time and space with us did much that is not recoverable by historians. Moreover, we are with equal surety entitled to suppose that some of this may be beyond historians' grasp not only in fact but in principle.[20] That any event that actually happened in time and space must be able to appear in a proposition of the form "On the available evidence, it is very likely/unlikely that x occurred" is a metaphysical doctrine that carries no certainty on its face. It is a doctrine deeply embedded in modernity's habits of thought, but not more necessary for all of that.

The phrase "however we find . . . out about" the historical Jesus points to a decisive circumstance for the project of this book. For we now have to note that believers' grasp of *this* historical Jesus has never depended only on the evidence to which "historical-critical" scholarship has confined its efforts—the New Testament, a sparse offering of other very early mentions, and a more or less arbitrary selection of other "gospels."

Besides the New Testament, there are two bodies of testimony to which believers have in fact turned for information about Jesus. There is the messianic witness of the Old Testament; and it does not matter to the present point how we understand that witness to have been made. And there is the spiritual tradition of the Church. Thus, two phrases from Isaiah, evoking a "man of sorrows, acquainted with grief," and the Church's iconography these phrases shaped, have doubtless more determined what believers know as the Jesus who came from Nazareth and had a mission in Israel than have any five pages of the Gospel. To be sure, it is a founding dogma of modern exegesis that believers' reliance on such sources is a native mistake; but whether this dogma is true is the very question at issue.

20. If Jesus did "miracles," perhaps these belong in this epistemological category. The resurrection itself is of course the key and central matter.

Believers' ordinary procedure is of course as preposterous as modernity thinks it is—*unless* it is indeed true that God is the specifically triune God; that Jesus, just as the historical Jesus, is the second identity of this God; and that this God is the Creator, so that what is true for him is all the facts there are. I have just listed two dogmas straight and given Cyril's construal of another. Our troubles with the historical Jesus—and historical Paul and historical whomever—were inaugurated by thinkers who exploited modernity's historical consciousness specifically and intentionally to escape "the yoke of dogma." But what if the Church's dogma were a necessary hermeneutical principle of historical reading, because it describes the true ontology of historical being?

Because the Church Fathers worshiped the specifically triune God, they understood the word of the Old Testament as the Word who is eternally with God and is God, and who has as the very same Word appeared among us "in these latter days"; they heard the testimony of the Old Testament as the voice of Christ and indeed *could* not hear these texts as otherwise. And it is of course a commonplace of churchly awareness that the gospel-word in the Church is Christ speaking. Now then, whose testimony to the historical truth about Jesus might the scholarly reader more want than that of the very person—remember, there is just one identity here—whose biography she or he is pursuing?

The question must of course arise, Are there then no limits to what believers may rightly say they know about the historical Jesus? It is here that we should in my judgment see a role for "historical-critical" research. There is undoubtedly much more to the historical Jesus—as the term is here used—than such research can recover; and I have proposed that other parts of Scripture and the Church's tradition can discover some of this to faith. But we should not claim to know anything about the historical Jesus that plainly conflicts with what we at any time take to be historically-critically established.[21] To be sure, "the assured results of critical research" are notoriously not all that assured; today's certainty may be the victim of tomorrow's new research paradigm. And indeed, what occasions reexamination of an accepted bit of historical-critical reconstruction may be precisely its clash with what believers think we know from, say, Isaiah. Together with the general probabilism of historical-critical knowledge, all of this means that we must carry our working picture of Jesus with a certain tentativeness—which is a theological good thing.

21. We must remember that such negatives as "Jesus did not do miracles" or "Jesus was not raised in the body" are *not* results of research and could never be.

VI

So what indeed if the Church's dogma were a necessary hermeneutical principle? What if we did take seriously those backflips that the resurrection performs on "Who is Jesus?" It will, I think, be much the best if we finally abandon sheer abstraction and display the consequences by doing an actual piece of exegesis. I choose the scene of Gethsemane because the mutual impact of dogma and text is in this case not far to seek, and because the question the mutuality raises are formidable and important.

The story by itself immediately provokes a question of dogmatic proportions: Could Jesus in Gethsemane have chickened out? Could he have said, "Father, you want this coming confrontation but I do not," and fled to Galilee? And a reader with even the most minimal theological concern cannot help asking also, "If he had, what then?"

Neither simple answer to the first question seems satisfactory. If we come to the text from a usual churchly catechesis, we are likely to say that since Jesus is God he could not have given in to fear; but this answer ruins the Gethsemane story, turning the prayer and anguish into pretense.[22] If, on the other hand, we are unbothered by the claim for his divinity, or suppose that we can bracket it out methodologically,[23] we are free to say that the story clearly supposes he could have fled, choosing his wants over the Father's. But this reading also turns out to ruin the story. For the Gethsemane scene has its drama only as part of the larger Gospel narrative; and this narrative, particularly in its presumably earliest canonical version by Mark, is shaped by the sense that Jesus' life is governed by a certain divine necessity, and that this necessity is not external to his personhood.

Indeed, it would appear that the only answer that preserves the narrative integrity both of the pericope itself and of the story of which it is one incident is that he could have fled and that this too, if it had occurred, would have belonged to the divine necessity that determined his life. That is, crudely, that he is God and could also in that capacity have ceased to be godly. But where does that leave us theologically?

There was some discussion among participants in this project whether attention to dogma might limit the range of readings available for a particular text, and whether this would be a good or a bad thing. In the present case, dogma clearly does exclude some readings: precisely the two readings initially considered. If we follow Church dogma, we cannot say that Jesus

22. A path that all too many preachers and teachers have taken, great thinkers among them.

23. I do not think we can do that, but of course the exegetical establishment has for centuries thought we could.

could obviously have decided for what he himself wanted, thus reading the story simply as a dramatic turning point in a human life; for dogma insists on his inseparable deity. And we cannot say that he could not have decided for his wants rather than God's; for dogma insists on his humanity—and since even if Jesus did not in fact sin, as the tradition has maintained, the whole point of noting that he did not sin is that he was genuinely tempted.[24]

Thus, the readings excluded by concern for the Gospels' narrative integrity and those excluded by dogma coincide. Perhaps this observation can teach us something both about the *way* in which dogma should guide exegesis and about the root of dogma itself.

The Gethsemane pericope narrates one side of a conversation. A conversation between whom? Since the conversation is in prayer, and since Jesus is a Jew, the one partner must clearly be the God of Israel, whom Jesus here as elsewhere addresses as his "Father." But who is the other partner in the conversation, the speaker of the side that we hear? Who says, "Remove this cup from me; yet, not what I want, but what you want"?[25] The obvious—indeed tautologous—answer is the man Jesus of Nazareth, shortly to be in deadly conflict unless this Father relents. But if we follow standard christological teaching, that answer poses a problem—or rather a whole nest of them.

Who prays here? According to Church teaching defined by the Council of Chalcedon (451), the protagonist of all scenes in the Gospels' narrative is a single person, who is truly God—the Son—and truly man—the individual Jesus of Nazareth, the Christ of Israel.[26] If we say it was simply the man Jesus of Nazareth who prayed, and observe that he did so in such fashion as to distinguish what he wanted from what the Father wanted, where does that leave the Son? Outside the conversation? Or, supposing that the Son agrees with the Father, are we to suppose a diversity of wants between God the Son and the man Jesus, internal to the one person? Is this supposition intelligible at all? It should be noted that we cannot rescue it by invoking psychological phenomena such as "being of two minds," since God the Son does not inhabit Jesus as a fact of his psychological structure[27]—indeed, the Son does not "inhabit" Jesus at all; he simply *is* Jesus, as Jesus then simply *is* the Son.

---

24. Heb 2:18; 4:15.

25. Mark 14:36 NRSV. The crudity of this translation, over against earlier English versions, rises almost to confessional significance. But it is the translation in use, and it answers to my needs in this essay.

26. Council of Chalcedon, *Definitio fidei,* 1:86.14–87.2.

27. The great attempt to solve the christological puzzles on that line was made by Athanasius' overzealous disciple Apollinaris and was quickly found wanting.

Should we therefore instead say that it is God the Son who says to the Father—by himself or jointly with Jesus—"Not my wants, but yours"? But is a divergence of wants between the Father and the Son, who with the Spirit are supposed to be but one God, thinkable? Jürgen Moltmann has made it an axiom of his theology that it is. His chief proof text is the so-called cry of dereliction on the cross, which he understands as marking an actual abandonment of God the Son by God the Father, a rupture of the concord between them. For my own part, I can only say that I am always tempted by such dramatic excess but cannot persuade myself that it is here justified by Scripture as a whole.

We have been noting ways in which dogma can constrain our reading of a text, in the case of the present text in considerable part by making it a puzzlement. Yet at the beginning of this essay we noted how the same or related puzzlements emerge from the narrative structure of the text itself, suggesting that our use of the dogma as a hermeneutical principle is not an imposition from outside. And now we may begin to perceive how the text can, vice versa, exert pressure on dogmatic thinking: is there indeed any way out of the questions the text poses but the frightening one earlier mentioned, that at Gethsemane—or over against the temptation to summon the angels and come down from the cross or at a hundred other points of the Gospel narrative—the triunity and so, by the dogma of the Trinity, the godhead of God was somehow at risk? We will come back to that.

The Gethsemane pericope narrates, besides a conversation, the making of a decision: that Jesus would do what the Father wanted rather than what he wanted. Who made this decision? The man Jesus of Nazareth? God the Son? Both? If we say just Jesus, and if we presume the concord of God the Son's will with that of the Father, this posits two possibly differing wills in one person of Jesus the Son. Does that make sense—psychology again not being the point? If we say God the Son, as somehow other than the man Jesus, either this means that Jesus has no will, or it results in the same antinomy.

This last quandary was the issue in the most decisive of the christological controversies that racked the ancient Eastern Church in the aftermath of the Council of Chalcedon's decisions: the monthelite/dyothelite, the "one-willite/two-willite" controversy of the later seventh century.[28] Chalcedon had laid it down: Christ is a single integral person, who does and suffers all that the Gospels narrate about their protagonist; and given what the Gospels

28. By this time, the Western church was not up to much theologically. It should be noted that the controversies and settlements after Chalcedon are customarily dismissed in Western seminary education as nit-picking. Looking into them, one discovers the contrary: only with them do the christological questions really become interesting.

in fact narrate about him, this person must be God and man at once—in the formulaic language of the decree, he must have/be "two natures," deity and humanity. So far so good, and this is the dogma we have been invoking. But the more abstract part of the council's text is patient of, and sometimes seems to invite, a construal of the Gospels' story that in effect says that in Christ's life and work deity and humanity each does its own thing, that is, that Christ is not a single dramatic protagonist after all.[29] Whole regions of the Eastern Church, followers of Cyril of Alexandria who had been put on edge by recent history, read the decree with suspicious eyes, decided that this is what Chalcedon would indeed turn out to mean in theological practice, and rejected it. As the dispute widened into schism, these became known as "monophysites," "one-naturites," for their insistence that the incarnation once given, the distinction of two natures is a distinction of concepts only and not of actual entities. Theologians of the imperial Church set out to find formulas that would entice the monophysites back,[30] and succeeded only in triggering a series of further controversies. The last of these provoked one of the last great intellects of the ancient world, Maximus the Confessor, to strenuous thought.

The imperial theologians proposed: we must indeed think of two natures in Christ, but the legitimate monophysite concern may be accommodated by saying that there is only one *will* in Christ—they proposed "monothelitism," "one-willism." One can see why they thought this proposal had to carry even those loyal to Chalcedon: what, after all, would a person with two wills be?[31] Appealed to for his judgment, Maximus refused to back off from the simple observation that clearly there are *two* wills in play in the Gethsemane story, and that on the side of the one who prays, it will not do to say either that this is just a man praying to God or that the struggle is pretense.

Within the terms of the imperial proposal, the two wills would not simply be the wills of Jesus and his Father. For the imperial proposal assigned having will to "nature" rather than—for a possibility that might occur to moderns—to "person"[32]: it is "natural" to "humanity" to have will. Moreover, if will were not assigned to nature, positing one will would give noth-

---

29. To this, the reference easiest for me to make is Jenson, *ST*, 1:127–33.

30. They wanted to do this for two reasons: sincere concern for the unity of the Church and concern for the unity of the empire, toward the end, in the face of Islam's military advance.

31. Again, psychological abnormalities are not relevant.

32. The dominant term in the East was, indeed, not "person" but "hypostasis"; and a hypostasis does not have qualities other than those of the nature of which it is a hypostasis.

ing to the one-naturites. To the consternation of the imperial theologians, Maximus perceived that if the terms of their own proposal are maintained[33] and the plain sense of the text honored, a "dyothelite" position results. One of the wills displayed in the story must be the one that belongs to the Son's human nature. And since the Son's other nature is the divine nature and since divine will is assigned to divine nature and not to divine personhood, the divine decision displayed in the story must belong to this other one of the Son's "two natures." Which gives two wills in Christ, one for each nature, one divine and one human.[34] But however are we now to construe the story? Surely blatant mythology is just around the corner?

Maximus' attention to the story compelled him to maintain that in Gethsemane the man Jesus made a hard human decision in fully human fashion. What then of the divine decision? To lay out Maximus' solution in his own language and follow his dialectics would take more space than could be justified within the purpose of this essay; what follows is my rewriting of Maximus' suppositions and argument.

Human nature and divine nature are ontologically asymmetrical.[35] Human nature is individuated, so that according to Jesus' human nature he is one individual of the human race, who thus makes his own decisions. But the divine nature is not individuated in *this* fashion; the Son has the divine nature only by and in the mutual relations of Father, Son, and Spirit—as likewise the Father and the Spirit each have the divine nature only in these mutual relations. Therefore, precisely because will belongs to nature, the divine decision made at Gethsemane must be thought of as made not by any one divine person but only in the mutuality of the Three.

Then Maximus makes his most daring move: since Jesus and the Son are but one person, it is the very decision made by the man Jesus that constitutes the Son's concrete role in the triune decision. Perhaps we may put it so: the man Jesus' human decision is the content of the triune decision—as, perhaps, the Father is its absoluteness and the Spirit its freedom. If we let Maximus—or anyway what I take from Maximus—guide our vision, we will see in Gethsemane a man making a hard decision, and we will see this very

33. Martin Luther arrived at a position remarkably similar to that of Maximus, with far fewer dialectics that follow, by implicitly denying the terms in which the old debate was conducted.

34. This sabotaged the imperial politics, over against monothelites, but now over against Islam as well, for which treason Maximus was tortured—apparently unintentionally—to death.

35. This is standard thinking in the tradition.

event as an event in the triune life, as nothing less than the triune deciding that this man will in fact be faithful, that is, that there will be an atonement.[36]

Could Jesus have fled? No, because his life, like all else, is governed by the triune will, here by the triune decision that he will be faithful. Yes, because his human decision is itself the Son's presence in that triune decision.

I would have thought this result an exegetically very good thing. The hard dogmatic thinking just sketched did not, as generations of critical scholars have supposed it must, lead way from the text but rather to discovery of the text's own power, in its plain reading.

Part of that power is the pressure that, vice versa, a text can exert on the understanding of existing dogma and perhaps on an eventual necessity of new definition—or, since in the situation of a divided church, formulation of dogma becomes problematic, perhaps we should rather say on dogmatic thought.

It does not seem possible to take the Gethsemane pericope—or the temptation in the wilderness or the passerby's challenge to Jesus on the cross or the Akedah or Joshua's question to Israel at the Jordan or . . . —seriously without thinking a thought forbidden by the weight of theological tradition: that at such junctures in God's scriptural history, the godhead of God is somehow at stake. Trying to specify that "somehow" would be altogether too audacious an attempt to penetrate God's mystery.[37] But the "somehow" alone is sufficient challenge to our metaphysical prejudices.

God is undoubtedly beyond any threat we or any creature might pose to his omniscience and omnipotence—or to any of the *omni*-s that enjoy at least quasi-dogmatic status. But without positing any actual rift in the divine unity, we can ask whether the triune life may not encompass something that if it occurred among *us* would surely be at least the *threat* of rupture. Jesus could not have fled Gethsemane—but his own free human decision belongs to the triune decision that he could not. It seems, therefore, that in some not-further-to-be-penetrated sense, God's unity, which is inseparable from his godhead, might not have been sustained.

What if Jesus had fallen? A metaphysical style more dramatic than most can approve would perhaps say: then precisely *nihil*, then the world would have been precisely what postmodernity takes it to be. Even more à la Heidegger: Being held its breath between "Remove this cup from me" and "yet, not what I want . . ." But enough of such extravagances.

36. It should be recorded that I know two eminent authorities on Maximus, one of them a member of this consultation. One of them thinks my use of Maximus goes too far; the other supports it.

37. Though one may perhaps remark that with God necessity and absolute contingency are the same thing.

Because there is the plain sense of the Gethsemane text and others like it, we must ask, not indeed *whether* God is "impassible," to use the word that sums up the *omni*-s, but *how that works* in the case of the specific biblical, triune God.[38] It would lead far beyond the confines of this essay to go any more deeply into that.

VII

There is much current discontent, among both exegetical and systematic theologians, with the hegemony of "historical-critical" exegesis. A variety of other modes of reading are therefore proposed: rhetorical, reader-response, literary, and so on. It is not, however, at all clear that either supplementing or replacing historical-critical reading with some other sort of reading will in fact reach the true cause of the discontent—or indeed satisfy our responsibility to truth.

It will be seen from the above that restoring the ancient mutual dependence of dogmatic thinking and exegesis is another matter altogether; their relation cannot be contained within modernity's ontological assumptions and so requires us to rework them drastically. Just so, in my judgment, the interdependence goes directly to the deep cause of our discomfort. To be sure, such a metaphysical fruit-basket-upset is uncomfortable to live through.

---

38. Thus, God surely knows everything, which does not itself say how he knows it.

10

Ipse pater non est impassibilis
(The Father Himself Is Not Impassible)
(2009)

I

What I hope to offer in this paper is a suggestion or two that may help to avoid stalemate between such supposed antithetical groups as "passibilists" and "impassibilists" or "traditionalists" and "revisionists." And in this connection let me take occasion to regret that Fr. Weinandy chose to deliver his attack on my previously published proposals outside the framework laid down for contributors to the symposium. For who knows? Openness might have led to some rapprochement.

It would in general be good if we could get past polemics of the kind that determines for someone—without asking him—what he must *really* mean, in order then to denounce it. From Weinandy's paper, I will instance only one central case. He writes that according to me God "actualizes himself . . . through his actions within history." I have not said any such pseudo-Hegelian thing, nor do Weinandy's citations from my work entail the proposition. Or rather, they entail it if and only if one invincibly presumes as the conceptual framework precisely the construal of time and eternity that I want to overcome—that is, only by a remarkably comprehensive *petitio principii*. In response to the editors' gracious and repeated requests that I clarify a little the issue with Weinandy and those who in this matter are like him, I will add a few paragraphs here—but only with the urgent plea that the actual beginning of *my* concern in *this* paper is at the number II.

It was, is, and, until the Lord comes or the Western Church disappears, will remain a chief intellectual labor of the Western Church to respond to the profound questions posed by pre-Christian Greece's religious thinkers, and in responding to transform them.[1] Encountering the new gospel, they asked: "What sort of 'being' does this 'Son of God' have?" "By what title is he 'God'?" "What, indeed, do Christians mean by 'being'? Or 'God'?" We have been working on answers ever since. The temptation that regularly besets us is fundamentalist longing to think that this conversation has come to a satisfactory rest at some point in the past, whether with the Fathers or Thomas or Luther or Barth or whomever, so that we are dispensed from its labors. Pointing out that this is indeed a temptation should not be regarded as an attack on the tradition; for—as especially much Catholic theology has recently insisted—the tradition is fundamentally the continuing enterprise itself, encompassing but never identical with its achievements to date.

Parmenides and Plato and Aristotle and the Stoics did not know the Incarnation or the biblical distinction of creature from Creator; thus their vision of deity necessarily differed greatly from that of Scripture. For them, the great distinction was between the temporal world and the atemporal realm of deity, the latter conceived as an abstract sheer other. Plato's deity is the geometric point at the center of time's circular mobile, that as merely geometric is itself immobile. Aristotle's deity is an "unmoved" mover,[2] an utterly self-contained substance, that attracts and so moves temporal almost-substances precisely by its obliviousness to them and their temporal troubles. For both, deity is pure timelessness.

It is apparent that this theology and Scripture's portrayal of God cannot both be true. The great labor begun by the Fathers and carried on through the centuries has been so to converse with Greece's pre-Christian theologians, as to rejoice in areas of agreement, to be energized and enlightened by their insights, and to overcome their pagan assumptions about being and God. Is my "being"—what it means for me to be—persistence in what I am from the beginning, and so am timelessly, à la the Greek thinkers? Is it not first anticipation of what I will be at the End, and so am *in via*, à la Paul? And if God is the Being of which my being is a participation, what then of him?

My own attempt to carry on the work may prove to make a minor or no contribution. But in the nature of the case *all* contributions—past, present, or future—to this effort must be partial and incomplete, including those

1. Adolf von Harnack notoriously taught several generations of theologians to suppose that what the Fathers were doing was the hellenizing of the Gospel, whereas what they in fact were working on was the gospelizing of Hellenism.

2. Or movers. This theology can accommodate a relative polytheism.

of the Fathers or Thomas or whomever; and to suppose that any of them provides a sabbath rest leads to ideology, not theology. I confess that in some critiques of my writing I detect yearning for such respite, and discern more remainders of Greek paganism's construal of deity than is tolerable at this stage of the theological enterprise—notably located in nervous insistence on God's utter impassibility. I am moved to say, as a theological hero of mine said of the neo-Arian devotees of impassibility:[3] "[L]et them rather . . . find the mark of deity in endless futurity . . . ; let them guide their thinking by what is to come and is real in hope rather than by what is past and old."[4]

II

I return now to what I wrote for the symposium, the "suggestion or two" announced at the beginning. Let me start with the simpleminded beginning of my own problem. If indeed the christology is true whose slogan is that "one of the Trinity suffered in the flesh," then the God here referred to by "the Trinity" is not impassible, in any use of the adjective that would occur to a native user of Greek, Latin, or English—or at least not to any such user who had mastered the relation of subject and predicate.

It is indeed important that the sentence ends with "in the flesh," but this adverbial phrase—adverbial also in the Greek—does not displace the subject-object relation: with or without "in the flesh" the subject of "suffered" is God the Son/Logos. Until 325, theologians alarmed by the suffering the Bible attributes to God, could exploit the seeming need to *specify* the deity of the Son over against that of the Father—who was taken to be God without specification—so as to construe the Son as ever so slightly less God than the Father, and so as one to whom the salvifically necessary suffering could be assigned without alarm. But Nicea stopped that bolthole. After Nicea the ground shifted, and from then until 451 the move was to intimate—never more than that—that there are two persons in Christ himself, one to be untouched God and the other to do the suffering, but Chalcedon's "one and the same" plugged also this escape—or did where the whole decree was taken seriously and not just its technical terminology and one of its attachments. Cyril's famous *apathos pathoi* is on the right track, and the subject of "suffers" remains the same also in this formulation. Let me add that the suggestions I will offer might well be taken as attempts to unpack Cyril's formula.

3. That was the real content of their "ungenerate".
4. Gregory of Nyssa, *Against Eunomius*, 1:672.

I am more or less aware of the subtle qualifications and real insights involved in the tradition's sophisticated massaging of the notion of impassibility. But in any sense of impassibility perceptible on the *face* of the word, it will not do as an attribute of the God of Scripture and dogma. The difficulty is that the face values of the words we appropriate can creep back into the structure and tone of our discourse.

There is another simplicity: neither can we say that the biblical God is "passible." Jürgen Moltmann's theatrically suffering God, or the God of "open theism," is no more biblical than his contradictory, and certainly no more coherent with dogma. Pagan gods have sometimes been given to suffering. "The God whom men call Zeus," the abstracted deity of high Hellenic theology, could not suffer, but the actual old Zeus himself had his Hera, and between Osiris' divine lot and that of Sisyphus there is little to choose. Which is why none of that crowd is the Lord. If it is permitted to mention Martin Luther here, his outrage at Erasmus was in considerable part driven by insistence that God is not going to react to our bad behavior by withdrawing his promises, that he cannot be affected in this way.[5] The Lord can say by the mouth of Ezekiel that Israel's unfaithfulness has broken his heart (Ezek 8:6)—which is certainly an affect. But throughout Ezekiel's book the Lord's concluding insistence remains: without tenses, "I am the Lord."

What then are we to do? We are of course dealing with paradox.[6] But if someone asks "How do you *mean* this paradox?" it does not help simply to repeat, "It is a paradox."

When both answers to a question posed between contradictories seem wrong or both right, the question may be wrongly posed. That is the possibility this paper will explore. Perhaps, *in divinis*, "*x est passibilis*" is not the right contradictory to "*x est impassibilis*." Perhaps "*x non est impassibilis*" with the double negative is, *in divinis*, the precisely right stipulation.

III

My title is, of course, a famous line from Origen's homily on Ezekiel 16.[7] The two contexts are important: one is Ezekiel's allegory of foundling Jerusalem, and the other an argument Origen constructs. Origen stipulates "pity" as

---

5. Luther, *WA*, 18:619.

6. And my own discussion of these matters in the *Systematic Theology* begins with Melito of Sardis.

7. Origène, *Homélies sur Ézéchiel*, 229–30. Since Origen's homilies are preserved only in Latin translation, we cannot always be sure what "the historical Origen" may have written. Here, I mean by "Origen" whoever is responsible for the text I adduce.

the *caritatis passio*, a dispositional affect necessarily present in anyone who displays *caritas*, as the Lord in Scripture does to his people. This affect must be in God, and indeed eternally antecedent in the Father, as the ground in God for involvement *in conversatione humanae vitae*, an involvement centering in the Son's *passio*. Hence not only the Son but *ipse Pater* is not-impassible. Origen constructs his argument as exegesis of Ezekiel's allegory of foundling Jerusalem,[8] in which the Lord's pity is evoked as he, on his way to some unspecified destination, happens upon the discarded infant. That is, the Lord's pity appears during an incident on the divine way.

It is the notion of a divine way, and of a dispositional *passio* in God as the possibility of certain incidents on that way, that I suggest may be developed to offer some alleviation of our problem. Many, I think, of our difficulties stem from a subliminal supposition that passibility or impassibility would themselves be statically possessed—impassible!—characters of God.

Let us suppose that a narrative can be told of God's life with us creatures, that is true of God himself—that is, that the Bible and the doctrine of Trinity are true to God. Narrative goes in waves, and its waves overlap and intersect in indefinitely many ways. Perhaps passibility and impassibility—and indeed other such abstractly stated attributes—appear with different waves of the narrative—or, as I will shortly suggest, with interactions between hyperbar-levels of the narrative's music. Perhaps the question is not whether God is or is not impassibly possessed of the abstract character of impassibility, but where he is in his story with us. And it is indeed his story with us—the "economic" Trinity—that is the locus of our problem and of most of the following discussion; though we will come to brief evocation of the "immanent" Trinity.

Narrative time—that is, the time that actually obtains, the time traversed in Scripture's narrative—is neither linear nor cyclical, nor is it accommodated merely by talk about *kairoi* or such. Narrative time is the ordering of events by their mutual reference, and the narratively-temporal extension of an event is thus its relation to other events in a set. Let us suppose a set of events A, B, C, and D. C may very well embrace A and B, and D be the event of the succession itself. Let us suppose a unitary subject of A, B, C, and D. Perhaps this subject may truly be said to be Y as the subject of D, but -Y as the subject of C, Y as the subject of A, and -Y as the subject of B.

And now let me make a main move of this paper. The pure actuality of narrative time can most sharply be seen in Western music as it was from the 16th century through most of the 20th. That music can be invoked in discussing such matters is of course not an original idea: when Augustine

---

8. Which he does not allegorize, since it already is an allegory.

wanted to model the time of his confessional narrative, he turned immediately to the sequence of semantically empty sounds we call a melody.

Nor is it any accident that our music has this narrative character. What in the West we know as music appeared within a culture that supposed history was getting someplace, that it had a plot, and that plotted sequences—subplots—could therefore often be discerned also in shorter sequences than universal history. A piece of Western music is the semantically emptied mode of such a sub-narrative—or even, in occasional Promethean intention, of the whole universal story. When the culture lost faith that history has a plot and subplots, our music promptly morphed into an antithesis of its original self.

Recommending theological attention to the way time works in Western music, Jeremy Begbie[9] has pointed out that a Western composition's total plot of tensions and resolutions has a bottom temporal level of meter-bars, and as many superimposed levels of ever more encompassing "hyperbars"—phrases, themes, movements, etc.—as the music's sophistication requires. What time it is in a piece of music thus depends on which level of bars or hyperbars you are asking about. And—much to our point—thrusting bars or hyperbars at one level may, for example, be embraced by dragging hyperbars at another level. Which then is the piece, vital or foreboding?

In Ezekiel's/Origen's story of God and foundling Jerusalem, was God passible when he felt pity for the exposed newborn Jerusalem? With Origen, we will have to say "Yes," since in fact he was affected and so manifested this dispositional property.[10] Was God impassible in his commitment to the wayward foundling? With Luther we will have to say "Yes," since at this level of the narrative's hyperbars he simply over-rides all challenges to that commitment.

Is God, considered as the subject of his total history with us, impassible? By the testimony of Scripture, he is indeed—in any plausible sense of the word. Is God, happening upon a lost sheep, passible? By the testimony of Scripture he is indeed—in any plausible sense of the word. Is then God, abstracted from all such tales, passible or impassible?

But that last is a pseudo-question, since the abstraction cannot be performed on the biblical God. Which brings us to the trinitarian ground of all this—where some here were anyway sure I was heading.

Whatever we find to say about the "immanent" Trinity is derived from the revelation we call the "economic" Trinity, that is, from a certain constellation of bars and hyperbars in God's history with us. Both in that

9. Begbie, *Theology, Music and Time*, 29–70.

10. Whatever it may mean to say that God has such-and-such a property.

constellation and in the derivation, much that occurs in God's whole history with us, taken with all its notes and their sequences and other relations in bars and hyperbars, is omitted: for example, the specific wording of the Son's prayer to the Father in John 17 is not revelatory of an inner-triune relation, only the fact of his prayer with that import—or anyway, this holds so far as we can know and so for the doctrine we can propound.

But while trinitarian doctrine is *derived* from the full biblical tale of his life with us, with all its levels and intersections of time-markings, and while the derivation elides a great deal, teaching about the immanent Trinity is not and must not be *abstracted* from the full tale. Whether or not a theologian thinks it wise to deploy the notions of narrative or history in an account of God's immanent life—analogously of course—if he is orthodox he cannot deny the hypostatic identity of one *persona* of the immanent Trinity with one *persona* of the saving history, and therefore cannot deny the hypostatic identity of the inner-triune relations, all of which have the Son as a pole, with narrative relations of the saving history.

IV

Thus there is in the immanent life of God something like what I have called narrative time. Or rather, there is in the immanent life of God that which narrative time is something like. In his immanent narrative time—begging permission to call it that—God to be sure transcends any conceivable "linear" time—as the partisans of divine impassibility rightly insist. *And* by the same token he also transcends any conceivable mere negation of our time— the negation on which partisans of divine impassibility seem to insist. If "eternal" is with the Greeks taken to mean simply "not temporal," it cannot be used of the real God.

The life of the biblical God cannot be located on any "time-line"; *that is*, it cannot be laid out on any story's bottom level of time-bars. Thus it makes no sense to ask what was happening "before" the inner-triune begetting of the Son, as was recognized at Nicea. And by the very same token, it makes no sense to ask what things in God were like "before" Mary conceived—even as it makes perfect and necessary sense to ask what eternity must be like for the Son to be born in time of a woman.

Nor can the biblical God be located at a point equidistant from all points on any time-line; our narrative/music does not circle endlessly around him. Thus the assertion that all points on any time-line are simultaneous for him, and the assertion that they are not simultaneous for him, are equally meaningless.

What then is the narrative time—or whatever you choose to call it—
that God has in himself? It is marked out by the well-known "innertrinitar-
ian relations"—though perhaps the traditional list needs some additions.
For example, the Father begets the Son and is begotten by no one; here is a
clear before and after—as those who lost at Nicea had insisted—which however can be plotted on no straight timeline—as those who won had insisted.
After Nicea, we may take it as determinative for God's narrative time that
the spatial language involved in all our images of time cannot constrain it.
This does not mean God's time does not obtain; on the contrary, it means
that it is the archetype of all times.

V

As the general assignment of our conference supposes, our attempts to construe the fact of providence are indeed a chief place where difficulties with
God's impassibility/passibility impede our efforts. According to Thomas—
whom I should doubtless forebear to cite in this company—God's universal
knowledge and universal will are in such sort one that God's foreseeing
determines what is seen. He is the cause of all things *per suum intellectum*,
and in this context that holds precisely with respect of their ordering to their
good.[11] The pre/provision, moreover, extends to every item and single event
of creation.[12]

It is apparent that this doctrine must provoke some questions. One is
the so-called problem of theodicy. In my judgment, this problem is in this
life insoluble: faith in God's universal ordering of creation to the good—that
is to himself—will remain a great "Nevertheless . . ." until the final vision.
Another is the question with which Thomas ends the *quaestio* just cited:
Utrum providentia rebus provisis necessitatem imponat. This he disposes of
elegantly and so far as I am concerned for good and all[13]—though folk do
have some trouble keeping his answer in mind.

In my view, however, the really difficult question concerns the meaningfulness of petitionary prayer—which is, after all, the kind most recom-
mended and practiced in Scripture. Suppose I pray for someone's recovery.
If the Lord foresees from all eternity that my friend will/not recover, and if
that foreseeing determines the event, and if he thus already knows what he
ordains and ordains what he knows, what role does my petition have?

11. Aquinas, *Summa Theologiae*, 1 q. 22 a.1. [See *Summa Theologiae*, 5:86ff.—Ed.]

12. 1 q. 22 a.2.

13. 1 q .23 a.4.

It is a question every pastor regularly encounters. And the answers offered are in large part evasions. Prayer undoubtedly "opens" the soul to God, but is the content of the utterance irrelevant to its benefit? Praying is undoubtedly salutary obedience to the Lord's command, but why this particular command in the first place? Petition is undoubtedly—and this has been my own mantra—the appropriate utterance of a creature to the Creator, but if we remain with this formalism how does that construe the Creator/creature relation? Not, I fear, conformably to Thomas' resolution of determinism.

It is the "already" two paragraphs back that is the Jonah, for its appearance presupposes that God's history with us can indeed be laid out on a straight time-line, on a sequence of meter-bars without hyperbars, without phrasing or melody or development or . . . ; that is, it presupposes that "already" and "before" and their like are univocal when used of God's time with us. What, however, if the temporal relation between God's determination and my prayer is not exhausted in any one before-and-after? What if there is a section through the bar-and-hyperbar-structure of God's time with us, in which his determination precedes my prayer, *and* one in which my prayer precedes his determination?

How does time work when in obedience to our Lord's command, we address God as "Father," and tell him how we children think the universe should go? With assurance that our opinion means something material to him, as it would to a good parent? We address this Father, after all, in unison with the One who by birth has that right, and who is himself one of the eternal Trinity whose joint knowledge and decision[14] determine the event. Prayer is *involvement* in Providence.

If prayer is anything less, it is simply a pitiful delusion. Perhaps if we were more straightforwardly to consider the biblical necessity of the two sentences just previous to this one, discussion of God's relation to our time, and so of his passibility/impassibility, would make more progress.

14. For will and intellect belong to nature, not hypostasis.

11

Can Holiness Be a *nota ecclesiae?* *(2006)*

I

The *sanctitas* of the Church begins its conceptual career as one of what came to be called the *proprietates ecclesiae*, the characters the Church has just because she is the Church—as rationality is a character I am supposed to have just because I am a human person. The question posed to our gathering is then: "Can this *proprietas* also be a *nota* of the Church?" That is, an ascertainable character by the presence or absence of which it can be determined whether or not some community is church?

The standard list of *proprietates* is creedal: the Church is singular, holy, catholic and apostolic. We together confess: a community totally lacking one of these attributes would be some other entity than the Church. But this doctrine leaves some questions open—and particularly the epistemological questions that are much of our concern. Thus, for an instance from another—though closely related—context, to say that rationality is an essential attribute of humanity, does not necessarily make rationality or its absence a sure sign of humanity's presence or absence. The newspapers are full of horrors caused by our supposition that we can use rationality as a dispositive *nota hominis*.

In the polemics following the Reformation, precisely the epistemic status of the Church's *proprietates* became controversial. The parties differed about whether the *proprietates* could indeed function as *notae*, that is, whether they were *ascertainable*, so that you could look around for them and if you found them in a community know that you had found the Church, and where you did not find them know that here was something other than the Church. Is, for example, apostolicity ascertainable, perhaps as a known continuity of bishops in place? So that where you can show such succession you can insofar be assured that you have located the Church? To our specific matter: "Can you look about for evidences of a community's holiness—perhaps the presence within it of persons of demonstrable holiness—and discovering such be one step of the way toward knowing that this community is church?"

It should be already plain that the matter is especially delicate in the case of holiness. For holiness is a remarkably mysterious attribute. In the case, for example, of apostolicity, we can if we choose simply define it in such fashion that it will be visible as institutional or official succession. But however you define holiness—a matter to which I must eventually come—it remains elusive. Who says that someone is holy? Let it be granted that holiness is sometimes indeed visible, but then it must also be granted that the saints have clay feet as well, even the greatest among them, and that these too are assuredly visible. It appears that perceiving holiness must be in this life a matter of balancing appearances. Who then is to adjudicate the needed preponderance of gold? Perhaps only God can adjudicate whether created human phenomena balance out as personal or communal holiness. It is at least in part for this reason that Catholic practice demands miracles worked by or on account of those who are to be canonized saints: they are God's testimonials. But again, who is to judge whether miracles have in fact occurred? There seems to be no one to do this but the Church. But if we are invoking the holiness of members within a putative church as a visible holiness of that church, the claim becomes circular. This discussion of the elusiveness of holiness has been at a superficial level. After a little I will try to probe deeper. But now I have to turn to another matter.

II

We think we need *notae* of the Church to tell where there is church and where there is not. We will not have this problem unless we encounter two or more communities claiming to be church, that so teach and live that at least one of them cannot be true church if one or more of the others are.

That there *could* be false church has been obvious from the beginning. Thus Jesus warned the disciples about those who would say "Lord, Lord" and nevertheless be no disciples; and Paul's fear for the Galatians was that in turning to "another gospel," that is, to a construal of Christ's work that varied decisively from his, they were in danger of undoing their reality as church—a warning which the "Judaizers" presumably returned. And indeed if we were willing to apply rigorous logic to historical entities, we would have to say that if two bodies claiming to be the Church of Jesus Christ so differ in teaching or practice as to be unable responsibly to break the bread and proclaim the word together, at least one of them must not be church at all. We should not in my view judge historical communities—even the Church—by so rigid a logic, but surely we must indeed suppose that where there are mutually excluding claimants to be church some of them must be at best gravely compromised church. In this context the Protestant scholastics spoke of "false particular churches," by which they did not mean entities that were straightforwardly *not* church, and current Roman Catholic language sometimes speaks of "wounded" churches or classifies separated bodies under such rubrics as "ecclesial communities." This logic has been obvious from the beginning, and the situation to which it applies has been exemplified from the beginning. (I am aware that some Eastern Orthodox theology does not take schism quite that seriously, and is willing to be out of communion with bodies whom it nevertheless regards as true church. Thus Moscow and Constantinople were recently out of communion, with no suggestion on either part that the other was less than one hundred percent church. I have to say I think this less a proposal than a bewilderment, occasioned by an implicit ecclesiology that is dysfunctional in any emperor-bereft historical situation.)

As soon as we recognize the possibility of true church and false church we seem to have the question of how to tell the one from the other. As both sides of the post-Reformation contention came to use the phrase, *notae ecclesiae* were certain alleged marks by which what the Protestants came to call a "particular church" could be recognized as "true" church—or not. The not very well hidden intent of each side was, of course, to devise a checklist of *notae* by which the other would be disqualified.

Catholic theologians like Bellarmine drew up their lists of *notae* by developing and expanding the *proprietates*. That is, they took the line we have so far been following. The true Church, they said, could be recognized by the attributes listed in the creed or by attributes implied by them. Protestants responded by exploiting such problems as I have just noted, generally claiming that unity, holiness, catholicity, and apostolicity—and any characters entailed by these—were precisely not perspicuous, and so could not be *notae* of anything. Each in its own way was, they said, not to be observed but rather to be believed. Thus the Protestant scholastics taught that the *proprietates* constitute the *hidden* truth *of* a "particular" and so visible true Church. A true particular and visible church certainly contains true saints, and is in that capacity holy, etc. But only God sees who those saints are, and so only God sees the Church's holiness, etc. As *notae* the Protestants instead proposed the two/three *minima* of the Protestant confessions. Right proclamation and sacramental practice/discipline appropriate thereto are, they said, audible and visible phenomena and can therefore supply the needed *notae*. To which Catholics responded by asking how one was to know that a body of proclamation or practice was in fact right? Without consulting the Church? Whereupon, they observed, we are in a circle.

Viewing the matter with some dispassion, it would seem that Catholic critique of the Protestant proposal and Protestant critique of the Catholic proposal are both decisive. Which leaves us with no *notae* at all. It is time to consider holiness itself.

III

Religionswissenschaft often identifies holiness as a or indeed the constitutive element of "religion," taken as a universal and universally realized propensity of humankind. And there is no reason to suppose that Scripture uses *kadosh* or *hagios* differently than other religious texts use these words or words so translatable.

We are religious as we are confronted with what we cannot manage in the ordinary way, but which we cannot leave alone either—with what is both *fascinans* and *tremendum*, in Otto's famous phrase. That is, the holy is the ineluctably exceptional—whether in the orders of power or of worth or of beauty. By following general rules, we can deal with the power of beasts or fires or politicians or whatever, even if we are defeated in the contest, indeed even if it can be foreseen that defeat is inevitable. But then there appears a power that offers nothing for us to grasp, against which we cannot even manage to be defeated. By hard looking, in the way we in any case must to survive, we can with dedication take in the beauty of an anemone or a Vermeer. But then there appears what Kant called the sublime. We can honor the worth of those like or not too different from ourselves. But then we somehow apprehend a demand for honor that we cannot even tell how to offer or refuse—we encounter an other in the drastic sense demanded by some recent French philosophers.

And immediately having said that, we must note an inner contradiction. For the holy is indeed the general mark of the encompassing and pervading fact of religion. How then is its appearance extraordinary? Consider the case of the Polynesians whose vocabulary anthropologists have found so useful: as tabu spreads, dealing with tabu becomes a science—indeed the paradigmatic science. Who needs to be afraid of the big bad *numen*, if all you have to do is go round by the designated path, or get the queen to come with you, or know the right gesture? Precisely the odd pervasiveness of the exceptional gives us purchase on it after all. We are back where we started, in modernity we call that purchase "religion." Religion—as has been noted by many—is both evoked by holiness and erodes holiness.

It is this that makes self-aware religion self-critical. For what the religions finally want is a holiness they cannot grasp; and if they are aware of themselves will know that in their every act they renew the attempt to grasp it. Undoubtedly Judaism and Christianity are the great experts of self-criticism; but they do not—as once I supposed they did—have a monopoly of it. What biblical faith may indeed have to itself is the possibility of carrying religion's self-critique to the bitter and just so triumphant end.

What then would be the end of the religious confrontation with holiness, as it is driven to debunk the very *numina* by which it is called forth? It would be a meeting with an exceptionality that was exceptional within no order at all, that was *sheer* exception, *totaliter aliter*, that offered no grasp even for religion. Otherwise put, that was exceptional in the order of being. Such being would be the one true holy.

Is exceptionality in the order of being conceivable? Thomas thought that it was: only in God, he said, are existence and essence the same, which is to say, God *is* in a way unimaginably different from the way in which anything else is. It may be, however, that Thomas makes this point in a way itself too generally applicable, that is, that he does not specifically develop it as a point about the *triune* God.

Moreover, just at this point we encounter yet another possible antinomy. For how is being constituted in *totaliter aliter* fashion ever to meet an other? So as to be fascinating and tremendous to someone?

IV

Perhaps a clue can be the appearance of *hagios* in Gabriel's discourse at the Annunciation. Mary asks how she can have a child without being impregnated. Gabriel responds that a descent of the Spirit will make it possible; and that therefore the one to be born will be holy—that is, the Son of the Father. The child is holy because his existence is an inconceivable exception to the conditions under which children come into being, and because this exceptionality—which might otherwise of course be attributed to demons or magic or divine fornication—is attributed to that Spirit of the Lord who throughout the Old Testament is the historical intervention of the one God. And it is a creature, a human child, that is this exception. Thus holiness as here invoked occurs in the mutual action of Father, Son, and Spirit; and is the holiness *of* a human creature. Holiness here is a trinitarian character and occurs as Incarnation.

The triune God's otherness is not some metaphysical distance from his creatures. It is exceptionality within itself, exceptionality—if you will—*a se*. The inner order of the Trinity is an order of origin; but the Father is unoriginate. The inner order of the Trinity is an order of glorification, but the Spirit is glorified of none. The inner order of the Trinity is an order of uncreated spiritual transparency; but the Son is personal as a created body. Thus the subsistence of each of the three is exceptional. And since there is God at all only as there is each of the three, exceptionality is the very being that the triune God is. The triune God does not need to be an exception to anything; he is three times an exception to himself.

Otherwise stated, the triune God is absolute self-referential contingency. He is that in that he is triune. No god otherwise subsisting could actually be holy. Moreover, actual holiness and the triune God are, by an extension of an ancient theological rule, the very same thing. From which it follows that creatures can be holy only by sharing the triune life. Which very thing they can do; for what is can be, and the interior mutual exceptionality of the triune life is in one aspect constituted in the presence there of a creature, indeed of the Son with a created body. I do not say that there could not have been the holy triune life without the Incarnation; with von Balthasar, I am convinced we have no warrant to say anything at all on that topic. As it is, there is this one holy creature, who is the Christ, body and soul.

By the will of the Father and in the futurity of the Spirit Christ is present to the Church, precisely in his holiness. The *viva vox* of the gospel, heard in the Church, is his voice. The loaf and cup seen and given in the Church are his body. And however we may determine the *possibility* of these identity-propositions, we may at this stage of ecumenical discussion perhaps agree in their truth. In the remarkable doctrine of Paul to the Corinthians, because we eat of the one loaf we are one body—which is identified in the next chapter as the body of Christ. Again, perhaps it may now be generally accepted that although Paul can secondarily use the notion of the Church as Christ's body as a trope, the proposition itself is not a trope. Thus, in the time of the Church and by that very decree of the Father and power of the Spirit instanced as the Annunciation, the Church *is* that body by which the Son is exceptional in the triune life.

V

So we finally arrive at the point. As with God and as with Christ, the Church and her holiness are the same thing. Thus indeed the holiness of the Church cannot be a discreet marker of the Church. It is not a *nota* of the sort which Catholic and Protestant alike wanted.

But the Church's holiness may still perhaps be visible, and so *notabile* in another and better way. The question is: Just *how* are the Church and her holiness the same thing? The Son is exceptional within the triune life because he is a creature with a body, so that this embodiment is one aspect of God's holiness and so of what holiness is. As this body of Christ the Church lives within the holy triune life. Therefore everything about the Church's holiness will depend on how we construe the christological "is" between "the Son" and "the man Jesus."

We come to my proposal. I suggest that our problem with locating the visibility of the Church's holiness derives from a fundamental christological error. I could father some of the following observations on, for example, Karl Rahner, but will make them on my own responsibility.

For Western theology, "Chalcedon" has effectively meant Leo. In our long labor to work out the implications of Chalcedon-according-to-Leo, we have created a remarkably sophisticated but also remarkably pusilanimous standard construal. The great medievals may be our paradigm here.

Skating over a multitude of nuances and differences, perhaps one can say that the medievals came to regard the hypostatic union as a sheerly metaphysical fact with no direct consequences at the level of "physics," that is, of natures. The Son is indeed personally identical with the man Jesus. But what this does for the man Jesus is to mark his humanity as that to which those created powers, "graces," are to be given which he needs to carry out his mission. The pattern has been persistent. Thus we may note that the extreme degree of this sort of christology was reached not by a medieval catholic or in the language of scholasticism but by Oliver Cromwell's chaplain, John Owen, whose thought is enjoying a revival in England—sponsored indeed by a student of mine.

As with Christ so with the Church that is Christ's body: in our ordinary theology the Church's holiness, apostolicity, etc. are thought of as created gifts of the Spirit, given her to enable the mission. It is precisely this created holiness that we found so elusive, and that escapes all parties' efforts to place it.

But what if we were to dare a somewhat riskier—but possibly more biblical and early-patristic—christology? What if we were to say that the man Jesus, in his relation to the God of Israel whom he called Father, simply *is* just in that relation the eternal Son? However we then worked out the metaphysics—with such strange questions as that about a *logos asarkos*? So that whatever created gifts may be given Jesus' humanity, his holiness—the man Jesus' holiness—is precisely his location as one of the three who in their mutuality are the holy God"? And what if we were accordingly to say of the Church that whatever gifts of the Spirit she may receive, as the body of

Christ her holiness is not other than the triune holiness of God? Which she has in that the same Spirit who gives himself to the Son gives—not only gifts but—himself to her? Can *this* holiness be perceived? Yes, as God gives himself to our perception, that is, *sub contrario*. The hour of Jesus' glorification, of the manifestation of his holiness, turned out to be the crucifixion. Were the body and blood of the holy Eucharist to appear in their risen glory, their touch and sight would destroy us. Were a preacher ever so to utter "Thus says the Lord" that we could have no doubt, that would be our end. Had Moses seen more than the Lord's backside, he would not just have glowed a little but would have blazed up and been gone.

The Protestant scholastics were right, but not as they understood themselves. The holiness of the Church is invisible as God is invisible. But the invisible God gives himself to our sight, sacramentally and *sub contrario*. The Catholics were right, but not as they understood themselves. We do indeed perceive the holiness of the Church, when we experience one another—in all our sin—and when we experience suffering and temptation—temptation not to be holy—and when we see and touch the bread and cup—which look like anything but resurrected body.

It is a key question just at this point. Can we rightly call the Church *peccatrix*? Plainly not in the way I call myself *simul iustus et peccator*, for the *peccator* in this phrase is "the old Adam," and the Church has no such antecedent fallen existence. Nor therefore can we call the Church in her own singular entity "a" sinner, since she is not a singular entity except as the body of Christ. But we can and must say something even stranger: when we see the sins of the Church as a people, and they are many, we *just so* see a holy community. We do not—as the Protestant scholastics seem to have thought—know that the holy Church is there when we see other marks; we do indeed see it.

VI

My answer to the question posed is no doubt disappointing. Holiness is not a mark by which true church can be located. Indeed there are none such. What there are are *normae*, measures of our labor to live the Church's unity and holiness and apostolicity *and* catholicity and possession of right teaching and right practice *and* whatever other *proprietates* may plausibly be proposed. And the only surety we have of success to date, the only surety we have that "true church" is extant, is trust in the Spirit. "It seemed good to the Holy Spirit and to us."

12

You Wonder Where the Spirit Went *(1993)*

I

Karl Barth is the initiator and model (the image, in his own sense!) of this century's renewal of trinitarian theology. He is moreover a giant of the Reformed theological tradition, famous always for its witness to the Spirit. The near-unanimity is therefore remarkable, with which a recent meeting of the Karl Barth Society of North America agreed that long stretches of Barth's thinking seem rather binitarian than trinitarian. What can be the explanation? This paper is the result of the Society's assignment, that I should seek one.

There are at least three modes of trinitarian reflection in the *Kirchliche Dogmatik*. First, Barth so locates the doctrine of the Trinity systematically as to make it identify the God whose ways the *Kirchliche Dogmatik* will seek to trace. The biblical narratives claim to identify a particular God, and therefore claim to be true of him in a way that specifies his hypostatic being. Barth sets his analysis of this phenomenon in the prolegomena of his dogmatics, to make it plain that it is this God of whom also his subsequent dogmatic propositions are to be true. Barth's observation—so easy to make once he had made it—that the doctrine of the Trinity is Christianity's identification of its God, and the amazing resolution with which he exercises that insight throughout his dogmatics, would be epochal theological contributions had Barth made no other.

Second, in I/1, §§8–12, Barth develops a full technical doctrine of Trinity. This locus is, I think, problematic in part. §8, "God in his Revelation" has been itself a revelation for many: the way in which the trinitarian mandates are laid one upon another, by each time asking what must be true if God is truly to be exactly as he is in revealing himself, has burned itself into the thinking of serious late 20th-century theology. But the §§ in which Barth then develops what he calls the "churchly doctrine" itself, are perhaps less rewarding as a whole. Though they are of course filled with remarkable individual insights, it cannot be said that they are either as creative or as knowledgeable as we expect from Barth.

Barth says that the three in God are foundationally to be understood "from their . . . variously specific genetic relations to each other,"[1] but in the actual development of the doctrine he makes little or no use of this principle, in practice substituting "analogy" for "relation"—that analogy is itself a relation does not change the point. Again, Barth takes the traditional founding of the three in their mutual relations as a reason for preferring "modes of being" to "persons" for the three. Surely, however, precisely "persons" are constituted in mutual relation—exactly according to Karl Barth!—in a way harder to grasp for "modes of being." My suspicion is that these questions are not unrelated to the question which directly occasions this essay.

Third, throughout the *Kirchliche Dogmatik* Barth indeed uses the Church's and his insight into God's triunity. This paper is devoted to a problem encountered just here. But that is only to say that the paper is devoted to nit-picking. For Barth is the theologian and the *Kirchliche Dogmatik* the book by which Western theology rediscovered that the doctrine of Trinity, while indeed a mystery, is not a puzzle, that instead it is the frame within which theology's mysteries can be shown and its puzzles solved. If some of his own solutions are incomplete or even misleading, that remains a secondary matter. To be sure, if the nit I will pick turns out to be the one biting it is a sizeable varmint, and lively on the ecumenical scene.

II

The *Kirchliche Dogmatik* presents a smorgasbord of cases in which the doctrine of Trinity, as used, seems to be rather a doctrine of binity. Let me mention three, at this point merely to instance the problem. Of these, the latter two are especially alarming.

The Karl Barth Society's attention was drawn to the problem by the case of Barth's trinitarian grounding of female-male community. As the Father and the Son are to one another, so therefore are Christ and humanity to one another, and so therefore within humanity are male and female to one another.[2] Since there are only two sexes—at least in the strange world

1. Barth, *KD* I/1, 382.
2. Ibid., III/2, §45.

of the Bible or of Barth—it is plain that the Spirit's appearance as a party in these analogies would be disruptive. But a theology's power at any point is perhaps best shown by its ability to profit from disruptions.

A second instance of apparent binitarianism occurs in IV/3, §69, 1, 2, 4. In these daring and in many ways even beautiful pages, Barth conducts a probing and systematically way-breaking discussion of the "objectivity" of the proclamation. Surely he is right: to be faithful to the logic of the gospel, we must think of the gospel's occurrence also *pro nobis* as itself a salvation-historical event antecedent to its sounding in any set of our ears, as itself an "external" reality. Perhaps we will be especially sensitive to this logic, if we have been attending to Orthodox ecumenical initiatives. Both common teaching and Orthodox urging will then make us expect Barth to designate the Pentecostal coming of the Spirit as the event just posited. Instead, Barth conducts some of the most tortuous dialectic in the *Kirchliche Dogmatik*, in order to locate the proclamation's objectivity in the Resurrection of the Son. Does Barth suppose that an act of the Spirit cannot transcend subjectivity?

Barth's more specific location of the proclamation's objectivity in the "universal prophetism" of the risen Lord would then, to be sure, more than recoup the pneumatological loss, if in Barth's description of this prophetism itself, the Spirit had the role which surely he should have in description of a "prophetism." But despite the title of §69, 4, *Die Verheissung des Geistes*, the Spirit hardly appears in the story.

Our third instance occurs in the same volume,[3] under the title "The Holy Spirit and the Mission of the Christian Congregation." Barth here undertakes nothing less than an exegesis of the novelty which the Church presents in universal history. The piece is a marvel. But he manages to write it entirely without mention of the Spirit—which must be an equal marvel, given who and what the Spirit is in Scripture.

III

I must turn to diagnosis. The present section is preliminary.

It is regularly observed that Barth's developed doctrine of Trinity is, despite the new insights on which it is based and despite some new insights scattered also in it, thoroughly Western-traditional in its general contour. The triune God as such is personal in a modern sense, while the three are otherwise characterized. The filioque is used systematically. Of the classic heresies, modalism is the temptation.

3. Ibid., IV/3, §72.

Notoriously, traditional Western teaching has its drawbacks, in my judgment one principally. Any theologian for whom the doctrine of Trinity is more than a relic, that is, any theologian who uses the doctrine of Trinity outside its own locus, is repeatedly led—indeed, compelled—to treat the three as parties of divine action, and that also "immanently." Not only those with a "social" doctrine of Trinity do this sort of thing—for my own part, I was initiated into the possibility by my orthodox Lutheran and otherwise adamantly Augustinian *Doktorvater*, Peter Brunner. The problem with the Western form of teaching is that it offers little or no justification for this necessary practice; indeed, it seems actually to have quenched the practice in Western theology.

Notoriously also, difficulties of this sort are especially severe in the case of the Spirit—whether or not Eastern attribution of all Western problems to the filioque is correct. Augustine himself felt and remarked a special difficulty with the Spirit, and so have many successors.

The general problem is plainly present in Barth. The three in God are not to be regarded as "persons" in a modern sense, but rather as the "modes" in which the one God "is three times differently God" (*dreimal anders Gott*);[4] in this systematically decisive definition Barth moreover intends the "is" as an active verb with the one God as its subject, so that the being of three is adverbial. Such a doctrine of Trinity can offer no better support for the actual use which Barth elsewhere makes of God's triunity than Western teaching in general does for such use. For also Barth's use invariably depends on taking the Father and the Son as parties of an action in God.

The drawbacks of Western-style trinitarianism are not necessarily fatal to theology that labors under them. That not every conceptual practice that a theologian finds necessary is fully supported by his/her general system is probably, indeed, a distinguishing virtue of theology. Moreover, Eastern forms of trinitarian teaching present equal if different drawbacks. So probably would any such future revised or ecumenical form as Pannenberg or I have been working on.

But within Barth's system, Western hindrances may obstruct more mischievously than elsewhere, just on account of his achievements. Barth envisions the entire history of salvation as eternally actual in God, in whom it is divine history posited in God's triunity. Therefore the way in which the immanent Trinity is interpreted must more directly determine the way in which God's triune work is grasped, than is usual in Western theology. This is profoundly to the good. But therefore again—and this is my preliminary diagnosis—in Barth's theology, Western trinitarianism's common difficulty

4. Ibid., I/1, 380.

in conceiving the Spirit's specific immanent initiative in God must become a difficulty in conceiving the Spirit's entire salvation-historical initiative.

It is not, of course, that Barth wants to conceive such a salvation-historical personal initiative of the Spirit and is hindered from doing so. He denies that there is any such thing to conceive: "The New Testament knows . . . of only one coming of the One who has come. . . . It is not thereby excluded that this . . . occurs in differing forms, at times he . . . chooses and in circumstances he orders. . . . It occurs . . . in the time of the Church . . . also in the form of the sharing of the Spirit. . . . And it will again occur in other form . . . as his coming to inaugurate the general resurrection. But in all these forms it is one single event [*ein einziges Ereignis*]."[5] What Barth is hindered in, is supposing that he ought to conceive a specific salvation-historical initiative of the Spirit.

IV

I will now concentrate my analysis on a decisive mark of Western trinitarianism and principle bone of contention with the East. In normal Western trinitarianism, characterization of the Spirit as the *vinculum amoris* between the Father and Son is systematically central. Barth is no innovator or exception at this point. Indeed, his great attachment to this theologoumenon is his stated reason for supporting the *filioque*.

Barth writes, "The *filioque* expresses our knowledge of the fellowship between the Father and the Son: the Holy Spirit is the love that is the essence of the relation between these two modes of God's being."[6] Confirming Orthodoxy's worst suspicions, he continues with the explicit proposition that this "perfect consubstantial fellowship between the Father and the Son" is "the being of the Spirit . . . ," and that precisely these propositions make the point "on which everything seems to us to depend . . ."[7]

The "inner-divine" fellowship of Father and Son in the Spirit is explicitly described as "two-sided," since the Spirit is the fellowship itself. Precisely this merely two-sided fellowship is then the eternal ground for there being fellowship between God and humanity,[8] first between God and the Son Jesus and then between God in Jesus and Jesus' sisters and brothers. But that is to say that this merely two-sided fellowship is the eternal ground of all salvation-history. Moreover, the way this grounding works is that each

5. Ibid., IV/3, 338.
6. Ibid., I/1, 504.
7. Ibid., 505.
8. Ibid., 504.

two-sided fellowship is the archetype of the thereby next grounded such pairing,[9] so that the two-sidedness reproduces itself at every ontological level.

One passage must be quoted *in extenso*: "The Holy Spirit is the power and its action is the work of *coordination* between the being of Jesus Christ and that of . . . his congregation. Just as he as a divine 'person' i.e. mode of being, as Spirit of the Father and of the Son (*qui ex Patre Filioque procedit*) is the bond of peace between the two, so in the historical work of atonement he is the constituent and guarantee of the *unity* of the *totus Christus* . . ."[10]

According to Barth, the triune reality of God is actual as the event of election, of the decision made "before all time" in God. And that is to say, the triune reality of God is actual as an eternal meeting between the Father and the Son, a meeting in which, as in all personal meetings, something is decided. What is decided is that the eternal relation of the Father and the Son is in fact the relation between the Father and the man Jesus, and so also a covenant between God and Jesus' sisters and brothers.[11] I think this complex theologoumenon precisely and simply true. But again, it may be that just the precision and depth of his understanding make Barth's participation in the common difficulties of Western theology more than usually consequence-laden.

Some of the pressure on Barth's ability to identify the Spirit's actuality may come from a residue of the traditional Calvinist teaching of predestination. That doctrine, for all that can otherwise be said in its praise, described the event of election much in the protological past tense and little in the eschatological future tense. Within Barth's correct identification of the event of election with the actuality of triunity, Calvinist presuppositions about election must exercise a reverse pressure on the interpretation of triunity. And if the Trinity's actuality thereby comes to be thought definitively in the past tense, the Spirit is left without that mode of God's time in which the Bible locates him.

But my guess is that the *vinculum*-doctrine is the chief Jonah. Precisely in that the inner-trinitarian relations do gloriously become concrete and alive in Barth, so that the Father and the Son confront one another, the actuality of a *vinculum* between the two parties Father and Son must be their I-thou relation itself. Thus the very reality of the Spirit excludes his appearance as a party in the triune actuality.

9. Ibid., 505.

10. Ibid., IV/3, 870.

11. For all this, I may perhaps be permitted to refer to my first book about Barth, *Alpha and Omega*, especially chapters 3 and 5.

In formal doctrine, Barth calls all three hypostases *modi essendi*. In his *use* of trinitarian insight, he nevertheless speaks freely of the personal immanent intercourse of the Father and the Son. But the Spirit is condemned by the *vinculum*-doctrine to remain a *modus* only. The concretion of triunity is a history in God in which the Spirit does not appear as an historical party. Appropriately, the causative relation of this history to a reality *ad extra* is an impersonal principle, of image-analogy.

It is again tempting to speculate that the pressure may work backwards, here from a merely two-sided understanding of human community and so of historical reality, inherited from the "I-Thou" tradition of nineteenth-century German philosophical anthropology, to a merely two-sided understanding of trinitarian community and history. Were this the case, it would be the symptom of a deep flaw indeed. It would mean that Barth's use of the image-analogy principle had opened a channel in his thinking for projection of perceived human value onto God, for theological analogy in which a human phenomenon is the primary analogate also in the order of being. I will not pursue this horrid possibility.

V

It is surely with the doctrine of the Church that a discussion of this matter must terminate. The discussion of the Church in IV and particularly in IV/3 finds its warrants at every step in descriptions of a meeting in God between the Father and the Son. An alternative possibility of course would be to find such warrants in description of a meeting between the Spirit on the one hand and the Son with the Father on the other.

The ecclesiology which would result from this alternative move has the recommendation of ecumenical urgency. For it is precisely that currently being pressed on the Western Church by Orthodoxy and increasingly found salvific also in Catholic/Protestant dialogues—though not often by Protestant churches reacting to the dialogues. What according to Orthodoxy must be apprehended is that the Pentecostal coming of the Spirit is "a new intervention of the Holy Trinity in time . . . ," and that on this occasion the intervention "issues from the third Person of the Trinity . . ."[12] When this specific role of the Spirit is not grasped, the Western pendulum between Catholic institutionalism and Protestant spiritualist individualism must, according to Orthodox polemic, necessarily ensue. When it *is* grasped, an ecclesiology of *communion* ensues.

---

12. Nissiotis, *Die Theologie der Ostkirche im ökumenischen Dialog*, 74f.

This leads to a final speculation—which I offer with quite intense suspicion that it is true. Perhaps the final reason for the whole web of Spirit-avoidance in the *Kirchliche Dogmatik* is avoidance of the Church. For if the Pentecostal creation of a structured continuing community were identified as the "objectivity" of the gospel's truth *pro nobis*, then this community itself, in its structured temporal and spatial extension, would be seen as the *Bedingung der Möglichkeit* of faith. Or again, if the Community between the Father and the Son were himself an *agent*[13] of their love, immanently and economically, then the Church, as the community inspirited by this Agent, would be the active *mediatrix* of faith, in precisely the way demanded by Catholics and resisted by Protestants in every chief dialogue.

Catholic commentators have notoriously found many approaches in the *Kirchliche Dogmatik* to Catholic patterns of thought. The point at which approach would become arrival has been defined by no less than Joseph Cardinal Ratzinger: "For the Catholic, the Church is itself comprised in the deep source of the act of faith: it is only in that I believe with the Church that I share in that certitude in which I may rest my life."[14] Union with the Church constitutes a "new and wider self" of the believer; and it is this self that is the subject of faith, "the self of the *anima ecclesiastica*, that is, the self of that person through whom the whole community of the Church expresses itself . . ."[15] May Karl Barth's impulsion to practiced binitarianism be in fact the last resistance of his Protestantism?

I must finish by considering the chief passage in which Barth states the ecclesial reality of the Spirit theoretically, IV/3, 867–72. The mystery of the Church is the "identity of her being with that of Jesus Christ."[16] But this identity obtains only as it happens; that is, insofar as it is "work of the Spirit."[17] So far, one might think, so plain. But then two phenomena appear.

The personal agent of this work in fact turns out at every step of Barth's argument to be not the Spirit, as advertised, but Christ; the Spirit is denoted invariably by impersonal terms. The Spirit is "the power of Jesus Christ's being";[18] "the Holy Spirit is the godly power [*Gottesmacht*] unique to the being of Jesus Christ, in the exercise . . . of which he lets his congregation become what it is";[19] the Spirit is what happens when "Jesus Christ makes

---

13. I do not yet know how to work out this proposition conceptually.
14. Ratzinger, "Luther und die Einheit der Kirchen," 575–76.
15. Ratzinger, *Église, Oecuménisme et Politique*, 173.
16. Barth, *KD* IV/3, 867.
17. Ibid., 868.
18. Ibid.
19. Ibid., 869.

use of his power . . ."[20] This work in itself is the *coordination* of "heavenly and earthly activity . . . ," in which their difference is—in good Western fashion—strictly maintained. And then we discover that the earthly activity in question is the "*subjective*" side of the knowledge of God.[21]

It seems unavoidable: in Barth's system, the Spirit is precisely the *Geschichtlichkeit* of "the relation of the being of Jesus Christ to that of his congregation . . ."[22] The Spirit is the capacity of God as archetype, at whatever ontological level, to evoke an echo in some subjectivity. When does the Spirit disappear from Barth's pages? Whenever he would appear as someone rather than as something. We miss the Spirit at precisely those points where Bible or catechism have taught us to expect him to appear as someone *with* capacities, rather than as sheer capacity—in the archetype/image scheme, as himself an archetype.

It is of course a generally unsolved problem, felt from the earliest days of Christian theology: How is the Spirit at once his own person and what "all three" hypostases actively are together? How is the Spirit at once one who has power and that power itself? It is no general refutation of Barth, that he too has left a few problems unsolved. But interaction between this unsolved problem and Barth's particular achievements produces an especially painful set of symptoms.

20. Ibid., 870.
21. Ibid., 871.
22. Ibid., 868.

13

Once More on the *Logos asarkos* (2011)

In what sense, if any, was there a *Logos asarkos*? A "pre-existent" second identity of the Trinity who was "not yet" the creature[1] Jesus? My attempt to answer that question seems to be known mostly for its negations—nor do I intend now to depart from these. But the pressure of the discussion and my own continued reflection—the two intertwined of course—have led to some further thoughts, which the following will sketch. The technical difficulties which readers may encounter in the concluding proposals are perhaps due to the still only partially digested character of my thoughts at that time. The essay is hardly a retraction, but it does attempt to ameliorate an inadequacy of my previous discussion.

Certain maxims have governed my thinking on the matter, and I continue to insist on them. I will give a paragraph to each of four.

1. The very earliest christologians had it right. Jesus is the Son/*Logos* of God by his relation to the Father, not by a relation to a coordinated reality, "*the* Son/*Logos*." The Apologists' creation of the "*Logos* christology," which presumes the *Logos* as a religious/metaphysical entity and then asserts its union with Jesus, was an historic mistake, if perhaps an inevitable one. Great genius has subsequently been devoted to the task of conceptually pasting together God the Son/*Logos* and Jesus the Son/*Logos* of God, and we may be thankful for many of the ideas posted along the way. But the task itself is wrongly set and finally hopeless.

2. In whatever way the Son may antecede his conception by Mary, we must not posit the Son's antecedent subsistence in such fashion as to make the incarnation the addition of the human Jesus to a Son who was himself

---

1. In this usage *sarx* simply means creatureliness.

without him. By the dogma, Mary is the mother of God the Son, she is *The-otokos*, and not of a man who is united with God the Son, however firmly. Thus the Church confesses that God the Son was himself conceived when Mary became pregnant—even if theology often labors to evade this confession's more alarming entailments. That Mary is *Theotokos* indeed disrupts the linear time-line or pseudo time-line on which we Westerners automatically—and usually subliminally—locate every event, even the birth of God the Son; but that disruption is all to the theological good.

3. The sentence "How would the Trinity have been the Trinity if God had not created a world, and there had therefore been no creature Jesus to be the Son, or had let the fallen creation go, with the same result?" is often taken for a real question. And here I do have a retraction to make. In the past I have sometimes responded to the supposed question, saying that God would presumably have somehow been the same triune God that he is, but that we can say nothing further about that "somehow." I now think that even this response concedes too much to our unbaptized notion of time, by supposing that the collection of words quoted at the beginning of this paragraph actually makes a question which one can answer, however sparingly. It has now dawned on me that the putative question is nonsense, and so therefore is my previous attempt to respond to it.

4. Occam's razor is a liberating and necessary tool. Indeed thou shalt not posit metaphysical entities beyond necessity. The ground of this commandment is theological. In Christian theology the warrants of ontological necessity must finally be scriptural, and we are not allowed to proceed past what they can support. In the present case, belief that there is the Son is indeed mandated by Scripture. But what mandates belief in an intrinsically disembodied metaphysical entity that is "the" *Logos*? The passage often cited is the Prologue of John. But "*ho Logos*" there is God's creative utterance from Genesis 1, which John glosses; even if middle Platonism's deity of that name lies somehow behind John's usage, it is the text and not its possible background that is to be read.

So much for my characteristic maxims. But then there is a maxim of a different and even overriding sort that is also not negotiable: the eternity of the Son/*Logos*. In whatever sense "was" and "when" obtain within the life of God, there indeed never was when the Son was not; and it is vital to remember that in the "pre-" folk worry about there is nothing *but* the life of God. Some critics have seized on my insistence that the *Theotokos* means what it says, to claim that I am a crypto-Arian; they have forgotten that point.

The problem is how to unite these two sets of non-negotiables. In the traditional language, how are we to conceive the "pre-existence" of the Son who Jesus is? How are we to read the Prologue of John's Gospel *and* the narrative it introduces as a coherent whole? Or indeed read the Prologue itself as a coherent whole?

In my *Systematic Theology*[2] I advanced three more or less related proposals. I continue to think that what I wrote on those pages is true. But the proposals are insufficient to one part of their joint task, and my language was intended to show that I suspected as much. I should have explicitly said so. A quick look at each of the proposals follows, differently ordered than in the *Systematic Theology*.

My exploitation of Romans 1:3–4 is—I dare to suggest—a necessary and significant corrective to the tradition's usual way of thinking about the Son's divinity. These two artful verses—whether they were devised by Paul or found as an existent confessional formula—are perhaps the New Testament's closest approach to a "two-natures" doctrine. The Son is, "according to the flesh," that is, as a creature, constituted as such by human descent, and indeed by specific descent from David. So far so easily read within the standard tradition. But then note what is paired with this! He is "determined"[3] to be "the powerful[4] Son of God" by action of the Spirit; and so not by divine origin as the christological tradition might make us expect, but rather by the resurrection, the supreme act of the Spirit who is "Giver of Life."

Within the mystery of the triune God's specific eternity, the Son's subsistence must therefore be as much from the Spirit as *telos* as from the Father as *arche*. Or anyway, so the Scriptures' pervasive eschatological-pneumatological orientation suggests—an orientation scrupulously ignored by traditional doctrine of the Son's divinity. Thus attending to Romans 1:3–4 is in itself a much needed move. The only thing is: the passage is not about the Son's *pre*-existence, which is what people are worried about.

The second proposal is more directly about pre-existence, and is in my judgement again a needed observation and corrective. For the most obvious pre-existence of Christ attested by Scripture is his active presence in old Israel: as the Glory of the Lord, the Angel of the Lord, and the Word of the Lord.[5] These appearances were recognized by the rabbis as one reality, God's *Shekinah*, God as his own "dwelling" among his people, as one who is other than God yet is the same God. Patristic exegetes even recognized in the

---

2. Jenson, *ST*, 1:141–44.

3. Not "declared" as in NRSV, ready as always to blunt Scripture's more offensive statements.

4. The phrase often translated "with power," as if there was or could have been the divine Son of God without power, is adjectival and should be translated that way. Just as "Spirit of holiness" is in the diction of this confession equivalent to "Holy Spirit."

5. And as other, more structural, phenomena.

Glory's "appearance" to Ezekiel[6] as "a man" the actual man who would again appear in God's Glory on the Mount of Transfiguration.

Without fully exploiting the fact of Christ's active and identifiable presence in Israel, and the scriptural testimony to the presence, doctrines of his pre-existence will always be biblically rootless. We must not merely note that Christ is present in the Old Testament; we must shape our understanding of his person and work to his life there. Still, we do indeed have to account ontologically for this presence. It would appear that a pre-existence of the Old Testament pre-existence is called for.

Here is where my third previous proposal fits—and fails. In the *Systematic Theology* I suggest a "pattern of movement" within the divine life. The problem is not that the suggestion is merely false, but that it is—as has several times been pointed out—hopelessly vague. It either gets us nowhere, or if it does may get us to a wrong place—though insistence that it *must* mislead is not quite warranted. So what to do? Here goes.

It is not as an individual instance of humanity as such, not as one among many who have the same human nature,[7] that Jesus is the second hypostasis of the Trinity. According to Aquinas—and to me—a divine hypostasis is "a subsisting relation," that is, a relation that is its own term, and so is not an *instance* of anything at all.[8] If then we obey my opening maxims, particularly the first, we will say that it is Jesus' *relation to* the Father—and not Jesus as a specimen of humanity—which is the second hypostasis of Trinity. The Father's sending and Jesus' obedience *are* the second hypostasis in God.

Next step: *this relation itself* can indeed subsist "before" Mary's conception, in whatever sense of "before" obtains in the Trinity's immanent life. For that life is constituted in nothing but the web of such relations, which as terms we are told to call Father, Son, and Spirit. In the divine life there is therefore no line on which the relation describable as God's sending and Jesus' obedience could occupy a position "after" anything. And again we must remember that antecedent to God's life, there is no realm in which the Son/Logos might "pre"-exist, or not.[9]

What in the triune life has ontological *pre*-cedence to the Son as subsistent relation, is the "monarchy" of the Father: his relation to Jesus is the condition of the possibility of Jesus' relation to him. Yet the Father himself does not subsist otherwise than as a relation to the Son—the circle is the

6. In the call vision, on which see discussion in Jenson, *Ezekiel*.

7. Whatever "human nature" is.

8. Except, I suppose, the class of subsisting relations—which is a small class, with three members.

9. Some of my critics seem not to have got it altogether into their thinking that time is created. Admittedly, it is a hard thing to do.

very point. Therefore, since there is no way in which anything could be precedent to the Father, there is nothing precedent to the Son as subsistent relation.

I am not sure whether or not this analysis fits what folk have in mind as the "pre-existence" of the *Logos*. But then, I have never been sure what anyone who is not an antecedently convinced Neoplatonist can actually have in mind under that rubric. I continue to regard *Logos asarkos*, used for something "before" the incarnation on any sort of line, as a *Vorstellung* in futile search of a *Begriff*.

Creation

14

On the Doctrine of the Atonement *(2006)*

The phrase "doctrine of atonement" is generally used to signify an account of why Jesus' death on a cross is important to us and specifically for our relation to God. "Atonement" is a deliberate coinage—though an old one, documented to 1513—meaning the act of putting things at one, particularly where a previous unity has been broken. In its theological use, the word thus presumes that what happened at Jesus' death was a reunion between God and us, which seems a biblically sound assumption. A *doctrine* of atonement is then an attempt to say how Jesus' crucifixion does that.

It is commonplace to observe that there is no dogma of the atonement, that although in christology there is dogma established at all seven ecumenical councils, no council—or pope or other plausibly ecumenical authority—has ever laid down a dogma of atonement. If you deny that Christ is "of one being with the Father," or that the Son and Jesus are but one hypostasis, you are formally a heretic. But you can deny any explanation of how the atonement works, or all of them together, or even deny that any explanation is possible, and be a perfectly orthodox believer. To be sure, if you simply deny that Jesus' death does in fact somehow reunite us with God, you are no Christian at all, but that is a different sort of deficiency.

Indeed, not even informally is there a generally accepted proposal. There is instead an inherited heap of proposals, classically if somewhat heavy-handedly and prejudicially sorted out by Gustaf Aulèn in his immensely influential *Christus Victor*. To be sure, in the West, Anselm of Canterbury's proposal—or rather a perversion of it—is often called "the doctrine of the atonement," but if we look to the full ecumene we observe that this identification is mere provincialism, Anselm having had at best a mixed reputation in the East. Some make a virtue of this proliferation of proposals and the absence of formal or informal consensus around any one of them; others see in it a historical failure and a challenge to do better. I am among the latter, which may be unwise, but there I am.

Those who make a virtue of our historical irresolution often say that the atonement at the cross is so profound a mystery that it can be evoked only by heaping up tropes. So it will be said that Anselm, with his "objective" doctrine, Abelard, with his "subjective" theory, and the ancient fathers who spoke of Christ as Victor over Satan and his powers—and any further contributions one might find—were not, in fact, doing what they each thought they were doing, providing a conceptual account of the cross's atoning efficacy. Instead, it might be said that they were putting forward "images" of what happened on the cross, and that now looking back we should say that this is just fine, and indeed the more such images are heaped up around the cross the better. The language of "images" has even become a standard way of *referring* to doctrines of the atonement.

This move has its followers, including folks I respect, but I get nervous whenever someone says that something is too mysterious to talk about with concepts. Images have their own grip on reality and are indispensable, but getting along *only* with images is problematic. True "mysteries" in the biblical use of the notion indeed often *break* our concepts and may even confront us with truth whose conceptual description obeys Gödel's maxim that truth cannot be proved, but mysteries in the biblical sense do not reduce us to exclusive reliance on images. Thus, the Incarnation is indeed a *mysterion*, in that it is in itself an irreducible contingency, transforms other reality, and is to be known only if God reveals it—and I have just recited three perfectly conceptual and coherent things theology has said about it. So also the cross as atonement is a mystery in that proper biblical sense, which by no means excuses us from clear conceptual discourse about it and about its mysterious character.

Thus, I am instead inclined to say that the historical record simply displays a theological question that we have so far not been able to answer in a fully satisfying way—which would, after all, not be the only such case. The notion that Anselm and the Fathers and the rest were proposing not theories but images or metaphors—and that the more of these we heap up the more we celebrate the mystery—seems to me a rather plain case of making a virtue of a failure. And I am even so rash as to think I have a theory as to *why* the Church's thinking has so far failed at this point.

So my first endeavor will be to present my theory. Very early, Christian theology of the cross made two paired errors, which are of a piece with wider errors. The Bible made sense of the cross by narratively and rhetorically locating it in history, as told in the Bible, and by conceptualizing the linkage. The twin errors I am about to discuss did their damage in concert by cutting away the event of the cross from its location in the biblical story.

The first error cut the cross off from its *future*, in the Resurrection, without which, in the Bible's general view of reality, a crucifixion would be anything but beneficial. The pattern of the primal kerygma of atonement is displayed in Luke's presentation of the first Christian sermon: Jesus was put to death by the hands of sinful men, but God raised him up; *therefore* a return to God and life in his Spirit are open to you. However, this is not the pattern of our inherited postbiblical theories; in fact, when theologians steeped in one of the inherited theories encounter this primal biblical doctrine outside the Bible, they sometimes do not recognize it.

The other mistake was to sever the cross from its *past*, in the canonical history of Israel. Without its specific location in Israel's adventure with God, the crucifixion of this one provincial celebrity, on suspicion of religio-political conspiracy, would hardly have been noteworthy amid the thousands of such Roman executions, even if he had thereafter "appeared to many." Nevertheless, the inherited theories discuss the Crucifixion in essential abstraction from Israel's history. It is not surprising that they prove unconvincing in the long run.

First, then, consider the separation of atonement and resurrection. In one way or another, the historically inherited theories of atonement presume that the action of atonement is finished when Jesus dies, so that the Resurrection then accomplishes something else, if indeed often no more than to repair collateral damage done by the Crucifixion. Anselm's doctrine is perhaps the most notorious in its ability to do without the Resurrection.

Anselm is, of course, regularly denounced on other grounds. Before proceeding to my own critique, fairness compels me to come to his defense, for many of those who attack—or affirm—"the Anselmian theory of atonement" do not seem to have read his text. Anselm does not say that Jesus' death satisfies God's wrath or that God punishes Jesus instead of us. Quite to the contrary, Anselm presents Jesus' death as God's *rescue* of creatures who are on a self-destructive path, which God accomplishes by *averting* a regime of punishment and instituting instead a regime of repair.

Nevertheless, Anselm's doctrine does have a fatal flaw: the Resurrection is not integral to achieving this result. Both in Anselm himself and in the bowdlerizations of Anselm, which are presented as "the" doctrine of atonement, God and humanity are reconciled when Jesus dies, and the Resurrection tidies up. It is very likely that Anselm, a devoted reader of Scripture, bishop, and regular celebrant of Eucharist, simply assumed that nothing theologically interesting works without the Resurrection, but his theory does not state this explicitly.

To grasp the second founding error we should remember that afore-mentioned exegetical commonplace: that the Gospels' own interpretation of the cross consists for the most part of embedding it in the Old Testament narrative. As is well known, hardly a detail of the Gospels' Passion narrative fails to invoke some Old Testament text or event. And Pauline and Johan-nine theology explained the meaning of the cross with the Old Testament concepts used in their original sacrificial and eschatological force.

Postapocalyptic Christian theology quickly isolated the cross from its biblical embedding in Old Testament discourse, especially at the dogmatic level, if not in preaching or in the liturgy. Both the early rules of faith and the baptismal and conciliar creeds that developed from them skip straight from Creation to the Incarnation, leaving out the whole of the Lord's history with Israel. To be sure, Marcion's proposal, to reject the Old Testament's God altogether, was too much: it was immediately seen that the Father of our Lord Jesus Christ had to be the Creator, so Creation got in. But for all the Creed's display, the Creator could just as well have sent his Son to reunite humanity with himself, without having called Abraham, or having led Israel from Egypt, or having dwelt in the temple, or having sent Israel into exile and having—sort of—brought them back, or indeed, without having done any of the works described in the Old Testament after the first chapter of Genesis. Think how the Roman creed goes: "I believe in God the Father Almighty, Creator of heaven and earth. And in Jesus Christ . . ."

The omission of the Lord's history with Israel in Christian theology is not accidental or explicable by circumstance, for it has been pervasive in other central aspects of the Church's life and theology, not just in the creeds. For a central location in the life of the Church, closely parallel to creedal formation, the Lord commanded us to give thanks to God in the style of Israel's table thanksgivings, sharing in the thanksgiving by sharing bread and cup, again in Jewish style. And most Christians have more or less obeyed. But our thanksgiving has routinely omitted the Exodus and the giving of Torah and the sending of the prophets, and indeed everything that must have figured in the thanksgiving Jesus himself offered. Most, not all, eucharistic prayers mentioned Creation and the Fall—which, I suppose, is some improvement over the creeds—and then went straight to Jesus and his cross.

As to systematic theology, many powerful systems make no use of the Old Testament except as witness to Creation and sin and as religious back-ground for Jesus. The systems of classical liberalism, fragments of which still dominate in this country, often do not even do as much. Indeed, classical liberal theology was partially powered by a desire to detach Christianity from the Jews and their Scriptures.

The isolation of the cross from the biblical history by which the Gospels and the rest of the New Testament make sense of it—from the Resurrection in one direction and from God's history with Israel in the other—has inevitably compelled theology to find some other framework that can make sense of the cross. If we come to the Gospels without an antecedent theory, what do we actually learn about the cross? The Gospels tell of a Jewish prophet and rabbi executed by Jewish and Roman authorities because he proclaimed and enacted the Kingdom with utter immediacy and so "made himself the Son of God." For the Jews, this meant blasphemy, and for the Romans, it translated to "pitiful would-be rival to the Caesar." The biblical witnesses reveal how they interpret the events mainly in the way they tell the story, the one event of a longer narrative. In the temporal direction, they report it as an incident within the whole scriptural history of Israel; in the other direction, it is recounted to trump and conclude the story of the execution with the message of the resurrection. Our inherited theologies of atonement, however, having severed these connections, must imagine some other framework and some other event within it.

So Anselm imagined a universal feudal system in which the good of each member is invested in the mutual giving of honor where due, construed sin as disruption of the universal balance of honor, and construed the atonement as creatures' rescue from disaster by God's restoration of the balance. I do not say that the resulting doctrine is altogether false or that one cannot make use of it in some contexts. The vision is detachable from feudalism and bears consideration for its own sake. But it remains that Anselm's transaction of honor is indeed *imagined*, that it has little resemblance to the narrative in Scripture, and that a free-floating imagination of this sort is indeed apt to become one trope among others, to be piled at the foot of the cross.

In contrast, Abelard imagined a universal divine moral pedagogy aimed at educating moral creatures in virtue—particularly in the virtue most lacking among fallen creatures, love. Then he construed the cross as the overwhelming display of God's love, which breaks our hardened hearts and moves us to love in response. Again, I do not say there is nothing in this, only that it is again the imagining of an event other than the one the Gospels narrate. Indeed, it is an evocation of love that could have been accomplished by some event other than the cross and even within the history of some nation other than Israel, and therefore, it will eventually work out as just another nice metaphor to heap around the cross.

So essentially, most of the Eastern fathers imagined—not to put too fine a point on it—a myth. Consequent on the fall of certain angels, they said, there had been continuous warfare between God and those now satanic powers, and the heavily veiled manifestation of that battle was the overt turmoil of earthly history. In this war, the Incarnation of God the Son and the giving of him over to crucifixion was a brilliant tactical move by which God gained final victory. Only on the surface was Jesus crucified by Jewish and Roman authorities. What actually happened was an attempt by Satan to kill what he thought was a human savior who turned out to be God the Son himself and who broke Satan's power.

Scripture does use mythic fragments and images in a variety of contexts and ways in telling of the cross. But it never tells a whole myth, nor does it convey this one. Scripture breaks up Eastern antiquity's mythic worldview, retaining some of its bits and pieces for its own quite different purposes. The fathers reversed this and made up a whole new myth from some of those bits and pieces, creating a frame within which to understand the cross. The resultant patristic imagery of conflict and victory is powerful and even spiritually transformative, but theology, born of the urge to *demy*-thologize, must eventually come to regard the patristic imagery as merely imagery, which, of course, is how we now handle it, even when declaring allegiance to "the patristic doctrine."

So what must we do instead? A first step is liturgical. We honor the way in which the atoning Crucifixion is indeed a *mysterion* in the proper sense when we recognize that its primal construal is recital and enactment of the Passion narrative in and by the liturgical celebration of Maundy Thursday, Good Friday, and the Easter Vigil, as well as by the condensation of that triple celebration in each Sunday Eucharist. We understand the cross as our reunion with God when we ourselves are made actors in the cross's story—a story that in the ancient three-day celebration is indeed complete with Israel and the Resurrection. The traditional liturgy of the three days incorporates us into the action by repeated communion, relates Israel's complete history through readings and prayers, and allows neither conclusion nor benediction until the Resurrection has been proclaimed.

It is undoubtedly this liturgical sequence, transcending the limitations of the creeds and the doctrines taught in schools, that kept understanding of the atonement alive for so many centuries. I suggest that it is the loss of this liturgy in most of Protestantism, and the concurrent loss of its Sunday compendium, that has slowly but inevitably delivered Protestantism over, on the one hand, to the grotesqueries of "blood atonement" and the like and, on the other hand, to a doctrine of the atonement that may be summarized: God loves us all regardless, and now let's get on to the real issues of peace and justice.

I have examined the liturgical knowledge of atonement in my *System-atic Theology*.[1] Here I want to consider something else—I want to develop a *theoretical* construal that in the systematics appears only *in nuce*. A doc-trine of the atonement is supposed to conceptualize our reunion with God. What I will attempt to do here—an effort that is hardly begun in *Systematic Theology*—is to show how the event of the cross, taken with its biblical past and future, does this. What is needed is a conceptual framework that does not substitute for the biblical history but rather exemplifies it. Just such a framework is at hand.

It is the *triune* God with whom we need to be reunited. Trinitarian doctrine's statements describing the relationships that make up the life of this God—that the Father begets the Son and breathes the Spirit, that the Son is begotten of the Father and sends the Spirit, that the Spirit frees the Father and Son to love each other—describe the plot of that biblical story I have been invoking. And trinitarian doctrine's identification of Father, Son, and Spirit as three in God names the carrying *dramatis personae* of that sto-ry. Thus a particular location within which the biblical story also describes a particular location in the life of God and a particular set of relationships to the three divine persons. A construal of how the cross, with its past and future, unites us with God must also say how this reunion involves us *in* the divine life *with* each of these divine persons.

For we can be reunited with the *triune* God only as we are fitted into the triune life. With some other sort of God, matters might stand differ-ently. But the biblical God is no monad; we cannot be reunited with him as one might reunite two pennies by stacking them. Nor can the specifi-cally triune God sustain any merely causal relation to the world, in any cur-rent use of "causal"; he cannot reunite us with himself by endeavoring to change us. The relation of creatures to this God is always a function of their *involvement* with the three who are God—or, in abysmal possibility, their disinvolvement.

So we must go triune person by person—remembering always that the kind of discourse that follows is a kind of sloganeering—that "the Father" is the God of Israel; "the Spirit" is the power of Resurrection, the power of God's future; and "the Son" is the Son Israel was called to be and who in the resurrection is that *totus Christus* that includes us. If this is not remembered, it may appear that in the following statements I do what I have rebuked

---

1. Jenson, *ST*, 1:256.

the tradition for doing: replacing the biblical narrative with a framework invented by theologians.

We need to be—and are—reconciled *to* the Father *in* the Son *by* the Spirit. Here and in the following, readers should pay heed to the prepositions. We need to be reconciled to the Father because we are at odds with him, at odds with the very one by whose sheer will we exist. That is, we are in rebellion against the Torah that tells us of the Father's will—it is in this patrological connection that talk of disobedience should appear in our doctrine of atonement. The Spirit—meaning the Spirit as the agent—reconciles us to the Father by making us one moral subject with Christ, who on the cross *is* obedient to the Father, even unto death. As both Luther and Jonathan Edwards taught, the Spirit so unites us with Christ that the Father's judgement, "You are righteous," is not fiction or a legal manoeuvre but a judgment of observed fact, although observable, to be sure, only by the Father. It is by cross and resurrection that the Spirit accomplishes this unity, when he enables the Son to cleave to us, even though we kill him, and enables us to cleave to the Son's risen presence.

We need to be reconciled to the Spirit, and are, *by* the Son—meaning the Son as the agent—*before* the Father. We need to be reconciled to the Spirit because we have backed off from the fulfillment to which he draws us, we have cowered before the utter transformation toward which the Spirit has prodded us since Creation, and we have not, in Bultmann's famous phrase, "been open to the future."

Thus it is in this pneumatological connection that talk of unbelief should appear in our doctrine of atonement. The Son reconciles us to the Spirit by entering that wonderful and frightening future before us, going through the end of this world on the cross and entering the Kingdom through the Resurrection, all the while appealing to his Father to honor his dearly purchased solidarity with us, just as, in the Resurrection, the Father does. Thus the Son brings us along as he follows the Spirit's leading. Indeed, as Paul taught, the Son so reconciles us to the Spirit that the Spirit even prays to the Father from within us, as so much our own voice that we cannot hear him.

We need to be reconciled to the Son, and are, *by* the Father, *in* the Spirit. We need to be reconciled to the Son because we have wanted to be individuals, a rebellion that is not uniquely modern. We have not wanted to be members of one body together, the body of Christ, to have our life within the *totus Christus*. In fact, we have not wanted to live within *any* personal whole other than that which each of us hopelessly tries to make for himself or herself. It is in this christological connection that a consideration of our being *incurvatus in se*, turned into ourselves, should be required in our doctrine of atonement. The Father, however, sends the Son into eternal identification with us, even unto Sheol, so that we simply cannot escape being one with the Son and so with one another. And in the Spirit we willingly live that identification, for the members of the Son's body are also his people and his spouse, which without our will we cannot be. So we are reconciled to the triune God by acts of each of the three over against the other two. Thus it may indeed appear that we are reconciled to God by his being reconciled in himself—but that is a matter for another essay.

15

Evil as Person (1989)

A Work of Penance

I am here to begin a work of penance. I—and, I think, perhaps some of you—have been wrong, and in no small matter. I—and maybe some of you—have supposed that it was possible to do Christian theology without explicit systematic reference to Satan; without systematic use of the concept of evil as person.

It has apparently taken me even longer than it did Luther to catch on in this matter. I could plead that we have a longer life expectancy now. And my difficulty has anyway been the reverse of Luther's. For Luther it was always clear that there was a devil, but it took him a long time to learn how thoroughly the devil was indeed ruler of this world. For me, on the other hand, it was always clear that the world lies in evil, but that evil could usefully and necessarily be conceived as a person, it has taken me some time to understand.

It is not that I have ever thought there was no devil. It has always been my principle that there is more in heaven and in earth, and presumably then also in hell, than is dreamed of in anyone's philosophy. I have therefore always acknowledged reality so abundantly testified in human history as angels and demons and so forth, even when I did not know what to do with them. But my soteriology has made no conceptual use of these acknowledgments; and that was a wrong procedure.

Let me begin by saying why I am now driven to take the devil with theological seriousness. It is because, first there is evil; and, second, there is God. It is confronting these two facts with each other rigorously and strenuously, that eventually compels one to think of evil as person.

The Personhood of God and Humor

What, one may ask, are the rock-bottom constituents of the affirmation that there is God? If it is the biblical God one has in mind? I suggest that there are two. First, to affirm God, is to affirm that all reality, and especially reality conceived as history, is embraced in a moral intention. It is to say that our apparently inescapable endeavor to do good, to choose the future, is in accord with that encompassing reality in which we find ourselves and in which we seek to choose. To affirm God is, at this first level, to say that there is moral order to the whole of things. It is to assert that the ground of being is a subjectivity, a will and an intelligence, that intends some futures and not others.

The question is: Is the world valued? Is the world loved? Are there intentions for the world? And is the world valued and loved antecedently to *our* valuings and loves? The one who says there is God answers that question "Yes."

But that is only the first question, and its affirmative answer only the first of two steps in the affirmation of God. For merely to say that the world is always antecedently valued, that the ground of the world is a subjectivity with moral intention, is not yet quite to say that there is God, at least, again, if with that word you mean something like what the Bible means. For it is not yet to assert that this subjectivity at the ground of things can be *addressed*, can be talked to; it is not yet to say that prayer is possible. A sheer moral intention at the ground of things is not yet to speak of what the Scripture calls God.

There are many ways, I suppose, in which one might stipulate the difference between a mere moral subjectivity and a person. But for this essay let me do it so: personal subjectivity has not only morality, but also humor. A person is moral subjectivity with a sense of humor. If God, therefore, is personal, He is not only the moral intention at the ground of things. He is also the laughter at the ground of things, the sense of humor at the ground of things.

We often ask why God takes such long ways around to his stated objectives. We wonder why He takes the long roundabout of crucifixion and resurrection, to his stated goal of reestablishing righteousness in the world. Given omnipotence, why not just do it? We wonder why He permits the fall, as an enormously painful long way around to the goal of showing mercy. We wonder why the history of His Church is so crooked. It does not, of course, answer those questions to say that God does it because He has a sense of humor. But it does, I suggest, precisely state the phenomena.

The difference between the impersonal moral world-ground and God is that we can talk to God, that prayer is possible. But prayer is, of course, a funny phenomenon, and in both senses: funny peculiar and funny ha-ha. Whyever, after all, would omnipotence enjoy our praises? And why do we need to petition omniscience? Surely God already knows what we want, and knows moreover what we need, and moreover knows what He is or is not going to do about it? If omniscience solicits our praises, if omniscience wants information from us, this can only be described as that peculiar kind of self-awareness and humility that we call humor. It is funny when God converses with us, paying real attention to our side of the converse. But He does do just that.

Evil as Person

The sheer assertion that there is evil pairs with the first of the assertions that makes the reality of God, that there is a moral intention at the ground of things. There is evil also. All history is embraced in a moral intention; that is part of the affirmation of God. And all history is also retarded by moral determinisms and amoral chances. It is not only our inescapable endeavor to do good that is somehow appropriate to the world in which we find ourselves; our equally inescapable moral confusion and incapacity, our flight from the future, is somehow also appropriate to that world. There is not merely disorder in general, along with order, in the whole of things; there is moral disorder in the whole of things.

As the ground of being, there is only God. As the ground of being there is only that will, that intention, that *values* the world. But somewhere in being, somewhere out there and in there and down there, there is a subjectivity that comprehensively *despises* the world, that *hates* all things. And that subjectivity, that hatred, that despising, is also antecedent to *our* hatings and despisings.

This assertion that there is evil is not, of course, a mere report of experience. It is an interpretation of experience. And it is an interpretation which is imposed by the affirmation that there is God. If we are embraced by moral intention, then our experience of moral disorder and reluctance can only be interpreted as I have just done. So far I had come earlier.

The affirmation of God is, however, not merely an affirmation that at the ground of being there is a moral intention. It is also the affirmation that this intention has humor. *Does not also this* aspect of the affirmation of God demand its correlate in the way in which we acknowledge evil? I have found no way to construct an argument that it does. I can only say that the force of the question itself has become compelling with me. It is somehow the mere symmetry that seems demanding. Since indeed it is only because we affirm the biblical God that believers interpret the moral disorder of the world as evil, as a hating subjectivity, must not also the second and decisive step in our affirmation of God have its correlate in the way we interpret moral disorder? If God has humor, as the subject that loves all things, must not the subjectivity that hates all things have also its humor, and *therefore* be understood as *person*?

Interpretation of the world's evil as personally willed, as intended, that is to say, by a subjectivity that like all persons has humor, seems at least to be in so far confirmed that it covers our experience. For surely it seems that evil not only impedes and derails good intention, but mocks it. Surely it does seem that there is someone out or in or down there, that is having malicious fun with God's creation.

We are about to elect a president of the United States. And for the moment, the great American experiment in democracy has come to this: our choice will be exercised though a mechanism which is constructed in every detail by utter contempt for the people. Now if that is not a *joke* on us, I do not know what would be. I know that this ironical outcome can be exhaustively accounted for in terms of impersonal historical forces. But is it not also a great joke? Are we not in fact arbitrarily resisting the most simple interpretation of the phenomenon, if we refuse to move on to such an interpretation?

Does not every divorce not merely frustrate but *mock* the couple? Again, while I was writing this lecture, Blanche and I were plagued with a series of frustrations that began to seem like a plot, and it is well known that the devil does not like to be written about. If the greenhouse effect proceeds as predicted, humanity will get a royal come-uppance; the maxim of being hoist with one's own petard will have been exemplified in mammoth dimension. Will *nobody* out there be laughing?

Or consider the kind of temptation of which Luther mostly talked. When the devil says to us, "Just because God wills your good, and has given you these commandments, and willed you to live by them for your own blessing—just because of all that, I've got you," is that not a prize piece of malicious wit?

What Ails the Devil?

Who is the devil? And what is he like? Better: what ails him? For the devil can only be described, according to long theological tradition, by his deficiencies.

The deficiency most immediately accessible is that the devil's humor is always mere wit; he is never truly funny. God is both witty and funny; and so sometimes, in God's trail, are we. The devil is only witty. Or, as Luther put it, he is a "sour spirit," a spirit at all because he like all spirits has humor, but a sour one. The devil's jokes are never on himself.

Indeed, if one were to speak more mythologically than even yet I am willing to do, and talk of Satan as a fallen angel, one could say that this is how he fell: he could not take God's big joke on him and the other great spirits. He refused to join Michael and the others in service to those mere animals, those humans down there, whom God impishly and foolhardily proposed to elevate unto himself, and in service to whom God proposed to assign the great spirits.

Thus the devil is indeed a person, but a sort of negative, mirror-image person. He is a parasite-person: the laughter which constitutes him a person is always on someone else. He never sees the joke on himself, as God does and as we sometimes do.

The devil is personal only in the passion of his refusal to be a person. The devil's jokes are never on himself because he has no self for them to be on. Or you could put it the other way and say, the devil has no self because he never sees the joke on himself. One could display the devil's negative personhood by contrasting it with our own, but that would be complicated by the fragilities of our own personhood. So I will go back to my opening tack and display the devil's deficiencies as a person over against the one fully personal reality, God.

God is fully and unconquerably a person. His humor is joyous. He always sees the joke on himself because he is *triune*.

Let me take some time with that last and decisive point, and let me use traditional trinitarian teaching, without arguing for it. The Father is no mere universal consciousness *because* he sees himself in and as the Son, because he has a partner other than himself in whom he finds himself. God is there *for* himself, and just so can be if he chooses there also for others than himself, for us. God, we may even say, is an *object* for himself. He can look at himself in the Son.

God, indeed, is a body for himself. There is something there that God looks at and says, "That is me." And the one then in whom he thus finds himself can also be an object for us. He can give us that one to look at and say, "That is God": the body on the cross and the body on the altar. And on that cross and on that altar, the joke can be on God. Since he truly finds himself in the thing on the cross and the thing on the altar, he has himself to laugh at. And his laughter is our salvation.

One step behind, we can do it too. I need you to help me out with it, which is the difference between God and us. Whereas God has his view of himself by himself, I have to get help. But nevertheless, with your help, I too can see the joke on myself. I can let myself be your object. I can let you have your view of me, as I have of you. And then I can take that Jenson as you see him, and find myself therein. Whereupon we must all, of course, burst out laughing. And indeed, only as I do this, only as I let the joke be on me, do I at all have, like God, a self, an object in which to find myself.

What ails the devil is that he will not give himself over to be anyone else's object. He will not allow himself to be defined by anyone else's gaze; no one is permitted to have their own view of him. He wants to be triune like God, to be himself the object in which he finds himself; only he is not, and so has no object in which to find himself; he has *no* self. He can never see the joke; he can only make cracks about others. Remember the prologue in heaven to the story of Job (1:6–12)? It is witty. And the devil *is* the great wit in the story, but the joke is always on someone else.

God is fully and richly embodied for himself and then for us, as Jesus the Son. Just so, he can give himself over to us and be maltreated by us. Just so his omnipotent rule is not tyranny. A purely disembodied consciousness, on the other hand, a consciousness that was always looking at us and never letting us look back, that always fixed us in its gaze and never let us see what he looked like, would be a universal tyrant. And it is, of course, that to which Satan hopelessly aspires. A disembodied spirit with no object to give to others, or to see himself in, would be, necessarily, a sort of universal hatred. Which is what ails the devil.

Temptation and Death

By not taking the devil seriously, I have done theology wrongly. What is to be taken seriously is a spirit with no sense of humor, better, a spirit with a purely witty sense of humor. How then should soteriology reckon with the devil? What I have been working on, and what I want now to lay before you, is a slow and so far minimal appropriation of that understanding of God's work among and for us as *battle*, as conflict with an opponent, which appears regularly in the Christian tradition and so strongly, almost bizarrely, in Luther.

Perhaps it is not too great an oversimplification to say that in the New Testament Satan appears above all as, first, the *tempter* of God's saints, and, second, as "he who has the power of *death*." I will organize my thoughts under these two rubrics.

First, how is Satan the tempter? Satan can *tempt* us precisely because he has no self of his own. He is thus protean in his emptiness. He speaks always in the person of someone else. Satan's voice is the voice of my conscience or of my friend or of my society. If in Luther's time the voice of conscience was his chosen mask, perhaps in our time the voice of society, in its own impersonality, suits him best, and vice versa.

As society or my friend or my own inner voices suggest evil, they *tempt* me. That is to say, I do not see through this stupid idea that my conscience is suggesting to me, or just say to my friend, "Cool it." I am instead tempted because there is really no one there to respond to, no identifiable enemy to arouse my suspicions, with whom to discuss or argue the suggestion.

We are, after all, created good, and it would be expected that we should see through suggestions of evil, that we should find them merely laughable. But we do not, because the suggestions of evil we encounter are no one's, because there is no way to talk them over, no one to answer back to, no one to laugh at.

There is a spirit afoot who has no self. When there seems no way to answer back, then it is that he is at work. His suggestions are actually laughable. He is the one who can never see the joke and is therefore bound regularly to be ridiculous, but we are bereft of the laughter that would save us.

The devil often speaks even with the voice of God—above all with the voice of God. For in his protean presence, he mimicks God's omnipresence. We hear him everywhere, and just therefore he can speak not only with society's voice or our inner voice; he can mimick God's voice. And the temptation he brings in that guise is the one great temptation, the temptation of which Luther was the expert: the temptation to despair in the face of God's holy will or to false confidence in the face of God's holy will, the temptation to unbelief, the temptation to let go our grip on reality, to join the devil in his own lack of being.

It is plain, therefore, what we need to save us from the tempter: we need to be able to *identify* him, to tell how the voice of society is sometimes the communal discourse by which we live and sometimes his, to tell how conscience is on the one hand inner discipline and on the other his sly permission to please ourselves, even if only by wallowing in despair at our iniquities. We need to be able to tell, above all, how religion is service of God and how it is the devil's service. No more is necessary. Once the devil is identified, he is too laughable to be taken seriously, but we have to know in what direction to throw the inkwell.

It is this identification that is accomplished by Jesus' cross and resurrection. In the cross and resurrection, in the Incarnation of the Son of God, the self as which God knows himself is there for us, that we too may know him. The body that God has for himself, is a body in our world, before our eyes and ears. Jesus' cross and resurrection is God's unambiguous self-identification to us. It is God's act to say and to show, "This is who I am." And just so, Satan too is identified and unmasked. Knowing God on the cross, we can distinguish. As our society tells us what we can do, we can distinguish between the commands of God and the insinuations of Satan. As our conscience speaks, we can distinguish between the echo of God's law and the voice of self-delusion.

In the Incarnation, the commandments recover their simplicity. That man does not live by bread alone is obvious; everybody has always known it. And it becomes again obvious as Jesus meets the contrary sly suggestion. That only God is to be worshipped is obvious in itself. And on the cross God is clearly located, that we may obey. That those who make tests of God's goodness never find it, is obvious in itself. And when Jesus repels Satan, we see how to tell the difference between testing God and believing His promises.

Above all, as God *gives* himself among us, Satan's difference from God is unambiguously exposed. God gives. Satan can only suck reality into the vacuum at his own heart. God plays the great joke of sin and redemption on himself. Satan only has witty defensiveness. It is the sovereign test: When the voice in the night tells me, "You are hopeless," is it said with a laugh or a snicker? If the former, the voice is God's; if the latter, out with the ink bottle. When the preacher tells me, "You are acceptable just as you are," on whom is the joke? If the joke is on me and the speaker, then the preacher's voice is God's voice. But if the joke is on everybody around me, in that now they can no longer rely upon my good works, then it is that same bad comedian on the stage again, even if the stage is in church.

To unmask Satan's temptations, Jesus had to be tempted by them. He had to hear the suggestions of self-preservation, of religious playing with God, of idolatry, and of all the rest of Satan's goods. He had to hear them in all their plausibility and evasiveness, and reject them. Which is to say, the biblical description of Christ's saving work as a struggle with an opponent, in all its apparent mythological character, is literal reporting.

Moreover, the struggle goes on, and is called theology. For what theology attempts to do is to identify God, to say who God is, and just so, to unmask Satan. So drastic an apprehension of our position at the end of time as Luther had, was a phenomenon that perhaps only comes when history is indeed lurching on the verge of the abyss. Thus also the apprehension of theology as struggle with a personified liar for the truth, is uncommon. But that is what theology is.

How, second, has Satan the power of death? Satan's power of death is the power to make us be like him. Death left to itself takes my self from me. When I am dead, I have no self for you; there is no longer anything for you to look at and say, "Well, there is Jenson again." And then I have no self for me either, for I am not God and have no second person in my own being in which to see myself. I need you to see me. Nor would mere "life after death" help. To be a mere subjectivity hanging around watching the rest of you, with no way to be there for you, would only increase the torment. If I die before Blanche, I do not want to watch her getting along without me—and whether that were torment or relief for her would make no difference. Mere life after death would be the very sort of life that Satan has. It would be to fall forever into his shadowy domain. Death is Satan's great trick on us, a marvelous piece of wit, but not funny.

Christ's resurrection saved us from all that, for he has not evaded death or survived it, but has overcome it. That is, he is beyond death *as* his self, *with* his body. And his body is precisely his self, his body, *given* for *us*. Therefore we are now in a fellowship of selves with him, a communion of bodies, that is already beyond death. We need not fear the devil's fate of merely surviving subjectivity. Our life, despite death, is with him whose wounds we will touch and whose bread we already share.

Moreover, his body is not merely his self given to us. It is the very body of God. The fellowship into which we go is, therefore, not the mere continuation of that which we now know. It is the perfect fellowship of the Father, Son, and Spirit. In the body of the Church and around the body of the Eucharist, we may look forward to death, not as the loss of one another and so of ourselves, but to our perfected fellowship and embodiment in God.

In the Kingdom we will each see ourselves as the whole rest of creation sees us, with the clear sight of God himself. We will see ourselves as Father and Son see us, as their beloved fellows. And eternity will thus roar with good humor, which is the Spirit.

Also in this connection, Christ's work is conflict with an opponent. Christ died, and so he encountered that vacuum whose trick death is. Words lose their purchase here. But that Christ died means, somehow, that the devil's trick was played also on him, that he met the malicious wit of evil that is the devil's personhood. Somehow Christ's death was a personal contest whose outcome was the resurrection. And somehow also the contest continues, for we who are one body with him must each enter that battle of wits that is death and be brought through it.

Death has no more sting, which is the great last joke on the devil. If he could only see it, he too would be saved. Indeed, the joke is so finally on Satan that he is, at the end, a sad figure. The gospel's laughter is our great defense against him. But in the end, it will be kinder to ignore him altogether—which is what I started out doing, just a little too soon.

16

The Strange New World of the Bible *(2008)*

"Let him kiss me with the kisses of his mouth!" she says. And then she turns to him, "Draw me after you, let us make haste . . ." As she is drawn into love so she draws the reader; the opening of the Song of Songs invites us into a world of this passionate woman and her lover.

Their world does not seem strange at first; we think we know about kisses; we think we live in the world to which kisses belong. Even if we are deprived of kisses or have for religious or other good reason renounced them, we think we know what we are missing or have given up. And indeed, at least at first, the love-world of the Song is recognizably our world of bodily longing and bliss and deprivation and the rest of it.

Yet—as the Song then leads us through its world, its familiarity becomes evasive. In the Song, the contours of love prove sharper than are the contours of our loves—did ever an earthly tryst come off quite so flawlessly as the one the woman arranges in a countryside bower amid spring's blossoms? In the Song the antinomies and conflicts of love are often bizarre: What are we to make of this woman, who—to choose but one incident—on discovering her love missing from their bed rushes into pitch-dark Jerusalem to find him, confessing the while that she has no idea where to look, and on encountering a police patrol inquires after him in terms that guarantee they will not know whom she is talking about?

The world of the Song gradually opens as a love-world not reported, but *imagined* by a poet, a seemingly high-modernist poet devoted to strange juxtapositions and riddles with no solution—someone a bit like the poet of J. Alfred Prufrock's love song, with better luck.

And then, just as we have settled in to enjoy the poetry—or anyway what we can make of it—we come to the couplet that is usually regarded as the climax of the Song: "Love is strong as death, jealously fierce as the grave."[1] If we ponder these lines, we will eventually have to ask, "*Whose* love can be such love? Whose love can bind as absolutely as death, whose jealousy will no more give up its prey than does the grave? Whose love exactly has the Song been celebrating?"

And if we are brought up short by this question, we may then notice that the language of this couplet is playing with us: that Hebrew *moth* in the first line of the couplet can indeed be translated as "death," but is also the proper name of a Canaanite god, the enemy of the life-giving gods, the Hebrew *sheol* in the second line can indeed be translated simply as "grave," but is also the name for that grasping negation of being which so many psalms beg the Lord to avert. *Whose* love and jealousy can match the god of death and the power of chaos? The couplet teases us, veiling and unveiling itself as—theology.

And we may then even remember that in one passage of Scripture, "Jealousy" is a proper name of Israel's God.[2]

What love-world is it, then, into which the Song's celebration of kisses finally draws us? Who now is the poet? Can this any longer be a poet like that Catullus of whose most famous lines the Song's opening may remind us?[3]

Nor are we even allowed to rest in such theological figurations, for if we read on through the Song's remaining verses, we find ourselves plowing through what is unmistakably a harassed editor's dumping ground for left-over fragments. At the end, we are brought rudely back to the earth where editors slave.

          ↬

Another opening.[4] Ezekiel reports: "In the thirtieth year, in the fourth month, on the fifth day of the month, as I was among the exiles by the river Chebar . . ." He is at pains to nail down the earthly chronology and geography, and the political situation in which he finds himself—a situation of exile familiar throughout earthly history.

1. 8:6.
2. Exod 34:14.
3. *Da mi basia mille, deinde centum, deinde mille altera, . . .*
4. Ezek 1:1–28.

But then, "The heavens were opened, and I saw visions of God." More abruptly than in the Song, a new a strange world opens, the world called heaven, the part of creation that God has made for his own dwelling and in which he is seen and adored by his creatures of angels and saints, the world that would open to John on Patmos and to Dante at the climax of his journey.

And so in the proper fashion of such apocalyptic adventurers, Ezekiel sees what is to be seen in heaven, uniquely of course the heavenly throne itself and a Presence thereon, a Presence at first so sheerly other than anything on earth that its fire and beauty is said by Ezekiel to be but "the *likeness of* the *appearance of* the *glory of* God."

All very properly transcendent—except that this heavenly throne has wheels, and after its suitably spectacular appearance trundles along by that same river Chebar. As Ezekiel looks about at the environs of heaven's throne, it is after all earth that he sees under its wheels and under his own feet, the world that requires that if there are to be travelling thrones, they must have wheels, with however marvelous a four-wheel universal.

And yet another opening into a new yet not altogether discontinuous world, and this the strangest, last, and most briefly describable of my instances. When on the third day faithful women and then some of the disciples looked into the empty tomb, and one went in to check, what world beyond the entrance did they look into or indeed venture upon? It was a chamber cut into a rocky face somewhere in the vicinity of Jerusalem, the possession, it is said, of a man of earthly substance—*in which* death was swallowed up in victory, to make that hollow in the rock the very gateway of heaven. It should occasion no surprise that Mark gives us his doubly offputting ending: the women flee and readers are frustrated. That emptiness was enough to put off the hardiest. And then again a comedown, for what could be more banal, than the disciples' subsequent disorganization? Or indeed the disorganization of the reports?

II

It goes that way when the Bible is opened—my examples could of course be multiplied, though the empty tomb trumps all. A world opens that is at first our earth, and then is strange and new beyond our conceptions, and then again with all its novelty and discontinuity is somehow the world we truly inhabit. The love-world opened by the Song is at once the world of earthly kisses and the world of the Lord's love for his people. The heaven that opens to Ezekiel, and that displays the eternal throne, is touring earth tending to politics. And for all we know, the rock containing the gate of heaven is perhaps still somewhere near Jerusalem, maybe even where tradition says it is.

How are we to understand the identity-in-difference and difference-in-identity of divine love and human love, heaven and earth, human-made cavern and gate of heaven? Clearly, we will not be able to read the Bible coherently without some construal of the way its strange new world is our world. I have of course stolen my title from the young Karl Barth, and that was his discovered problem when he was assigned to preach on texts he did not choose, and so to be confronted with Scripture on its own terms.

III

I think that we mostly get that construal backwards, and that *therefore* we have such troubles with the Bible. For of course we do indeed have our troubles with the Bible. The scholarship devoted to explaining it, to interpreting it, to applying it, to devising hermeneutical metatheories about it, increases exponentially and becomes ever more desperate; while in the Church the Bible nevertheless becomes ever less accessible. I want to propose an explanation of this phenomenon. I think we read the relation between the strange world the Bible opens and our familiar world the wrong way around, and so are in a hopeless situation from the start.

We are socialized to suppose that the "real world" is a world outside faith's story of God with his people, outside the Church doors, outside the covers of the Book, a world "out there." And we suppose that we—preachers and teachers and worshipers leaving the service—are supposed to carry good ideas from the biblical world "out" "into" this "real" world. Preparing to preach or teach from the Bible, I think I must discover the "relevance" of my text to the world out there. Writing a piece on hermeneutics, I think I must ask: "What hermeneutical move will blaze the way from biblical narrative to real history?" "What," the devotional reader asks, "can I get out of this passage for my current actual situation?"

The "real" world of kisses—everyone tells us—is the world of *Sex and the City*; and it is the Church's mission to bring forgiveness to that world, to console the brokenhearted, and perhaps to work for some amelioration of the chaos. The real political world—we are all socialized to suppose—is the world of Babylon *as* Babylon conceived it, a world of rulers and armies and territories; and we believers are some citizens of that world who happen to have "peace and justice issues" with it. The chamber in the rock, with its demonstrative emptiness and heavenly messengers, feels spooky to us; indeed the disciples apparently supposed that anything that emerged from it had to be a ghost. What feels solid to us is the rock itself and the stone that sealed its entry.

I have described our delusions in terms imposed on us by the particular history of the West, but the delusions are inveterate. In some terms or other, fallen humanity has always gotten reality the wrong way around; it has regularly inverted the relation between the creation's stunning new reality as it opens in the Book, and that epiphenomenon we call the real world. Abraham supposed that realistically the king's power was more to be reckoned with than the promise, and abandoned Sarah to the harem. The last Judean kings supposed that Egypt had many divisions, and doubted that the prophets had any, whereupon the prophets mustered all Babylon's divisions against them—and Stalin repeated their mistake, to his empire's eventual undoing. The disciples feared that the risen Christ might be a dangerous illusion, but did not doubt the reality of the door with which they tried to shut fear out.

And *that*—I suggest—is why Scripture lacks force in the Church, and indeed has repeatedly done so.

If we preach from Scripture or teach it or read for edification, we cannot avoid Karl Barth's experience. And then the question is: Which is the really real world? This world that opens in the texts or the one we take for "real"?

When the Bible lacks force in the church, it is regularly—from the time of the apostles to post-Christendom–because we presume that the "real" world is some other world than the one that opens in the Bible, and that what we have to do is figure out how to make the Bible effective in the putatively "real" world.

The thing is: it cannot be done. The Bible is in fact ineffective and *irrelevant* in our so-called "real" world, because the Bible does not acknowledge that our "real" world deserves the adjective.

IV

We do of course have to note that there is another possible, neatly polar, false answer. It is possible to take divine love for real—and then to take *human* love for illusion, to take the prophet for real and Babylon and Egypt for irrelevancies, to take the risen Christ for real and the cross and tomb for divine misdirection.

Many would-be Christians have done that—and indeed, *mutatis mutandis*, entire world religions. Among would-be Christians there is a pretty clear line between the Church that stems from earthly crucifixion and the bodily Resurrection—the Church whose own inveterate mistake I have just been berating—and those prone to the opposite evasion, the "gnostic" evasion—if scholarship still lets me use that term.

If we proceed on the Gnostic line we will of course have eventually to drop the Scriptures, or edit them, or supplement them with some new gospels or whatever—projects on which folk who have wanted to be Christian without the bother of faith have been laboring since Pentecost. For the Scriptures do not work very well as guides into a heaven that is simply an alternative to our world; and when we discover this problem, there have always been some who have looked for a more uplifting religious wisdom.

The teaching that Jesus imparted to his disciples, as the synoptic tradition preserved it, is for the most part distressingly plain. Among apostolic theologians even Paul, for all his apocalypticism, keeps harping on about church suppers and traditional morality and hairstyles and such. He will have to be edited. Maybe we can keep John, if we can just interpret him in the light of those dominical sayings and acts that John says are not written in his book. Of course we will have to provide that material—perhaps by discovering yet again that there are gospels of what the Lord whispered to whomever, and really spiritual stories said to be recorded by this neglected apostle or that—and no doubt other titillations waiting in the sands, or waiting simply to be made up.

But if we are not to satisfy ourselves with religious imaginings, and yet also are not to repeat the Church's own millennial mistake, how do we avoid both? That is, how does the Bible hang together, as it neither simply fetches us out of the familiar world into an imagined alternative, nor yet bows to our putative reality?

V

The way the Christian Bible hangs together generally is as a single christological metanarrative; and if it is not allowed to do that it does not hang together at all. The Old Testament or *Tanakh*, the Scripture of canonical Israel, was in the first century just there, most consequentially for the disciples of the Risen One and for the successors of the Pharisees. Each provided that Scripture with a second volume: rabbinic Judaism the Mishnah and the Church the New Testament. Rabbinic Judaism's second volume is oral *Torah*; reading canonical Israel's Scripture back from it, Judaism reads these Scriptures fundamentally as Torah. The Church's second volume, the New Testament, is of a quite different character: it tells a *story*, of the Christ, with commentary and explanation. Reading canonical Israel's Scripture back from her second volume, the Church reads it too as fundamentally a connected narrative.[5] Thus the *Christian* Bible, Genesis to the Apocalypse, tells the one drama of Christ's coming. If it is not allowed to do this it falls quickly apart into Hebrew Scripture and sundry traces of Christian origins, that is, disintegrates as a single book, as a *biblios*.

This narrative-christological unity of the Christian Bible is now more widely acknowledged than it was in modernity—though not of course in those precincts of academia where no unity of anything is tolerated. But if that is how Scripture hangs together lengthwise, so to speak, then I suggest that also its strange-familiar *world* must hang together christologically, that also the ontology, the reality-picture, that the Bible displays is christologically constituted. I suggest that it is in Christ that the world of divine love, the world of heaven, and of heaven's gate, as this opens in Scripture, is one with the world of human love, of earth, of the rock outside Jerusalem, as this too in its way appears in Scripture.

I suggest that all Scripture's openings to a strange world that is somehow our world are openings into the reality established by the existence of Christ, the reality of the Occupant of heaven who is a creature. He is one person, who is at once God and creature, because his one life establishes in the first place what it is to be God and what it is to be creature.

In him divine love and human love, God's heaven and God's earth, the tomb and eternal life—and so on with all the strange world-pairings of Scripture—are one, and they are so because only as he is the one he is does either term of such pairings subsist in the first place. When he performs signs of the Kingdom the man Jesus opens heaven; and when he is buried in the tomb, God goes to earth. Without him is not made anything that is made, which does not only mean that he is an agent of creation. We are instructed that all things are made *in* him.

Put it this way, with the scholastic tradition: God is being and we are beings. And then let us be slightly more adventurous than the scholastic tradition usually is: the unity between us as beings and the being of all beings is not a general metaphysical principle but simply this Jesus, the Christ: we *are* at all just as we are in him and he in us. And so the Bible's world and this earth are one world, the world in Christ.

Every time the Bible opens a strange new world, we will understand how that strange world is nevertheless our "world" if and only if we see them as one in Christ. We have noted: if we make the Bible a collection of tales about a fanciful other world, it will have no power; and if we make the

5. Thus neither rabbinic Judaism's nor the Church's reading of the Old Testament/ *Tanakh* is more legitimate or original than the other.

Bible a source of advice about how to get along in this world, the advice will always prove unsuitable and will again have no power. But we certainly *will* do one or the other if we do not with every glance into the book confess the Christ of Nicea and Chalcedon.

What the strange beginnings of Scripture open to us is the mystery of Christ. And our preaching and teaching and reading from Scripture will have power as—and only as—the mystery of Christ is at every biblical step what we discover in the Bible and preach and teach and obey.

VI

So who are the lovers of the Song? The rabbis and fathers of the Church and the medieval and Reformation exegetes were unanimous: they are the Lord and his people, and the Christian exegetes were further unanimous that Jesus is that Lord. To be sure, our great forebears tended just a bit to what I called the Gnostic reading, often reading the human lovers right out of the story, and we should not follow them in that.

We will read the Song as the unique universal love-lyric, in which divine love and creaturely love serenade one another in canon. The love here celebrated, the preacher should say, is the love that is the very being of Christ, in whom the God who loves and we who are to love God are one body of love.

And then the preacher will invite us to enter that body, at once in the love-feast of the Eucharist and in our loves of this earth—for these too can be a "great mystery." And the preacher will proclaim the coming fulfillment in which there will no longer be a difference between them, no difference between Eucharist and created passion, the day when the Church, carrying all the created loves of her members, will enter the eternal love of the Father and the Son in the Spirit.

～

Or what is heaven doing traveling along our rivers, as in Ezekiel's revelation? A few verses further along, Ezekiel finds a clue. The glories shift a little, and he sees that the Presence over the throne has after all a shape: it looks—somehow—like a man. We may ask why that is so. And the answer of Nicea and Chalcedon is: because when we see face to face and no longer in a glass, when we are no longer blinded by all that transcendence, we will see that the Presence *is* a man, the man Jesus who is one of the Trinity, who of eternal right appears upon the throne.

The preacher should tell us that: our brother who loved us to the end is the very content of heaven, and this is why we can entrust ourselves to heaven. Indeed, the message is more immediate. The risen Christ's presence in the Church, in all its modalities, is heaven's presence. Martin Luther's favorite characterization of the Church was that it is the gate of heaven: when we enter it, we enter Christ and he enters us. We enter heaven's earthly gate and earth's heavenly atrium.

Which brings us to the ultimate mystery: that gate of heaven hacked from a rock outside Jerusalem. The Resurrection of the conclusively dead one to be the final living one—that is the unity which appears in all the strange unities in Scripture. And here I will shortly cease talking, as I think exposition and explanation of Easter's world-opening should be very circumspect, should efface itself in mere service to other modes of the word.

The Bible opens twice in the Church's gatherings: once read as text, without the addition of anyone's opinions or—if readers are well trained—even too much of the reader's expressivity, and then, surely after a pause, through the efforts of the preacher. Telling the *Resurrection*, the book can open heaven with little help from us. At Easter the Bible fulfills itself: the text *is* the message.

That identity is the famous hermeneutical principle for which we have spent so much time looking. At Easter, if the Bible recruits anything to its voice, it is not so much exposition and explanation as music. Once I introduced a lecture by breaking into song; I once thought it would be clever to end here that way. But I shall wait until the world comes clearly together and we are in better voice.

17

Creator and Creature (2002)

I

What makes the difference between Creator and creature? One way of answering this question is to map the Creator/creature pair onto some other conceptual pair of commonsensical or philosophical discourse, which is then thought to be so well known or indeed obvious, that no further justification or unpacking is required. The Creator is infinite and creatures finite, or the Creator is timeless and creatures are temporal, or the Creator is omni-something and creatures are not, or the Creator is "transcendent" while the creature constitutes the land of "immanence." This procedure is especially invoked in polemical contexts, where it will be said that such-and-such a systematic construct "blurs the difference between Creator and creature" in that, for example, it "fails to safeguard the Creator's transcendence."

It will be the initial contention of this article, that this procedure is radically mistaken: that the pairings onto which the Creator/creature difference is customarily mapped are themselves far from obvious, and that in any case the pairings are mismatches. And it will be the further contention of the article, that to the extent that we indeed need to move conceptually outside the biblical narrative as such, to a more conceptualized and metaphysical discourse, the difference between Creator and creature is displayed precisely by the sort of christology against which the pair-matchings are most frequently deployed.

II

Perhaps we may take it as given, by the grammar of standard theological usage and by the biblical passages on which the grammar rests, that the Creator is one who does something, and that creatures are what he does, in respect of a certain aspect of his activity. So Creator and creature are indeed two. So far so good. But every move to close the deliberately open ends of that given position—"does something," "what he does," "a certain aspect"—heads into disaster, meaningless abstraction, *or* more adventurous christology than is typical in the West.

Let me take just one aspect of personal doing as an analytic theme, without suggesting there are no others: in Scripture's narrative, creating is something God *wills* to do. And it is at least possible that some "creatures" also do things willingly—we have, anyway, no way to deny this a priori. So we have, or may have, will on both sides. Let us use this circumstance to test various pairings thought to specify the Creator/creature difference. What is the difference between the Creator's willing and ours?

Is it the difference between infinity and finitude? But the notion of an infinite will undoes itself. Someone who wills something not only chooses that the world shall be one way and *not* another, he identifies himself as will with the chosen way and not with the other. Which is to say, he sets limits for himself. Which is to say he is not infinite, a contradiction which has been often explored by philosophers. Or has he to some extent "withdrawn" his infinity? This is a move made by too many gnostics before us to be attractive.

That is not to say that God is not infinite, in some uses of "infinite,"[1] only that the finite/infinite conceptual pairing cannot as such fund the Creator/creature difference. Once the difference is established, divine infinity can be a wonderfully fruitful and decisive notion.

Or is the difference between Creator and creature the difference between eternity and temporality? To make this work, eternity must be taken as the simple contradiction of temporality, since mere contrariety or more subtle distinctions will not set up the desired disjunction; if time and eternity are only contraries, there is room for some things to be neither. But what would be a simply timeless act of willing? It has always seemed to me that a sheer contradiction of eternity to time is the notion lurking in the background of many construals of the Creator/creature difference, also among some who when considering the relation of time and eternity more thematically do not want simply to define eternity and time as A and -A.

1. Thus the "temporal infinity" of God is a central notion of my own systematics. See Jenson, *ST,* 1:215–21.

It will not do at this point to evoke mystery or the analogous character of predicates applied to God. According to a proper doctrine of analogy, to say that, for example, God is good is to say that God is the formal cause of what we call good in creatures, though we can give no further specification of what it is about God that so qualifies him. But if we make time and eternity contradictories we define the difference between Creator and creature in such fashion as to make the posit of a cause in God of, for example, goodness in others itself simply inconceivable;[2] and then analogies cannot be posited.

That we have constantly said, "There is in God something, I know not what, but it is something," has been the path at the end of which postmodern atheism stands, which does not propositionally deny God but rather merely finds no actual thought to match with the word. An act of will, however divine, demands a before and after of some sort, that is, something analogous to time rather than simply opposite to time, as Karl Barth surely should by now have persuaded us. But if time is analogous to eternity, rather than contradictory to it, then the difference between them is not the conceptual knife some think they are wielding.

Or is the difference that God "transcends" all creatures? There is indeed a harmless and often convenient use of "transcend" in which it merely says that the transcendent reality is one or another way "beyond" certain conditions or limitations of the transcended reality. So we may say that God transcends space, meaning perhaps that if he is present at one place he is not necessarily absent from any other. But this tells us very little about God's actual relation to space, certainly far from enough to form any decisive part of the distinction between Creator and creature. Particularly, it does not even exclude the analogical attribution of space to God, as in the dictum formulated for all subsequent theology by John of Damascus, that God is his own space. The Creator/creature distinction, on the decisive other hand, is not patient of analogy: we are not analogously the Creator nor is God analogously a creature.

If on the other hand we take the proper notion of transcendence seriously, a transcendent *willing*, as against a willed act of transcendence, is a mere oxymoron. To transcend is always to transcend *something*, it is to move beyond something at which one starts. Thus to transcend, in the case of a willing agent, will be what is willed, not a character of the will.

Moreover and more straightforwardly, God does *not* transcend the creation, since he does not start from it. It may be meaningful to say that *we*

2. As some "Christian philosophers" endlessly rediscover, as they struggle with "divine causality in time."

transcend the rest of creation, whether we actually do or not, since that is indeed where we start. But a god who needed to transcend anything would be precisely an idol.

Finally on the usual list of suspects, is the difference between God and creatures that his will is omnipotent and creatures' are not? Or if we were working with some other obvious character of the Creator, that he is "omni-" something else? Neither does this work. The extension to God of concepts like power, signalling the extension by modifiers like "omni-," has place within *Christian* theology only as analogy. And we must and can speak analogously of God only because the Creator/creature difference is already in place.

III

In Scripture itself, the difference between the Creator and his creatures is not laid out conceptually at all, but rather narratively. The verb "create" appears in the caption of Genesis 1–3, and what it means appears in the following story. Moreover, commented narration remains the fundamental and the only indispensable way of telling the difference between Creator and creature. The story tells what God does, called "creating," and creatures are what result other than God.

The tale of Genesis 1–3 has, however, been many times retold, as I have done in my *Systematic Theology*, and I will not here repeat what I have said there. Here I want to explore a slightly different and probably more perilous line.

There is one conceptual specification of Creator/creature that works, or comes very close to working. According to Thomas Aquinas, the difference between Creator and creature is that in the case of creatures, existence and essence are distinct, whereas they are not in God. Essence is, of course, *what* something is; existence, in Thomas' here innovative use, is the fact *that* something is. Simplifying greatly, we could know absolutely everything about what a putative creature would be, without knowing whether the thing so described actually exists. Not so with God: could we—as short of the Kingdom we cannot—know what God is, we would merely therein discover that he is. God contains within what he is the reason that he is; we do not.

In my view, Thomas' brilliant move must surely suffice for all ordinary theological purposes, and I invoke it regularly. Yet I am haunted by the feeling that it also is too abstract to quite fit the biblical narrative. For Thomas himself, the non-distinction of existence and essence in God belongs to his doctrine that God is Being. I agree, but I note that the Eastern doctrine that God is above Being seems to exegete Scripture with equal plausibility, which suggests a certain loose fit in both cases.

So let me try to move on even from Thomas. I do so, of course, with some fear and trembling.

IV

I begin with a dictum that will sound very Barthian, though I did not come to it from him. It is *God*, we must acknowledge, who distinguishes himself as Creator from all else, which just so is creature. *We* do not set up the Creator/creature difference by pairing it with or spreading it out on *any* set of concepts. The difference between Creator and creature is one which God *enforces* by taking action.

If there is God and anything else, the anything else must find its goal in God or find no goal at all. If we affirm the latter of ourselves or our world, we have dropped out of the discourse here being considered. Nihilism is not a Christian option.

Taken, therefore, in the purest abstraction, what is other than God necessarily has God as its final and formal cause. Its being must be participation in God who is Being—or in God's ever-renewed transcendence of being. And moreover, its salvation must be return to God, reunion of its shared being with Being. It is these considerations which have led the movement of "Radical Orthodoxy" to its insistence that some form of the Platonic great chain of being is a required moment in the doctrine of creation, that some modification of the Platonic notion of "participation" is indispensable in Christian theology, indeed that the faith's movement through the world of late Mediterranean antiquity and its emanationism was a necessary *preparatio evangelii*. And the considerations which lead John Milbank and others that way do indeed obtain.

But an entity that in Proclean fashion emanates from God and so is drawn back to God, must if left to itself seek to melt into God—if God were, *per impossibile*, the kind of God something could melt into. We may see this acknowledged and indeed celebrated in all pagan versions of post-Plato Platonism.

The fundamental proposition maintained in this section is then: God establishes himself as Creator and everything else as creature by actively stopping *this sort of return* from happening. To say that God is Creator and we are creatures is to say that God takes a certain preventive action.

The great visions of emanation from and return into deity are intu-itions of what reality *would* be if God did *not* determine himself as Creator. Such visions, of course, can come to us only because of the incident nar-rated in the third chapter of Genesis, where—absolutely inexplicably—the difference between Creator and creature is what the creature tries to deny. Whether the one true God could have determined himself over against an other than he otherwise than as Creator is, of course, another question alto-gether—to which, while we are at it, the answer is "No."

What then does God do, to prevent his act of originating from being an act of emanating? To understand this—so far as it can be understood at all—we must start precisely with that one unitary agent who is, just as such, both Creator and creature. And we must start with him not in the abstract, as some God-man or other, but as the concrete protagonist of the story told by the Gospels.

In the protagonist of the Gospels we see one who answers prayer and prays; who interprets the Torah as only its author should do and obeys it as so interpreted; who glorifies others—including his "Father"—and is glori-fied; who heals, even healing death, and suffers death and more trivial ills; who is born of a woman and sovereignly determines who are his mother and his brethren; who knows what is in all hearts and does not know the Hour or the Day. We see two very different agencies.

The question is: Are there two agents here, or one? The Gospels them-selves depict only one, and fidelity to that simple observation is the starting-point of all christology in the line from Cyril. But the history of theology has from first to last been shaped by attempts to evade such simplicity, the archetype of which is, of course, Nestorianism. Nestorian protests were pro-pelled precisely by the supposition that we know in advance what is suitable to the Creator and what is suitable to the creature. As Nestorius said, to trigger the great controversy, "The Logos was not raised, he raised the man with whom he was united."[3]

But, Nestorians to the contrary, it is precisely when we deviate in the slightest degree from the observation that the protagonist of the Gospels is but one, that the difference between praying and answering prayer, knowing and not knowing, becomes blurred. For then we must posit some media-tion between the two supposed agents, and then of course the difference between the two observed kinds of agency also is mediated. And then we get that middle realm. It was not the "neo-Chalcedonians," who labored to construe Chalcedon as Cyril would have wanted, who needed to posit a Jesus whose agency was so much *like* the Son's, that for our purposes it is

---

3. It would have been, he was sure, irreverent to suppose otherwise.

the same, but their Antiochene opponents. It was not the Cyrilleans who needed to speak of a Logos who attenuated himself to allow co-operation with his partner, but those from Antioch.

It is the same with such things as the doctrine of real presence. If we take "This is my body" straightforwardly, the divine decree and the human reality are hard up against each other, and just so the difference is established. If we make it mean "This is an effective symbol of my body," the decree becomes something a *philos anthropos* might say, and the body becomes just a bit ghostlike.

As Israel moved from the Exodus and Torah to the affirmations of Genesis, so may we from christology. Staying with will as the thread of our argument, the Creator's willing differs from creatures' willing precisely as Jesus' unity of will with the Father in the Spirit differs from his acceptance of what is decreed in that unity. Again, the Creator's willing differs from creatures' willing precisely as Jesus' *fiat*, "But I say unto you . . . ," differs from his obedience to *Torah*. It is one story of God and his creatures that Scripture tells, and one defining step of that story and its unity is the incarnation. In that story we cannot sort out what God does and what creatures do so as to obtain two stories. Just so, we do not need to mediate the two in order to save God's relation to the world. And so it is, and not otherwise, that the "middle realm" that Barth decried is in fact cleared out, that the idols, the supposed beings who are not quite God and not quite creature are swept away.

To keep his creating from being an emanating and absorbing, God does the incarnation. It is christology that is not intimidated by foreign notions of the difference between God and not-God that must represent this act within theological systematics. And just so it is such christology that in fact and not merely in supposition can function as a critical instance to undo within theology our desire to melt into God.

There is thus a perhaps quicker and simpler way to lay out the situation than that followed above. God acts to block the possibility of emanation/return by being in his second identity an actor who acts always as Creator and creature, and by just so seeing to it that there is *only* that one. Theology that describes *such* an actor, without ifs, ands, or maybes, is the theology that truly guards the difference between Creator and creature. Theology that seeks from our side to enforce the distinction with conceptual pairings has throughout Christian history been an invitation to the appearance of demi-gods and demi-creatures.

18

An Ontology of Freedom in the *De servo arbitrio* of Luther *(1994)*

I

The title of this essay may well seem far-fetched, since *de servo arbitrio* is an extended argument *against "liberum arbitrium,"* as attributed to creatures (I will throughout leave the phrase untranslated, to avoid prejudicing the investigation by choice of translation). Just so, however, the work provokes the question: What exactly did Luther mean by *"liberum arbitrium"*? And indeed by "freedom" itself? Since, as we will see, Luther is reluctant to call anything "freedom" that is *not liberum arbitrium!*

It would be possible to pursue this question by invoking external texts, whether from Luther himself or from his intellectual and spiritual milieu; and indeed this has often and usefully been done. But as it happens, the text of *de servo arbitrio* not only provokes the question but if read by certain strategies provides a considerable part of an answer. It is this method which will be here followed—which accounts also for the lack of notes, that could increase only the bulk and not the plausibility or import of the essay.

Luther's *De servo arbitrio* is often read as an ad hoc collection of debating points against Erasmus. Yet if read with our question in mind, the text may instead impress upon us a rigorous systematic of freedom, created and uncreated. This systematic power is obscured by the work's form as a line-by-line refutation of another writing and by Luther's rhetorical energy. But the systematic once noticed, its presence is relentless. The effort of this essay is to trace what has indeed to be called an ontology of freedom, an ontology that constitutes the conceptual structure of Luther's contrapuntally entitled essay.

II

Notoriously, Luther in this work insists that *"liberum arbitrium"* is "flat-out" a "divine name." And, as we will see, Luther is extremely reluctant to call anything less than *liberum arbitrium* freedom. Therefore, insofar as freedom becomes thematic in *de servo arbitrio*, this must at least initially be *God's* freedom.

The overt purpose of Luther's tract is to overthrow the presumption that creatures do or can have *liberum arbitrium*. Sheer recognition of God's *liberum arbitrium* as Creator is without further ado the "thunderbolt" by which this is essentially accomplished,[1] and which could, except for the requirements of debate, rest Luther's case against Erasmus. There cannot be two *libera arbitria*. If there is one that one is God, so that were there two or more there would be two or more Gods.

The "thunderbolt" is intuitively compelling. But it does not by itself tell us much *about* what God has that therefore we do not, and that Luther denotes with *"liberum arbitrium."* Searching for further information, we learn from *de servo arbitrio* two things directly about God's freedom.

First, God's freedom is his capacity to make and keep promises. A promise is a communicated decision not to decide otherwise later, and so is an exercise of decision covering the whole of the promiser's future, which in God's case is all the future there is. And for someone always to *keep* his promises, he must be sovereign over all contingencies.[2]

Second, if creatures recognize such freedom in God, their apprehension of God is thereby sundered, and, short of the Kingdom, irreparably.[3] On the one hand, experience both worldly and theological confronts us with God hidden precisely by his utterly free sovereignty. On the other hand, the free action of God at the cross confronts us with God in the hiddenness of love.[4]

To detect more of Luther's interpretation of divine freedom, we must adopt an oblique strategy of reading. We will gather Luther's arguments *against creatures'* possession of *"liberum arbitrium,"* and take them the other way around: asking what it is that we do not have because God does have it,

1. Luther, *WA*, 18:615.
2. Ibid., 18:619.
3. Ibid., 18:684–90.
4. Ibid., 18:685–86.

for which Luther reserves the phrase *"liberum arbitrium."* By this tactic we discover more of what is attributed to God by this one of his names.

III

Luther's arguments against created *"liberum arbitrium"* can for our purposes be put in two groups.

Those in the one group may be jointly summarized: we cannot get behind what we in fact choose, we cannot choose what to choose. We should note that in the passages devoted to this sort of contention, Luther moves back and forth between denouncing attribution of *liberum arbitrium* to creatures as blasphemy because it must be attributed solely to God, and arguing that the notion of such self-transcendence is in itself incoherent; the possible antinomy thus presented will be taken up later. We will here instance two such arguments.

The first. Luther develops the same position that Jonathan Edwards would re-invent to counter both the Enlightenment's theological repristination of Erasmus and the Enlightenment's scientist determinism. The freedom that can reasonably be attributed to us is the "willingness" with which we act when we are doing what we have chosen to do (*libentia seu voluntas faciendi*). If we are contingently permitted to pursue what we have chosen, this action is said to be done "willingly" (*volendo et lubendo*), and that should suffice us. We can have no powers by which to alter the choices by which our powers are directed.[5]

The second. Attribution of *"liberum arbitrium"* depends upon supposing that "between the two, being able to will the good and not being able to will the good, a mean is posited, that is an absolute willing" (*inter haec duo, posse velle bonum, non posse velle bonum, dari medium, quod sit absolutum Velle*), that is, that there is in us a "pure and mere willing" (*purum et merum velle*). Here Luther's argument is thoroughly modern. The positing of a *merum velle*, an actual but uncommitted will, is a "dialectical figment," resulting from "ignorance of realities and attention to words" (*ignorantia rerum et observantia vocabulorum*), from the metaphysician's besetting sin of assuming that things are always "disposed in reality as they are in words." If we consult experience, we will find only our determinate choices to do such and such, and external support for or resistance to our doing it. "*Velle*" is but a word we use in speaking of our determinate choices to do or pursue some real thing; like logically similar words it does not, merely because it

5. Ibid., 18:634.

exists, necessarily denote anything by itself, and in this case experience in fact offers no denotation.[6]

So—if these passages display what we do not have that would be our *"liberum arbitrium"* if we had it, what does God have in that he does indeed have *"liberum arbitrium"*? God, it seems, *does* choose what to choose, *is* somehow will antecedent to his own determinate will.

IV

In the second pigeon-hole is a form of argument developed in one passage[7] but pervasive in the work. If we are bound and determined somehow to use the phrase *"liberum arbitrium"* of humans, Luther says, we could by such usage only denote a sheer dispositional property (*dispositivam qualitatem et passivam aptitudinem*). It indeed belongs to humanity to be "apt" to be free: the question, "Is *x* free in this situation?" is meaningful when *x* is a human whereas it is not meaningful when *x* is a log or a goose. But—and here is a key point for our whole investigation—this disposition is the anthropological place of actual freedom only as I am *"rapt"* (*rapi*) into free action, by *another* than myself.

It is important to note that this anthropological fact would obtain also in an unfallen creation. Were not sin given, we would be and always have been rapt by God, and the problem of moving or being moved from one rapture to another would not appear, nor then would anyone dream of positing an unraptured *velle*. The soteriological problem is set by the circumstance that we are in fact rapt by Satan and so not by God[8]—Luther wisely attempts no explanation of how this can be. And either way, whether rapt by Satan or God, in such rapture we act "willingly"[9] in the sense noted above.

So—again—what is that we do not have because God does? It seems justified to say: to have *"liberum arbitrium"* is to be rapt into freedom without dependence on alien freedom. We earlier obtained the proposition that God can choose what to choose, that he is anterior to his own self-determinations. Now we add the proposition that God is himself the other by whom he is rapt into freedom. Since we are talking about God, the maxim must hold that these two differ only *per rationem* and not *in re*; and Luther plainly deals with them just so.

6. Ibid., 18:669–70.
7. Ibid., 18:636.
8. Ibid., 18:635–36.
9. Ibid., 18:634.

V

And now an observation, that is a main point of this essay: only with inclusion of the classic doctrine of Trinity does the teaching just described make the coherent system it urgently seems to be. God is freedom antecedent to himself as determinate free will. He can intelligibly be said to be this as the Father is the source of the Son and both are freed in the Spirit. God is rapt by another without dependence on an other than God. He can intelligibly be said to be this as the Spirit, as the lively future of God, is himself the very same God.

I do not claim that Luther said to himself, "Let us work out this question about God's freedom in trinitarian fashion." At his time of history, it was still the mark of a genuinely trinitarian thinker to need very few explicit trinitarian statements. I do claim that what Luther says about divine *"liberum arbitrium"* hangs beautifully together said of the triune God and as part of one conceptual structure with propositions asserting his triunity, and if said of any other sort of God makes a mere collection of disparate debating points—and it may well be the personal unitarianism of most modern historical scholars which has so often led them to see *de servo arbitrio* as just such a farrago.

Moreover, we should consider the apparent antinomy earlier suggested. If it is logically incoherent to say that someone chooses what to choose, then it is logically incoherent to say this of God. And then it is no blasphemy to attribute it to creatures, since it is not in fact a divine character. The antinomy dissolves if God is not *a* someone.

VI

Finally, we should briefly consider that Luther does after all, also in this work, speak of creaturely freedom. What is interesting is the reluctance with which he does so until he reaches one point.

It would, as a first step, be possible to say that our "freedom" is the dispositional property which distinguishes humans from other creatures with respect to free action, that we are apt for it. It is, after all, a remarkable property. But Luther sees in our pride over this (in his eyes) paltry property only an evidence of our bondage, and in the possibility of calling it *"liberum arbitrium"* an evidence of the phrase's emptiness when used of creatures.[10]

Next step. If we are in fact freed, rapt into actual choice and so into action dictated by that choice, this action is uncoerced and *lubendo.* Edwards

10. Ibid., 18:636–37.

and others—including myself—regard this *voluntas faciendi* as itself the proper and only possible referent of "freedom." But while Luther does call it *"libentia,"* further he will not go.

Next step. It fits the tone of *de servo arbitrio* that when "freedom" (*libertas*) does appear as a predicate of humans, it appears only negatively in the phrase "when freedom is lost." But of course, only that can be lost which at least might have been possessed. And the invariable context of the phrase makes plain the conditions under which Luther can think of our possessing freedom. So, for example, "Neither God nor Satan . . . allows a sheer will [*merum velle*] in us . . . ; rather . . . , when freedom is lost we are compelled to serve sin . . ."[11] Luther's willingness to speak of created freedom thus will depend, it seems, on by *whom* we are rapt.

This leads to the final step. Luther finally is forced, in a parenthesis, to attribute "freedom" (*libertas*) also to us, even "royal freedom," in the case when the *raptor is* God: God *"rapiat"* us "into his booty, by his Spirit we are made his servants and captives (which is just so royal freedom), that we willingly may will and do what he wills" (*nos rapiat in spolium suum, rursus per spiritum eius servi et captivi sumus (quae tamen regia libertas est), ut velimus et faciamus lubentes, quae ipse velit.*)[12] We should carefully note the vocabulary of this passage: the familiar *rapere* and participle of *libere, and* the sudden intrusion from the tract *On Christian Freedom,* "royal freedom." And we should note exactly how God appears as *raptor,* suddenly to qualify our usual *libentia* of action as *libertas*: it is "by the Spirit."

We have to ask: "Why must it be God by whom we are rapt into freedom? Why is it not freedom if I am rapt by *you* into 'willing' action, in love or discipleship or communal concern? Or, for that matter, why is it not freedom when I am rapt by Satan?" There seems to be only one possible explanation: the rapture-relation is not causative but participatory. You cannot by your enrapturing me *make* me free; you could only *share* freedom, and this you cannot do because you do not have it yourself. This explanation is also supported by the observation that *de servo arbitrio* is devoted to arguing that *liberum arbitrium* cannot be a creaturely possession, and so also not the kind of thing that can be the result in us of causation.

Therefore when God "enraptures us" (*nos rapiat*), he frees us by sharing with us his own freedom, his *liberum arbitrium*. Human freedom, in the only sense Luther wants to talk about, is nothing less than participation in God's own triune rapture of freedom. We pick up the last thread: Luther's

11. Ibid., 18:670.
12. Ibid., 18:635.

usage in *de servo arbitrium* is invariant that God frees us "by the Spirit," by that personhood in which he is his own freedom.

Culture

19

Christ-Dogma and Christ-Image (1963)

I

That Jesus of Nazareth, the Christ, is a legitimate subject for art is theologically indisputable. If he was "true man, born of the Virgin Mary," then the artist with a representational style and a taste for historical subject matter is quite free to paint or sculpt him, if he chooses. Nor is such art, if it is good, irrelevant to the life of faith, either for artist or beholder. *No* art is irrelevant to the life in faith of the one who experiences it, for by its refusal to allow reality to remain imprisoned in our habitual ways of seeing it, art is a destroyer of false faith. And the piety of the believer may well lead him to seek the aesthetic experience in art with literary content so congenial to his *true* faith.

But it is not this general question that I wish to discuss. I am concerned with images of Christ used liturgically *as an integral part of a space created for worship*. I am concerned, for example, with the crucifix on the altar. There have always been voices in the Church that have branded such images of Christ idolatrous—and with considerable plausibility. For if Christ is not only man but God, then must not such liturgical images of him (where his status as the God to whom the liturgy is directed cannot be irrelevant) fall under the prohibition against representing God? If we nevertheless persist in creating and using such images, what justification do we give? It is, moreover, evident that whatever that justification may be, it will not extend to the liturgical use of *any and all* representations of Christ which might be offered (no one, for example, would consider erecting in the sanctuary a picture of Jesus with horns and a tail). If we have a justification for the use of images, we will therefore have also criteria for discriminating good ones from bad ones. The evident fact that in practice we have almost no criteria, that any monstrosity short of horns and a tail can be found in some church or other, shows that we also do not know if we are justified in using images.[1]

In asking for a justification and criteria of liturgical images of Christ, it must be clear that we are not asking directly on behalf of the artist. The artist does what he has to and that is an end of the matter. We are asking on behalf of the Church's *use* of the artist's labors. What ought we to look for when setting out to find a new set of windows? Or should we buy plain glass?

II

Since the eighth-century iconoclastic controversy there has existed a theology of images. This was derived from the basic conceptual framework of the learned christological theology of the Greek fathers, by extrapolating that framework out beyond its directly christological use. It was Origen, the inventor of learned and systematic theology, who had definitively worked out the fundamental conceptuality of Greek theology. For Origen the theological question of God and our relation to him took by historical necessity the form of the problem of the relation between the various steps in an hierarchical series of levels of reality, from God at the top to matter at the bottom.[2]

Origen grasped the relation between the levels of being by describing them as a descending series of *images* (*eikones*).[3] On the one hand an *image* is an expression, a manifestation of that of which it is the image, and precisely therefore has its origin solely in that prototype.[4] On the other hand, such an ectype can in turn be a prototype by the reflection of which yet a new image is constituted.[5] Each image is a revelation of that above, and reveals itself in that below. Thus we may also say that an image reveals the superior reality of which it is the image to the reality below (which is in turn constituted as the image of this image).[6]

1. I do not mean to imply that there has been no theological reflection on the matter, though such basic discussions as the fine one by Peter Brunner in *Leiturgia*, 291ff., are all too rare.

2. Cf. for example Koch, *Pronoia und Paideusis*; Faye, *Origène*.

3. Cf. for a superfluity of proof: Crouzel, *Théologie de l'image de Dieu chez Origène*.

4. The Son and the Father are "hypostatically two realities, but one in unity of thought, and in harmony, and in identity of will. Thus he who beholds the Son, who is the splendor of God's glory and the stamp of his nature, beholds in Him, since He is God's Image, God himself." *Against Celsus*, VIII, 12. *Commentary on John*, I, 17.

5. "For as . . . the Father is related to his Image and to the images of the Image . . ." *Commentary on John*, II, 3.

6. *Commentary on John*, XXXII, 29.

This concept allows Origen to state the doctrine of creation. As his images, all things other than the Father depend wholly upon the Father for their reality, indeed have their reality only in the Father. It also enables him to state the doctrine of salvation. For through the series of images we ultimately know God, and this knowledge is our being[7] (we too are images) so that the actualization of this knowledge is the fulfillment of our being, that is, salvation. Now all this is only the conceptuality through which Origen states a christological doctrine of creation and salvation. It is the Son who is the image of God. All other spiritual beings (we included) are the images of the Son.[8] But in a special sense it is Christ's humanity that is the image of the Son.[9] Thus when Christ comes in humanity to confront us and accordingly activates the image-nature in us,[10] we move in the knowledge of God through Christ's humanity to his deity,[11] and then with the Son to the beatifying vision of God, seen with the eyes of the Son himself.[12] In Origen, the image-concept serves to express faith in creation and salvation through Christ.

Where did Origen get this key concept of the image? Ultimately, of course, it is a fundamental myth quite probably co-temporal with the human race.[13] But the historical source was Plato.

Plato's great problem was the relation between our life and the perfection from which and to which it goes. Our present reality is real precisely in that it strives toward perfection, yet compared to that perfection it is worthless and unreal. It is this ambiguity of present existence which Plato struggled to grasp, and for which "image" proved the increasingly satisfactory myth—an image *is* something, yet *is not* that something.[14] "Image" comes from the language of craftsmanship and artistry, and is intimately joined with three other words: The "craftsman" "imitates" a "pattern" and creates an artifact which is thus an *image* of this pattern.[15] The culmination

7. Ibid., XX, 22.

8. Ibid., II, 2.

9. *Commentary on Romans*, PG 842A.

10. *Commentary on Genesis*, XIII, 4.

11. *Commentary on Song of Songs*, III.

12. "The . . . eyes of the Logos, with which he who participates in Him also sees . . ." *Commentary on John*, II, 7.

13. For the way in which this concept appears precisely at the mythic junctures of Plato's thought, cf. Friedländer, *Plato*.

14. "Then what we call an image, though it is not, yet is? Answer: It does seem that not-being has involved itself with being—which is paradoxical." *Sophist*, 240B, C. To this and the following cf. Willms, *EIKON*, 1–24.

15. *demiourgos, mimeisthai, paradeigma*. Cf. *Republic*, 401B; *Sophist*, 235E; *Cratylus*.

of Plato's development in the use of this concept is the *Timaeus*. Here all visible reality is seen as the image of eternal perfection, an imperfect yet true expression of that perfection. And the rooting of this term in the act of artistic creation comes to dominate the whole vision: God is the *Craftsman* who makes this world in the *image* of the eternal *pattern*. The world is an *imitation*, a product of art.[16]

In this conception the act of the artist-craftsman, namely, "imitation," is the act of reconciling in the artifact which he creates the actuality of our world with its transcendent perfection, in which he posits the oneness of what is with the fulfillment of what is. Plato did not invent this concept; it was the given reality of Greek art and understanding of art that he exalted into a cosmological principle.

In Plato, the notion of the image was reserved for empirical reality as the ectype of spiritual reality. But the subsequent platonizing thought seized on this notion of a level *between* being and not-being, and made "image" serve the overwhelming desire of later antiquity's religious crisis for *bridges* between God and us. Image came to be the name for the whole principle of mediation between transcendent and given reality and for the intermediary semi-divine realities through which that mediation was believed to take place.[17] This is the point where Origen picked up the notion.

What is important is that in adopting this framework of thought Origen was adopting a metaphysical ontology which had grown out of a "root metaphor" drawn from aesthetics, from the work of the artist.[18] "Image" is the product of the artist's work; that work is understood as "imitation." All that was necessary was for the apologists of later centuries[19] to extend the image-schema out beyond the use to which christological theology since Origen had put it and so to liberate it from its christological binding, to obtain ready-made a metaphysical explanation of the function of images and a religious aesthetic for their creation and employment.

The image made by us is justified as an extension through human means (like the baking of bread or the writing of the Bible) of the series of

16. *Timaeus*, 92C, 28–9, 48E–49A.

17. This history is analyzed and documented in Willms, *EIKON*, 25ff; Jaeger, *Nemesios von Emesa*; Crouzel, *Théologie de l'image de Dieu chez Origène*, 25ff.

18. "... the craftsman God, the imitator of this God. ... The first God is goodness itself. His imitator is the good Craftsman. ... His imitation ... the good cosmos." Numenius, as cited by Eusebius, *Praeparatio Evangelica*, XI, 12.

19. For a concise and most illuminating account of the whole history cf. Campenhausen, "Die Bilderfrage als Theologisches Problem der Alten Kirche." Cf. also Harnack, *History of Dogma*, 317ff; and for the secondary concepts used: Schaeder, "Die Christianisierung der Aristotelischen Logik in der Byzantinischen Theologie," 4.

images through which God descends to us. Thus it has sacramental significance; it participates in the divine self-revelation.

Such an image is the product of *imitation*, that is, it intends to grasp the identity of the portrayed reality with the fulfillment and perfection of that reality—in this case, the unity of the human life of Christ with that of God the Son. Therefore, such an image will make a deliberate attempt to *portray* Christ's divinity. Therewith is posited, to some extent, the typical stylistic elements of Eastern iconography: the flat surface, the rejection of perspective, the golden environment; all portray a human person existing in a transcendent space and mode. The typical concentration on Christ's person as a *being*, to the relative neglect of any specific acts done by him, that is, the concentration on *portraiture* of Christ, is also dictated by this aesthetic, for it is simply Christ's human nature as a being which is the image of God the Son.

III

Is this theology legitimate? Here I must be cautious. Eastern theology and piety, where these ideas have their home, move in a spiritual world radically different from ours. It is impossible for a Westerner to say exactly what the icons of the Eastern Church and the image-theory which supports them mean for the believers there. I can only speak of what these things seem to be to a Westerner—that is, of what they have in fact meant in the history of the Western Church. But with this qualification, it must be said that while the program of drawing guidance in this matter from christology is fascinating and, I think, the only possible one, the way in which Greek theology carried it out is untenable.

The fundamental postulate of this icon-theory is the ability of imitation's transcendence over the separation of the ideal and the actual to grasp and realize the union of God and man in Christ. But the whole point of the christological dogma is the confession of a *unique* relation between God and man in Christ. Therefore, imitation's unifying of actuality with its transcendent fulfillment is, in at least this one case, not among *our* possibilities—and the attempt to arrogate this possibility to ourselves is precisely that works-righteousness with respect to revelation which can only terminate in a graven image. The aesthetic of imitation is inapplicable to the God-man. It is remarkable that precisely this criticism was made by a council of the Eastern Church in 754. Under the bullying of the iconoclast emperor, the bishops declared the use of images to be heretical in that the unity of God and man in Christ cannot be portrayed, so that the attempt to portray it results instead in representing a mixture of the human and the divine.[20] The image created by *imitation* can never be an image of the God-man, but only of a divinized man—which is just what Christ is not.

This theology of images was a product of the Eastern Church and has always remained far more central to the life of the Eastern Church than to the West. But imported tags of it have provided such rationalization of our use of images as we have possessed. Thus the necessity of rejecting it (at least insofar as we understand it) strikes deeply into unconscious assumptions of our church life. Two main aspects of Eastern image-theory and practice have pervaded the Western tradition. The interpretation of images as possessing a sacramental function usually appears in Protestant circles in a washed-out version as the notion that it is the function of a Christ-picture to be "inspiring" or "educational." The creation of images of Christ as images of a divine man also appears, where you least expect it. For example, our recent and still all too extant sentimentalized Christs are based on a vulgarly psychologized version of the attempt at imitative portrayal of Christ's divinity. These must be removed from our churches; they are graven images. Where the pedagogical motif combines with this spiritualizing, we get the deadly "symbolism" so much in vogue.

IV

Meanwhile the christology of the Western Church, although often dependent on Eastern theology, has had its own path. The descending series of images has never been its main conceptual framework. If a christological rationale of *our* use of Christ-images is to be found, it is to possibly unexploited resources of this Western christology that we must look. Here I will be arbitrary and simply assert without proof that the christology of classical Lutheranism is the penultimate fulfillment of Western christology.

A first axiom of the Lutheran dogmaticians is that the union between the person of the Son of God and a human life is absolutely *sui generis* and quite beyond the possibility of our recapitulating in thought or otherwise.[21] We begin, therefore, with all the negations of the last paragraphs as a fixed position. But it is my belief that precisely the *peculiarities* (or the *advances*,

20. Cf. Harnack, *History of Dogma*, 4:324f.

21. So Gerhard, *Loci Theologici*, 4:115. I base the following on Gerhard's discussion. Cf. also the greatest work of old Lutheran christology: Chemnitz, *De Duabus Naturis in Christo*; and for a contemporary analysis: Elert, *Morphologie des Luthertums*, 1:195–223.

as I hold them to be) of classical Lutheran christology enable us to go beyond negations.

The old Lutheran dogmaticians taught (1) that the living existence of the eternal Son of God, the act and decision in which he is and becomes what he is, by which he creates his history as a person, not only involves the human reality of Jesus Christ but takes place in and through the story of Jesus Christ so that *this man too* lives and acts and creates historic reality— in an act and decision and creation which *is*, with no qualifications, that of the eternal Son.[22] They taught (2) that as a consequence the eternal Son is nowhere present apart from his human reality, that it is the man Jesus who is present to hear our prayers and who is present to direct history and to will the existence of the stars.[23] They taught (3) that as a further consequence the characteristics and acts of God the Son become characteristics and acts of Jesus Christ as a man.[24] To be sure, Christ's human reality does not possess the properties of God in or of itself, but Christ's humanity is never in or of itself—it is the life of God the Son which is the life and act of Jesus' humanity.[25] And so Jesus Christ, *as a man*, is omnipotent, omniscient, life-creating, the judge of the last judgment, omnipresent. He works miracles, redeems, sends the gospel and gathers the Church, gives the Spirit, forgives sins, raises from the dead, declares judgment, and glorifies the saved.[26] "Since the Son of God has taken human nature into the unity of his person in order *in and through* it to perform the work of our redemption and salvation . . . therefore he has enriched his flesh with divine powers to make it a proper organ of his divine works . . ."[27] There are several aspects of this christology which seem to me to provide the basis for a theory of images.

22. "Because the hypostasis of the Logos was made the hypostasis of the flesh, therefore the hypostasis of the Logos is communicated to the flesh. The Logos has this hypostasis in and of itself, the flesh has it as communicated, by virtue of the union . . ." Gerhard, *Loci Theologici*, 4:121. It is this doctrine of the *communication* of the Son's hypostasis that goes beyond the ancient doctrine of the an- and enhypostatic character of Christ's human reality. As the matter is put in the text, the peculiarly Lutheran emphasis is represented by the words "*this man too.*"

23. "Because the hypostasis of the Logos was made the hypostasis of the flesh . . . the Logos is in such a way present to the flesh and the flesh to the Logos, that neither is the Logos outside the flesh nor the flesh outside the Logos . . ." Gerhard, *Loci Theologici*, 4:121.

24. It is the (in)famous *communicatio idiomatum, genus majestaticum* that I refer to. This is defined: "The second sort of communication of attributes is that in which the divine nature of the Son communicates its glory and excellence to his human nature . . ." Gerhard, *Loci Theologici*, 4:201.

25. Gerhard, *Loci Theologici*, 4:201.

26. Ibid., 4:214–36.

27. Ibid., 4:201.

This whole affair is one grand insistence on Luther's refusal to "know any other God than the babe in the lap and at the breast of his mother." The concern of Lutheran christology is that God's acts by which he makes himself our merciful God take place and are historical realities as the human story of Jesus Christ, that the events which make up the personal history of Jesus of Nazareth are (with no qualification) God's history-creating acts by which we have a life with him.

If then we portray the human story of Christ as a human story, we are portraying the acts of God, we are portraying God-at-work-among-us. No transcendentalizing is needed. We can make and use liturgically significant images, images in which our history with God is posited, without the fake attempt to grasp in a work of our hands the union of God and man in Christ, without creating graven images of a divinized man. What images may we meaningfully incorporate into the space for worship? Simple images of the man Jesus of Nazareth.

But what then differentiates such images from those secular works of art where Jesus' story simply provides historical subject-matter? In the image itself—nothing whatever. Here a second characteristic feature of Reformation christology provides the clue. The old dogmaticians used the doctrine that the act of the Son's existence is made the act of this man's existence as the foundation of all other assertions. That is, the union of God and man in Christ is treated fundamentally in terms of act. Now the authorized reproduction of this act is the action of the preaching of the gospel and the eating of bread and wine and the pouring of water. Therefore it is the use made of an image within this liturgical action which can posit the fact that the life of Jesus Christ there portrayed is the history of God's saving acts. The image in which we may see God's history with us is an image of the man Jesus placed at a key point in the space for the liturgy. I think we may go further yet. The space created for the liturgy is not homogeneous. Some areas are more associated with our movement to God—for example, the nave with its aisles—others with God's coming to us—for example, the altar. The Godhead of the man Jesus, who is portrayed in a window or as the *corpus* on a cross, is posited by erecting this image of him in a spatial position associated with God's presence in the act of worship. The true icon is an image of the story of the man Jesus, but an image that comes to us from the direction of God—for example, the crucifix on the altar.

If it is in this way possible to show the legitimacy of liturgical images of Christ, what ought such images be like? That they must resolutely avoid all attempts at showing Christ's divinity by a spiritualizing of the forms has already been shown. But I believe that positive criteria can also be derived. It is inescapable that Reformation christology understands reality historically.

The "human nature" which the Son of God is said to take on is spoken of in a way which fits a story much better than a thing. It is the concrete personality and history of Jesus that God the Son makes his personality and history.[28] Our representations of the man Jesus ought, therefore, to be representations of events from the evangelical history, rather than portraiture. The typical "head of Christ" does not belong in a house of worship. It is the crucifix, the manger-scene, the cleansing of the temple, etc., which are the "human nature" we are allowed to depict.

Lutheran christology yields one more criterion of a good liturgical image. This christology insists to the point of monotony that Jesus' life as a man has absolutely no meaning, no fulfillment, no reality in itself, that the historic act by which Jesus lives is exclusively the act of the Son of God. In portraying this human reality for liturgical purposes we must therefore avoid all modes and styles of realization which suggest that this human life is finished and fulfilled in itself. Impressionism and the allied movements which grow out of the scientific impulse, which seek to be empirical and capture the present visual reality just as it is in the moment, will not produce liturgically suitable images of Christ. Nor will naturalism or realism, whether of the trick-the-eye or ashcan school—for here again it is what the subject is in and of its own reality that dominates. A good liturgical image will be distorted and abstracted, not to spiritualize the image but to break it, to open it, to destroy its self-contained sensuality. Even a strong dose of crudity will often be in order.

V

One question remains to be answered. If images of Christ do not have a sacramental function, if they are not a part of God's self-revelation, then, even if we can discover a justification and criteria for their use, why should we use them? The answer is that there is no command to create images. They are not part of God's revelation; they are part of the response of our piety, like music. Whether or not our places of worship contain images of Christ

---

28. The divine gifts bestowed in the human reality are divided by Gerhard into two series. The second and most important (see enumeration in the text above) is simply a recounting of the biblical history of Jesus Christ, with the various events confessed to be acts of God. The first series of "attributes" appears more abstract, but that the "nature" is a history becomes plain when we examine what is said in proof of Christ's possession of these attributes. For example, with respect to the most abstract of all, omnipresence: "... we prove this ... from the promise ... 'Where two or three are gathered in my name, there am I in the midst of them.'" Gerhard, *Loci Theologici*, 4:219. "Christ is present in the world according to that nature, to the presence of which the holy supper testifies."

is entirely in our freedom, is entirely a matter of whether they fit organically and inevitably into the expression of our piety. But it seems likely that in proportion as natural religious belief loses its power to give our lives shape and carry our religious response to the gospel, the shaping and forming aspects of liturgical worship will become increasingly necessary. What is important is that this development not be thoughtless and uncritical ("Why not a nice picture of Jesus on the communion table?") eclecticism, nor built on debased remnants of late antique theosophy, but an expression of faith in the Babe, the Healer, the Crucified.

20

Christ as Culture 1: Christ as Polity (2003)

The title of these Maurice lectures[1] is, of course, a rather too obvious parody. H. Richard Niebuhr's famous book, *Christ and Culture*, has many merits, but nevertheless has for some time seemed to me foundationally misconceived. The title presumes that Christ is one thing and culture another; and the book is about possible prepositions to replace the non-commital conjunction. Christ must be against culture, or above culture, or ahead of culture, or whatever.

But "Christ" is a *title*, and therefore is itself meaningful only within a particular culture, in this case the culture of Israel. The title "Christ," *Messiah*, has its use within Israel's politics, her cult, even her arts and architecture—only consider, for example, that the function and ideology of the Jerusalem Temple was sustained in part by its layout and even its decor, and that without the Temple and its ideology the distinction in Israel between those who are annointed and those who are not would have worked very differently than it did. "Messiah," if the word had become important at all, would have meant something different than it does, had the Temple had a different ground-plan, or not been decorated as a depicted garden.

Thus it makes a logical tangle to speak of Christ "and" culture absolutely, since by referring to Christ one is already invoking a specific culture, that of Israel. However Christ is related to other cultures or to the general human need to have a culture, the relation is *not* simply external; a relation between, say, Christ and Chinese culture is in itself a relation between Jewish culture and Chinese culture.

1. These three lectures on "Christ as Culture" were originally delivered as the 2003 Maurice Lectures at King's College, London.

Let me adduce two standard definitions of culture, from different branches of social theory. We may say that a culture is the mutual behavior of a group insofar as this behavior is sustained by teaching and not only by genetics and physical ecology. Or we can say that a culture is the mutual behavior of a group of persons insofar as this can be abstracted from those doing the behaving, as in itself a coherent system of mutually determining signs.

For reasons that will become clear, I will approach the notion of *Christ as culture* by first making a few points about the Church as a culture. For by either definition above, the Church obviously has—or rather is—a specific identifiable culture; an observation I think I need not argue here.

The first concerns the identification of the Church's culture. If the Church is, or has, a culture of her own, then the Church's claim somehow to *be* Israel must also be a claim somehow to continue the culture of Israel. To eliminate the "somehow" and the vagueness it introduces, we would have constructively to interpret the identity of the Church with Israel, and how to do that is notoriously disputed. But however we go about to avoid—or even justify—supersessionism, the Church's claim to be Israel at least imposes some questions about the Church's culture, which the ancient Church pondered deeply, but which the modern and particularly the Protestant church has mostly dropped. For example, does the Church, like rabbinic Judaism, have a constitutive relation to the erstwhile Temple even in its absence, indeed precisely to its absence? If so, what is it? Or again, are the purity laws *simply* moot in the Church? Are we permitted simply to skip over Leviticus? Or, do Christian ministers stand in some identifiable succession to Israel's sages and priests? If they do, how should that shape their office and their understanding of it?

Second, since the Church is a culture, there are limits on "inculturation." With any culture, there are some elements of other cultures that it can assimilate and others that it cannot without self-destruction. So, for example, the disastrous effects of the Churches' extensive assimilation of the Enlightenment ideal of autonomy are now widely perceived. Perhaps shortly we will also notice that this is why practices in church polity and in the Church's arts that embody that ideal have been so destructive. Thus it is not the case that there is all that great art being done out there, but that the Church has—alas—abandoned her old role as patron; rather, most art done in the West since the seventeenth century is disruptive when appropriated by the Church, as witness Catholic baroque decor and music—wonderful stuff, but a mere distraction of the liturgy and rightly reigned in by the magisterium—or the polar barrenness of a great many Protestant churches, built according to intrinsically rationalistic standards of beauty.

Third, if the Church is a culture of her own, she, like any community, is responsible to cultivate her culture, and can lose her identity if she does not. Arguments about music, discipline, language, ministerial style, architecture, and the like are not *in their ensemble* about "matters indifferent," though usually no one such decision is by itself fatal. Moroever, catechesis of new members, whether after baptism or before, is essential to their survival. Entry into so strange a culture as the Church is—that does not dispose of unwanted infants or elders, that gathers in spaces that let the populace into the God-chamber, that has a preference for the poor, that regularly contemplates images of a man being crucified, that require marital faithfulness also of men—can be a fatal shock to the moral system, unless carefully overseen. Of course the Church can lessen the shock by becoming more like the world, but then why not just rest content with the world?

Now—coming at last to the matter of these essays—if the Church is the body of Christ, that is, if the Church is the availability of Christ in and for the world, and if this body of Christ, the Church, is a culture, it follows that Christ is a culture. And the sense of the "is" in "Christ is a culture" will be the sense in which each of us must say that he or she "is" his or her body.

Now of course it may seem to make no sense to talk of an individual person as himself a culture. But Christ's individuality is of a peculiar sort, indeed he is an individual at all only in a sense unique to him.

Christ is eschatologically and so ecclesially what Augustine called the *totus Christus*: he is himself simply *as* himself *and* he is himself as one with his disciples, with the members of his body; and only as he is both is he indeed himself. His person, in so far like ours, is constituted by his vocation and its carrying-out; but his mission was precisely to give himself wholly to others—consider only, "This is my body, given for you." Now neither eschatologically nor any other way is there a *totus Robertus Jensii*; the structure we have just described is the structure of Christ's one personal life only, of the life that could and did empty itself by death into a community of disciples without therefore vanishing into the community. Christ is and remains the second identity of Trinity as one only; yet he and the community he brings with him into the life of the Trinity are again one and the same "whole Christ."

Christ has a body that is itself a community of bodies; while I have only this one thing that sits before the computer as I write. Nevertheless, the relation between Christ and the Church is the prototype of my relation to my body, so that analogies can be drawn: just as I am my body yet can stand over against my body to discipline it or harm it or suffer it or enjoy it, so Christ is the Church yet stands over against the Church to discipline and shape and suffer and enjoy it.

As Christ is the Church, he is in that same or a related sense a culture, the culture the Church is. And now, for how that odd "is" works in the case of "Christ is a culture," I turn to the title of this first essay. For I think the relation is better explicated by being displayed than by being theorized.

The West's use of the word "polity" has been directed by an of course much-idealized memory of fifth-century Athens. A group of persons is a polity if there is within it an arena of discussion and debate concerning its own shared moral future, and if such debate can be conducted with some view to its decisions having force. For example, "What shall we teach our children?" "Are there constraints on the community's use of force, within itself and externally?" Although our nostalgic model is momentarily democratic Athens, a polity need not be democratic: a monarch in council—or even just a monarch and a lover talking in bed—are still such an arena. An untouched tribal society with no joint moral decisions to make at all, or a perfect dictatorship—if there can in fact be such things—would not be polities, though we might still speak by extension of their "politics." We should further note that the questions a particular polity will deliberate will be posed by its own historically established identity: a *shtetl* in the pale of settlement did not worry overmuch about just war theory; and if indeed some South Sea islands had no clear institution of marriage, divorce did not pose a problem.

So to say that that Christ is a polity is to say that he is in himself a sort of gathering, around a historically specific arena of joint moral deliberation. There are at least two ways in which it appears how this can be so.

We may first observe that the biblical history of God with his people is from first to last a political history, and one with a specific institutional structure. And then we may put that together with a further observation, that the history of God with his people both *includes* the coming of Christ, and by classic teaching is as a whole *encompassed* in his coming.

The history of Jesus, if the Church's claims about him are true, did not begin when Mary conceived. According to Chalcedon, it is "one and the same" person who is born in these last days of Mary and eternally from the Father. Thus, however we are to construe the matter metaphysically, the "pre-existence" of Jesus the Christ is not simply that first there was a sheer divine entity who then became Jesus the Christ; somehow Jesus Christ, the God-*man* "pre"-exists himself, as has been noted with varying clarity and conceptual context by Irenaeaus, Athanasius, Karl Barth and others. Thus the antecedent of the pronouns in Colossians' great cosmological passage, "He himself is before all things, and in him all things hold together," is the phrase "our Lord Jesus Christ."

Now, once one has seen that, and however one solves the metaphysical questions it poses, one is at least open to notice a regularly unnoticed biblical phenomenon: that to the pre-existence of Jesus Christ there belongs among other factors his pre-existence in and as the nation of Israel. For Israel also is the human Son, whom God called out of Egypt as he would call Jesus the Son from the tomb—and if we ideologically insist on calling these predications metaphors, we still have to ask what must be true of those to whom these metaphors can be appropriate. If we would understand the relation between Jesus and the one he called Father, by virtue of which relation he is the Son, we must rehearse the whole relation between Israel and her Lord.

To our present concern: what in Israel is scattered, both in the way of history and by sin, is gathered up in the one Israelite; but just so, vice versa, what is compact in the life of the one Israelite is laid out in the history of Israel. The biblical story of God with his people both includes the coming of the Christ and is included in that coming. "In" Christ is the historical polity of Israel.

So—the polity which Christ "is," is the polity of Israel on its way to the kingdom, whose character is narrated throughout the Bible. The polity of this people manifested from the first two features that will occupy us through this essay.

First, its constitution, "the covenant," contained a promise, that among the nations, which all belong in one way or another to the Lord, this one should be the "kingdom of priests" for the others. Israel's polity was thus intrinsically eschatological from the start, in that the good she was communally to cultivate would if fully accomplished unify all nations in worship of the Lord, an event which when it occurs must indeed explode the parameters of historical continuity as we now live it.

Second, the moral arena at its heart was—to say the least—remarkable. On the one hand, jurisdiction belonged directly and exclusively to the Lord, who spoke through "men of God," "prophets" in the later terminology. When Israel eventually wanted to have a normal mid-Eastern monarchy, the Lord said to the prophet currently in office, "They have rejected me from being king over them." Yet on the other hand, prophets—or at least those in the legitimate succession of Moses, "the" prophet—spoke also for the people *to* God, indeed they reasoned and expostulated with God. Thus legislation did *not* belong exclusively to God; there was an arena of moral argument in this nation. That is, she was an actual polity.

The first Israelite constituting arena of moral deliberation had God and the people's representative, Moses, a human individual, for its members. The polity, we may say, was *theanthropikos,* divine-human. What then if one day there were one Israelite who was *theanthropos*? God-man? Would he not *in his person* be the public square of this people?

This last question becomes more urgent with the monarchical covenant that succeeded but did not supplant the desert covenant. A monarchy was in fact established, which eventually had all the appurtenances of a proper state: it policed and judged the territory it controlled, made war, conducted trade, and so on. Yet the dynasty's founder, David, could legitimate the succession only by being himself a prophet; his "last words" that effect the succession begin with announcement of prophetic seizure, "The Spirit of the Lord is upon me . . ." (2 Sam. 23:1–2). The kings, moreover, were subject always to harassment by prophets—sometimes from among their own household shamans—who intruded the Lord into the monarchical councils, and just so intruded into those councils the people also, whom in their office they represented and whom at least some of them did in fact deliberately represent.

The role established for Israel's kings, was thus in effect to be *theanthropos*; this was too much to bear and most of David's line did not even try. Notoriously, the hope developed for a king who would do what Israel's kings were supposed to do, for one who would be what *Moses-with-the-people and the Lord were together*.

The main event of Israel's political history after the establishment of the monarchy was its long drawn-out undoing. Contrary to what might have been expected, the decades of "the Exile" became the occasion of a final radicalizing of prophecy. The "something new" now promised by the exilic and postexilic prophets is a fulfillment of Israel's mission that is plainly and often explicitly beyond the possibilities of history in its present terms; in exilic and postexilic prophecy Israel's political hopes are openly eschatological. "Nation shall not take up the sword against nation, neither shall they learn war anymore" (Mic 4:3), which demands nothing less than that God "will destroy the shroud that is cast over all peoples . . . , he will swallow up death forever" (Isa 25:7). Finally, in the "apocalyptic" schemes cast in the last time of Israel's prophecy, the difference between "this age" and "the age to come" is explicit and indeed ontological. The age to come is none the less—or rather, all the more—envisioned as a polity.

Then—on the day appointed—the *theanthropos* came, preaching that this kingdom of heaven had "come near," so near indeed that following him was entry into it and to turn away from him was to balk at the gate. With that, eschatological polity appeared as a possibility for present citizenship. And when the God of Israel raised this Jesus from the death to which his radicalism had brought him, following him became a continuing possibility within this world, and a mission began to bring all into this citizenship.

This citizenship, it must for our purposes be emphasized, is membership in a particular community and just so in a particular person; to belong to the Church and to be "in" Christ are the same fact.

A polity is constituted in its discourse. In the case of the Church, the central discourse is prayer. And when the Lord's disciples asked how to pray, he invited them into his own discourse with the Father. That is to say, he invited us into a political arena that is constituted in his own relation to the Father, which is in turn to say, into his own being as *theanthropos*.

Thus as the Lord's sisters and brothers, as the members of the *totus Christus*, as corporately his body, we make a perfect participatory parliament of prayer. Were it merely a matter of common and even equal membership in a community that somehow belonged *to* Christ without *being* identified with him, that is, were the Church properly conceived as some Protestantism does, that would have the ironic consequence that Christ would be our polity in a way analogous to the way in which a pure absolute monarch would be a polity in sheer conversation with himself. But that is not the way the New Testament presents the matter.

The matter of prayer, and particularly of what we call petitionary prayer, leads us into what is perhaps the deepest mystery of membership in the polity that Christ is. The polity that Christ is, we said, is the polity of Israel when the *theanthropos* comes to be Israel. This polity like every polity deliberates its own future, both final and immediate. But the future of the *theanthropos* can only be the future of the universe, final and immediate. We call the *totus Christus*'s deliberation of the cosmic future, immediate and final, petitionary prayer. "Thy Kingdom come soon," we pray. "Cure my child tomorrow," we pray. Also believers have great difficulty believing that such giving of advice to the Almighty is a sensible procedure. But we are to consider that when we pipe up "Our Father . . ." it is not some little group of hole-in-the-corner creatures speaking; it the *totus Christus*, it is the second person of Trinity addressing the first; it is an inner-triune political deliberation.

I said there were two ways in which the sense of that "is" in "Christ is a polity" could be displayed. We come to the second. By his resurrection and ascension, Christ is a political fact among and in competition with the polities of this world. The members of his body proclaim that he sits at the right hand of God, that is, that he is the world's sovereign, and inform all earthly would-be sovereigns that they are merely his place-holders, his vicars, and that, moreover, they are extensively in rebellion.

Moreover—and here is the vital switch for our topic—we who make this claim, inhabitants of polities of this world, proclaim ourselves as together this universal sovereign's embodied presence in this world. That is, we proclaim *ourselves* as sovereign over against the polities we for the moment of this age continue to inhabit.

The papacy's occasional behavior as a government in this world, with ministers of state, ambassadors, even an army, was doubtless a perversion. But it was a perversion of something true. Christ's presence in this world is not a private phenomenon, an invisible interiority. It is, as Cardinal Bellarmine once famously said of the Church—and however dubious his ecclesiology may otherwise have been—"as visible as the republic of Venice."

Augustine's "polity of God" is not a polity only in heaven; it is—however imperfectly—a polity *now*, and just so *in conflict with* other polities, with what Augustine called the "earthly polity," the polities of this age as a class. Which is of course simply to say again that it is itself a polity, also in this age.

If we are in Christ we must expect to be involved in the political struggles of this world. In particular, we must expect other polities to make war against us, as China does and as most Islamic societies do, and as do the liberal democracies, in certain ways.

The *Letter to Diognetus*'s famous proposition, that Christians are citizens of all nations, and not obtrusive by their patterns of civic life, is only half the truth. Christians are indeed citizens of all nations, and equipped to be exemplary citizens. But this means that short of the End, Christians are saddled with plural citizenship. This does not make for peaceful lives; it means that the line between the polity of God and the polities of this world runs through each of us and through our community, and that we must expect to struggle in our own communal and individual lives with the conflicts between polities which in this age are inevitable. When the Chinese government persecutes Christians, the persecuted are instructed by Paul to be loyal also to the persecutors, precisely because the persecuted are in fact sovereign over the persecutors.

Once started on these lines, one could go on more or less indefinitely. But enough must be enough.

21

Christ as Culture 2: Christ as Art (2004)

Philosophers, social theorists, critics, inveterate writers to the editor, curators, the artists themselves—all have proposed definitions of art. So why should not I? Let me propose one that I think may be appropriate and that is suitable to the needs of this article: an artist is an experimenter with possible worlds.

This description will best be clarified by examples, which I will mostly draw from painting, though in the body of the article I will speak of music, dance, etc. as well. I do not intend in bringing examples to parade myself as an art historian or connoisseur, neither of which I am; what I am able to adduce is merely the result of fitful reading over the decades and of some acquaintance with the objects themselves, acquired as opportunity has offered.

Thus, for an example very amenable to my purpose, much painting and sculpture in Western modernity has construed a world of objects salient in space: looking perhaps at a seventeenth-century portrait, one often has and is intended to have the feeling that if one could contrive to move a bit sidewise in the space of the painting, one could see behind the figure, or indeed that if one could only get close enough, one could seize hold of it. But of course pictorial representation, even sculpture, can locate figures in space in quite other ways than as salient objects in a space projected as a subject's field of vision, and indeed in the long history of pictorial representation has mostly done so. Thus the figures in a medieval window are all confined to their flat surface, and are determined to remain so in despite of any maneuvers by an apprehending subject; nor will it do to explain this with an inability of the artisans to do it differently. Again, the world need not present itself in anything like so neatly *delineated* a fashion as most seventeenth-century portraiture does; as the impressionists were to teach us, the world can, seemingly with just as great fidelity to what is somehow there, be construed with only the haziest of internal boundaries.

Critics influenced by Marxism have had some worthwhile things to say about the way modern—not modernist—painting tended to construe the world. A world of objects salient in space is a world well adapted to *subjects*, that is, it is a world that can be got hold of and so perhaps manipulated: the Cartesian intellect arrays the world before it to be grasped and acted upon. This world of objects arranged for grasping by intelligent and active subjects is the bourgeois world; the artists of the bourgeoisie construed the very world to be inhabited by their clients with their activities and self-understanding. Just so, of course, the world typically proposed by the art of the West's modernity was precisely but one *possible* world, for there can be other ways of inhabiting a world than the way of the bourgeoisie—a class, by the way, whose achievements I have no desire to denigrate and whose fringes I am grateful still to inhabit.

Around the turn of the nineteenth and twentieth centuries, what we call modernism burst into Western modernity's world—and by the way, it clears up much confusion when it is noted that what happened in painting and sculpture then and is usually called "modernism" is more or less the same thing that happened later in some other fields and is called "*post*modernism." The high modernists regarded themselves quite explicitly as revolutionaries, also in politics and society; their very conscious vocation was to deconstruct the bourgeois world depicted by their predecessors—indeed, they were prominent among those who made the word "bourgeois" into an insult. Thus we again see how that world of modern—not modernist—depiction was only one possible world, for if it had been simply the "real" world, it could not have been deconstructed.

In the deconstruction other alternate worlds appear. So Cezanne's great pictures of "Bathers" present sheer sensual flesh, given shape on the plane of the canvas not *as* bodies, by virtue of their own shapes, but by patterning all that flesh on an abstract geometry constructed within the rectangle of the canvas. The bodies do not make the pattern as bodies: indeed one cannot always tell where one body ends and another begins, it is in one or two cases not even clear that a supposedly female bather does not have male genitalia. The pictures would be just a mess, were all this flesh not constrained by superimposed geometry on the plane of the canvas, by arrangement in balanced triangles, and the like of the sort people explaining a painting always tell us to notice, here laid on by the painter in blatantly hegemonic fashion. Thus these paintings also construe a specific possible world, which perhaps we may say is a world of sensual promiscuity rescued from chaos by centrally imposed rules, the very ideal of the social and political revolutions which the modernist artists wished to promote—the Bolsheviks, you will remember, were originally all for free love and for managing everything else.

Just one more example from my feeble store. Mondrian and his allies, who invented truly "abstract" painting, did so by inspiration of and in support of a formulated theology; they were theosophists—Mondrian was a formal member of the society. He espoused Pythagorean doctrines, that underlying the flux of the perceived world, which the impressionists and various "post-impressionists" had explored, is a world of pure, simple and changeless geometric archetypes. Painting, according to Mondrian, was to induct the viewer into this world, it was, indeed, to save the viewer's soul.

So there have been and no doubt will be plenty of possible worlds construed by art. A stark choice is posed at this point. *Is* there a world other than the multitude of possible worlds? Do artists simply create worlds, any one of which is as real as any other, there being, as it were, no standard world by which to judge them? Is the visible world simply the logical product of its construals? One should note the congruence of this question with that posed by postmodern theorists of *language*, who argue that texts fail to mediate any "presence" other than themselves, so that finally a text is only the indefinite set of its interpretations, there being no standard by which to rate them. And indeed, whether we are considering the good, the true or the beautiful, if there is no God then all is permitted.

Christians and Jews, however, know there is God, and even what he is like. And so they know there is a standard world, the one he, as we uniquely say, "creates." Or, looking from the other side, Christians and Jews know that artists are not creators, not even co-creators—whatever such beings might be.

The world as we perceive and so inhabit it is indeed always the world construed by a certain eye, bourgeois, Bolshevik, Hinayana Buddhist or whatever. Moreover and vice versa, this vision is always given to us by art, without which there is no vision. But believers know that there is indeed a standard of our experiments, because there is only one God and all reality is his creation.

Yet, and here is a decisive next point, in my view postmodern theory is in so far right that we are not in position to access this standard directly. For if the standard world were immediately available to us, there would be no possibility of our making art—God the Artist, as evoked below, would be the only artist—and we do in fact make art.

The sign that art's proliferating construals have indeed a standard, even though we do not access it directly, is that artistic production is *work*.

In a recently republished essay originally written in honor of Donald McKinnon, Rowan Williams argued that the chief component of a realist epistemology is recognition that at least some knowledge requires to be learned, to be acquired by labor. So also a realist understanding of artistic activity is recognition that an artist must labor to construe his possible world, that he cannot just decree it; he must work *on* something, that is, on a given world which indeed neither he nor we can see independently of this labor, but which nevertheless presents itself precisely in the necessity of laboring. We have in our living room a painting by a very gifted lifelong friend of Blanche Jenson. He says it is a painting of the harbor at Mykonos; for my part, I have never been able to see any harbor at all, much less a specific harbor of Mykonos, and refer to the shapes I do see as two whales kissing. The point is: he really did sit looking out over the harbor of Mykonos when he made the sketches, and the painting would not be what it is unless he had thus been working *on* something.

Were there no Creator and so no creation, no standard world, artists would need to do no work. It marked the end of high modernism, when the brilliant Marcel Duchamp simply lost faith in painting and sculpting, and picked up a urinal to hang on the exhibition wall. Why labor to sculpt or paint, when the world is full of things that already have interesting and complex shapes, such as an artist might work to create, and if there is no standard by which to prefer one shape to another? Much sold or exhibited as art in the last thirty years or so is the product of deliberate metaphysical nihilists, who explicitly do not think they need to work to make art, and who, if they can be said to construe an alternative world, construe a void.

It may, by the way, be an evidence that this nihilism is false, that is, an evidence that there is God, that this art is so very bad—bad, to be sure, by standards the perpetrators do not recognize. Blanche and I well remember the first time when a visit to a new exhibition at the Museum of Modern Art in New York, where we had for so many years gone to be exhilarated, instead simply bored us. When the American Academy of Religion met in Toronto last November, there was an exhibition somewhere in town with the title, "Any Asshole Can Make Art." We did not visit it, but one reviewer hinted that the works exhibited at least proved the point.

So an artist is one who experiments with possible worlds, by working on the created world, which neither the artist nor we perceive except by such experiment. Does this definition fit all "the arts," or just the visual art I have so far discussed?

Music is the obvious other art to be considered. The world presents itself not only as a congeries of sights but also and indeed first as a congeries of sounds. I say "first" as a congeries of sounds because we are disarmed to what we hear as we are not to what we see: we have flaps on our eyes to start and stop sight, but no such instant defenses for our ears—indeed the external ear structure is designed to channel sound in willy-nilly—and we direct our seeing as we cannot direct our hearing. Just so also, the world as heard is in more immediate need of construal as some specific world or other, than is the world as seen.

So we replace the buzz in our ears with rhythms and melodies and harmonies. There is, of course, a great difference between the visual arts and music. Whatever alternatively seen world a painter or sculptor may propose, it remains out there, a thing—not necessarily an object—other than the one who beholds it. But as Augustine long ago pointed out, a tune or rhythm exists at all only in memory and anticipation; which is to say it exists only within its hearer. Moreover, this has an at first sight paradoxical consequence: a developed piece of music is a world we can inhabit in a way we cannot inhabit a painting or sculpture. One lives in a fugue while it is going on.

Which brings us again to art as experimentation with possible worlds. For the world of a fugue is a different sort of world than the world of a so-nata-movement, to say nothing of a raga. It surely suggests something that, for example, Beethoven was a contemporary of Hegel; or that the vogue for "other musics" coincides with the rise of a sort of populist pantheism.

There are, of course, other modes of art that must be capable of this analysis, if the analysis is true. There is, for one thing, heightened language, and its nihilistic pair, deliberately debased language. One can say, "It's best for good folk to stick together," or one can say "Let me not to the marriage of true minds admit impediment," or one can rap out the pleasures of having a woman. The worlds construed by such utterance are very different, and not just by virtue of the propositions enunciated.

Or for one last instance, there is dance. When the waltz was regarded as indecent, it was because folk knew the sexual secret of dancing, and thought it both more appropriate and more fun to let it remain more a secret than it could be in the waltz. The church authorities who prohibited "social" dancing at the church colleges of my youth were misguided and in any case doomed to defeat, but they did not lack insight. A minuet, a waltz, a pelvic writhing to disco, a fertility stomp, a sequence of Martha Graham's poses, each construes the human world of male and female in its own way.

Now—if that is what art is, what about Christ? I know that order of questioning is neo-Protestant, but will plead that like Aquinas at the beginning of the *Summa Theologiae* my apparently neutral beginning was covertly christological all along.

Note that my title is not Christ as Artist, but Christ as Art. If the Son is art, the artist must be the Father.

The Son is the Father's experiment with a possible world. In his being as the Logos, as the sense in created things, the Son is the particular coherent shape which the world in fact makes, insofar as the world's behavior manifests knowable laws—if at the level of axioms knowable only to God. But just so he is precisely an experiment, for nothing binds the Father to make *this* sense *ad extra* instead of some other sense. The Son is not the sense which the world just has, for apart from the Son precisely as the sense of which he is the experiment, there would *be* no world. If we could abstract from the triunity of God, and imagine the Father before all worlds having a conversation with himself that was not the Son, we might imagine something like this: "Wouldn't it be cool to try an *extra* with awkward featherless bipeds that could talk and black holes and . . . ?"

Now of course we cannot thus abstract from the triunity of God, and so the conversation before all worlds is the conversation of the Father and the Son, whose import is again the Son. The conversation before all time does not in fact begin in the subjunctive mode, "Wouldn't it be cool . . . ?" Therefore—and this is the unlikeness between created artists and God—there is not a created world *over against* which the Son is an experiment. Like us, the Father does not know the standard world except as and by his experiment; but unlike us he is not at the mercy of the standard world, which does not exist except as he experiments. Unlike us, the Father does no labor between his experiment and the standard thereof.

Nevertheless, just here is where the analogy bites. For indeed we can also then say that the Son is the Father's labor on a real world which obtains just in that this experiment is conducted; and that the Father is indeed an artist, the artist from whom all artists take their name, in that he knows the real world precisely and only by the experiment the Son is.

What is this thing we inhabit? Our operative construal of the world is, of course, the one we work with before we stop to think, and in us Westerners that continues to be determined by the cruder versions of the Enlightenment. The world we presume before we stop to think is that of an inadequately nuanced modern—not modernist—painting. We act as though we inhabited a vast mechanism, whose basic structure and laws are changeless and eternal, and whose bits are discrete substances interacting in space, like the parts of an engine or clockwork; we act in accordance with this picture even though we have of course known—overtly—for decades that this is not so. And Christians should in any case always have known that if God is the Trinity the mechanistic picture of the universe must be false—indeed, some like Jonathan Edwards did know it. That recent science utterly contradicts it, is at most a pleasing Barthian "little light."

What is truly out there is, though we cannot access this directly, the standard of our experiments *because* it is the standard implicated by and never opposed to the one Artist's one Experiment. Why is there a creation, a standard of our experiments? Because there is an Experiment going on that determines its own standard world.

Thus the real world, the world we do not access except by our experiments, is free with the freedom of the Great Experiment. And that is the one great thing to know about it.

We inhabit a world that is as free as ever the world taking shape under Picasso's pencil and yet is not at all arbitrary, is not subject to deconstruction to make way for some other experiment. No created artist can ever be satisfied with any of his or her actual experiments—actual sonatas or actual canvases or actual poses—and with us that is a good thing despite the threat of futility that thus hangs over our creations, for when *we* are satisfied we stop. God however *is* satisfied with his experiment, he pronounces it good; and with God that is a good thing, for with him there is no dissonance between standard and experiment.

The lightness of being is intolerable, unless we know it is an artist's freedom. If we do know that, then the dogwood tree outside my study window, in its amazing thereness and its simultaneously amazing never-the-sameness is above all an occasion for merriment. Then the question, "Whyever should there be such a thing as a house, and in particular that perpetually-in-repair mansion across the way?" "Warum gibt es überhaupts Seiendes und nicht vielmehr Nichts?" is not a solicitation of *Sein zum Tode* but a solicitation of freedom, to join the fun of being something.

Believers, moreover and penultimately, inhabit not only the creation but before all else they are in Christ. That is, we inhabit the great Experiment himself. To be in Christ is to live—and here to make my point as directly as possible I find I have to think of music more than of other arts—to live in Christ is to live in the rush of the great fugue as God is composing it.

One does not readily sense that on most occasions when the *totus Christus* gathers. But sometimes one does. For me it happens when the preacher actually makes sense, and I am swept along in the melodious enthymeme of the argument. Or when the procession of folk to commune displays all sorts and conditions of humanity, all the notes of a chord too densely augmented for mortals to sort out. Or when the depicted spiritual universe in a Byzantine Church approaches the paradigm described in textbooks. Or of course by the eucharistic transformation itself, when the fruits of past labor are brought to the altar and God lets us taste and see how they are open to the final Climax.

Moreover and finally, the great Experiment we inhabit is not an improvisation whose shape we cannot guess. The Christ in whom we live and move is Jesus the crucified and risen rabbi and prophet in Israel; he is one of us, whom we know. The great fugue is still going, and we have no idea what inversions or other surprises are yet to come; but we know the pull of the final resolution.

A great many things follow from these observations, should they be correct. I have neither the time nor the wit to construct a nice sequence of such consequences, and will merely throw out several, from a variety of regions of discourse, that have suggested themselves to me.

For one. It is because Christ is the great Experiment, whose internal logic or flow or melody those in the Church are privileged to experience, that habitation in Christ is by faith rather than by works. For to have faith is to abandon oneself to a Freedom, which is yet so determinate that it can be trusted. It is to ride the great Painter's brush, to skip about between the great Composer's hands on the keyboard.

For another, from a quite different area of reflection. Our churches have architecture, and we dance and make music in them and—some of us anyway—paint and sculpt them. Do our observations suggest anything about such churchly art?

The Church's artists have no more direct access to the standard world on which they labor than do others. But we may indeed say that by faith a churchly artist lives the movement of the very Experiment which posits the creation. Must not then the churchly artist enjoy a certain surplus of freedom, of trust in the movement of his or her invention? And of purity, of freedom from dissonance between his or her construal and the standard on which it labors? It seems to me that we sometimes see that: in the direct gaze of some Eastern icons, in the straightforward power of the depiction of the harrowing of hell in the apse of the side-church of Constantinople's St Savior in the Fields, in the enormous economy of some contemporary liturgical music, such as that of Arvo Pärt, or in the ease with which Bach manages complexity, even in the uninhibited fun of some of the liturgical high-jinks of the 1960s, before lack of inhibition was confused with not having to think. This freedom is not the kind of thing which can be commanded, or for which directions can be devised. But I think we can recognize it after the fact; and perhaps much more to the point recognize when it has *not* been happening.

A last consequence. It does seem that something must be said in this article about liturgy. That each liturgical celebration is a work of art—good, bad or mostly indifferent—is a banality. The observation I want to make here is from a viewpoint looking the other way. If the Church's artistic working takes place within and indeed moves with the Experiment by which the universe exists and moves, then we have another insight into why prayer and sacrifice work: the Experiment that posits all things and their movements is the *totus Christus*, Christ as he embraces us. When we utter, "Save us from the time of trial," or "Give us this day our daily bread," within the whole sweep of the Church's great "work," our piping belongs to the free movement—the chorus, the mural-in-progress, the ballet—by which the creation occurs.

22

Christ as Culture 3: Christ as Drama *(2004)*

Drama is, of course, one of the arts. But the fact and notion of drama are so intimate to my understanding of Christ that I need to devote a special article to them.

Partly for that reason, I will not this time take the risk of the neo-Protestant order of questioning as in the previous article, or at least not in quite so blatant form. I will begin with the surely respectable theologoumenon, "Jesus is the Christ."

"Christ," as noted before, is a title. A further observation can launch our present reflections: "Christ" is a title for a person. And that is to say, we can understand a proposition of the form ". . . is the Christ," as a literary-critical remark about a story. For the immediate future of this article, I will be trying to elucidate that—perhaps rather unexpected—assertion.

What differentiates a person from a mere individual, is that an individual something need not have a story, while a person not only has but in my view *is* a story. Of course, a story of sorts could doubtless be constructed about the desk at which I write, but—*pace* Martin Heidegger—we know what the thing is without any such construction. But what is Robert Jenson? We may of course answer, a specimen of the species *homo sapiens*. Or, famously, a member of the only known group of featherless bipeds. Or so on. Thereby, however, we would not have said what the *person* Robert Jenson is.

And so soon as we move to even the most guarded of propositions about the *person*, we must begin to narrate. Even "Robert Jenson is a would-be theologian" or "Robert Jenson is a Norwegian-American" tell long and complicated tales. And if we were responding to any kind of real curiosity about what Robert Jenson is, we could do so only by becoming ever more biographical. What am I? I am a story that the moving finger will one day stop writing.

It is for me a fundamental insight and therefore one that some readers will have heard or read me expound before in various contexts: what joins the sequential events of my life together, to make them be *someone*'s life, my life, is dramatic coherence. I will bring in my favorite bit of Aristotelean insight yet again: a sequence of events has "dramatic coherence" if it fulfills the following conditions: before any one event we cannot say or could not have said for sure what will happen, yet after the event can see it was just what had to happen. And if with Robert Jenson there are relations of dramatic coherence sufficient to speak of him as a person, but nevertheless events scattered around that just do not fit, yet seem clearly to have happened to him, that only—in my view—shows that his personhood is fragile—which we already knew. A person is a sequence of events that before the event retains the capacity to surprise, yet after the event displays a coherent dramatic sense that has been tightened by that very event.

Now it may well be that to differentiate a person from, say, a fiction or a culture, we need further some further specification or specifications: perhaps that the sequence of events in question happen to the same organic body or to the same soul. It may be that there has to be an x identifiable by "Robert Jenson," that is not itself identified by narrative, to have this story. I myself sometimes think—and indeed have written—that the posit of this x is merely a necessary obfuscation: our finitude may ineluctably inflict it on our thinking, but we should not use its assertion as a warrant in other reflection. But so far as I can see, we need not now settle or indeed further pursue this question: so far as I can see, it makes no difference for what I want to say, whether or not an unnarrated x is a condition of a personal life's narrative-dramatic unity. When in the following I refer with such phrases as "the drama that is Christ," that "is" should be understood as allowing either position.

The Gospels are long versions of the fundamental gospel-statement, "Jesus, that is, the one who was born of Mary and baptized by John and called disciples and . . . , is risen." The Gospels' proposition is the resurrection of someone; their chief matter is narrative of that someone.

Now, the proposition with which I began says about the story named "Jesus," that it is the story of "the Christ." I said, perhaps with some glee in being oracular, that this was a literary-critical remark. But it is indeed the sort of remark literary critics make: it stipulates the *kind* of dramatic coherence, the *genre* of plot, which binds birth from Mary and baptism by John and healing paralytics and arguing with other theologians and getting crucified and so on to be a person. Let me mention just a few aspects of the "Christ"-story genre.

To be the story of the "Christ" is to be integral to a story not immediately referenced by "Jesus," the story of a particular nation, Israel. The story of the Christ therefore coheres only together with the story of Israel, and the hearer or reader is warned that the whole story told by the Old Testament is not only presupposed but included. The point has been demonstrated by experience of historical-critical exegesis. Whatever might have been the case, or might now become the case, historical-critical exegesis of Scripture was historically (!) driven by desire to detach Jesus from Israel—indeed often enough by crass and explicit anti-Semitism—and the result of this separation was that also Jesus fell apart in the hands of the historical critics: there was the Jesus of Mark and of Matthew and Q and of John and then the Jesus of various layers discoverable in each of these and so on.

Again, to be the story of the Christ is be an eschatological story, that is, one whose resolution lies beyond what the story itself narrates or can narrate. The story of the Christ therefore coheres only as it at every step refers beyond itself, only as the story itself is prophecy. This point too has been demonstrated by sad experience. The enterprise of the "Jesus seminar" was to draw a picture of Jesus immanent within conceivable—conceivable to the participants—history. They ended by providing another case for Schweizer's diagnosis, and depicting only their own California-guru selves.

To be the story of the Christ is, finally in this series, to be at once an earthly story and a heavenly story—in the Israelite sense of "heaven." The Messiah was never, contrary to some overly simple expositions, thought to be a purely earthly-political figure. Even remaining within the title's strictly political provenance, the Messiah was to be the one who would truly be what the Davidic kings were called to be; and that means as we early discussed, he was to be *theanthropos*. But we can at this point rest content with a perhaps less controversial observation: the Messiah was the one to whom the Lord would say as he said to earlier Davidic scions, "You are my Son, today I have begotten you," and have it prove true without reservation. If we suppose there was first an earthly story, subsequently interpreted as a heavenly story, we will discover no plot to the story at all.

There is, of course, yet a step to be taken. That every person is a dramatically coherent story does not yet say that some person is a *drama*. A drama has more than one *persona*; even a play like Beckett's *Krapp's Last Tape*, which seemingly does not, is presented precisely to establish that drama is impossible. There is thus a difficulty here analogous to the difficulty about a single person's being a polity; and the resolution of the difficulty is also analogous to that proposed in the first article.

There are two sets of other *personae* with whom Christ makes a drama: the divine Father and Spirit, and his human sisters and brothers. God first.

The Father begets and sends the Son; the Son is begotten and sent by the Father; the Spirit is breathed by the Father upon the Son; the Spirit frees the Father and the Son to love one another. This is an imminent drama, in which the Son takes his role *with* the other divine *personae*. But then there are two further standard trinitarian points: only as this drama occurs is there God at all, and then each of the three just *is* God. Which is to say that the Son is simultaneously a *persona in* a drama with the other triune *personae*, and that he is the God actually *as* this drama.

That point may seem merely clever or worse, but I will come back to its utility. First we need to look at the other set of *dramatis personae*, Christ's dramatic relation to us, which can be very briefly done.

The human drama Christ enacts with us, as told in Scripture, is clear and well-plotted, complete with development, crisis, turning and recapitulation. Clearly he is one *persona* in this drama with the rest of us. But then, we who are the other *personae* of this drama are by what in fact happens in it so taken into him and he into us, that we make his own body. We remember the relation of the person to his or her body, already evoked in the first article in this series: both are simultaneously true, that I am my body and that I act on my body. So Christ acts over against those who are his body—to make a drama—and is that body—he is the drama he makes.

And now we must bring together these two dramas that Christ makes, with the Father in the Spirit and with us. It is a central contention, indeed motivation of the doctrine of Trinity, that the story God lives with *us* and the story that is his *own* life, are not other than one another. We must indeed be able to speak of an immanent Trinity, in some distinction or other from the economic Trinity, but we must not think of them having differing characters or differing plots. However we are to distinguish the immanent from the economic Trinity, we must not conceive two different dramas. Rescuing Israel from Egypt, giving Jesus over to crucifixion and rescuing him from the tomb—these are determining events of the triune life as they are determining events of the history of our salvation. Indeed that they are the first is how they are the second.

About this simultaneity, I will only say that it is our salvation. And I will point out one further circumstance. As actors in the drama, we are like players in a play for which concluding scenes are not yet written. We have a working script for the parts we can already rehearse; we call it Holy Scripture. The author holds conferences with us, and we trust him. We know who the hero is. And we know the play is not a tragedy.

I have been speaking of the drama Christ is. It is time to consider other cultures and their dramatic reality. In the previous article I began with what is true of all artists, then considered the Father as Artist. This time I began the other way around: with the drama Christ is, and must consider the dramas other cultures make.

Could there be a culture that did not depict things for sight, or make any sort of music, or employ special language for special occasions? I doubt it very much; nevertheless, one can as a mental experiment imagine a culture with one of these deficiencies.

It is impossible, however, to imagine a culture that did not act anything out. An anthropologist coming on a group utterly devoid of ritual acting would simply refuse to call it a culture—and if that reduces the contention to tautology, so much the better for my point.

Why is a culture without drama inconceivable? The reasons, I suggest, are closely related to those which make a person inconceivable apart from the drama of his or her life. A culture's diachronic self-identity is—I am contending—dramatic; and in the case of a culture we, of course, need no profundities to discover that the necessary plurality of *dramatis personae* is to hand.

At the start, I defined "a culture" as a system of mutually enabling signs. The definition is illuminating. But it falls short in one decisive way: it abstracts to the semiotic structure observable at a momentary state of a culture. Such abstraction is often useful, and that it is possible doubtless tells us something about cultures in general, but it can also be misleading. For, of course, cultures no more than persons exist momentarily; they exist only diachronically.

That being the case, how, after all, should a culture subsist save as a drama? With a single person, there are at least some initially plausible candidates to be the supposed unnarrated substratum of the narratable events that make a life. An obvious candidate is the organic body; what we commonsensically call the person's body may indeed by a necessary condition of the person's continuing identity. But a culture *has* no single body, unless the culture is—as is true of the Church—the body of some single one of its members, who will then be metaphorically the head. When a culture dies, it leaves no corpse that is its own—though it may indeed leave a mountain of other corpses.

In the history of Christianity, the "soul" has, of course, most often been thought to be the diachronic identity of the person. And it does seem to make some kind of sense to talk about the soul also of a culture. But the personal soul is supposedly qualified to be the x binding the events of a life because it is thought to be independent of those events, to be indeed separable from all the rest of what constitutes the person. I suppose nobody thinks the soul, for example, of Norse paganism went to heaven—or the other place—when that culture came to its end.

Whatever may be true of persons, a culture, it surely would appear, has no diachronic identity other than the coherence of its plot-line. Which gets us back to the question: why is a culture without drama inconceivable?

At this point I have a proposed explanation. The proposal is apologetic: if it persuades, it constitutes reason to credit the particular Christian drama. The proposal may, to be sure, be rejected; in which case its apologetic force of course fails.

The first step of the proposal: the various dramas that may be performed *within* a culture are all micro-dramas of the drama the culture itself is, mirrors in which the culture can see itself; and such mirrors of the culture to itself are necessary to the culture's continuance. If within a culture we have no notion of its plot, if we have no image of the culture as a whole, we cannot induct into the culture or cultivate it or know which alien forms it can adopt and which it cannot. Whether it be a tragedy of Shakespeare or the endless improvisation of a group of imaginative children or a religious cultic enactment, every drama is a small revelatory micro-drama of the whole cultural drama within which it occurs.

And then the second step of the proposal. We have to ask how this is possible. A particular culture's drama is not a whole until the culture ends, and then no more dramas are performed within it. So how can a play or ritual within a culture mirror the drama that culture is?

In the last decades of the previous century, theology made considerable use of the notion of "anticipation"—often under other terminology and indeed sometimes in disguise. Doubtless the most celebrated development of the notion was Wolfhart Pannenberg's. Pannenberg used the notion only on the very largest scale: the whole creation's end is anticipated by the resurrection of Jesus. To my disappointment, he never did say how this was supposed to work metaphysically.

The latter does not seem to me particularly difficult to do. Created reality exists and exists with the characters it does, precisely and only because it is indeed created. And Scripture unpacks its unique concept of creating quite clearly: to create is not to make or emanate a something, not even a glorious something like a cosmos; it is rather to initiate, fulfill and just so carry through a history. But a history is a whole only by its conclusion; were it simply to go on and on it would never be one thing, and so could not be a creation, a single thing distinct from God. Having a conclusion, and being shaped by it, and in that sense anticipating it, thus belongs to the being of a creature. That is, anticipation is a fundamental metaphysical structure, and cannot be construed in terms of other supposedly more fundamental structures.

If then a culture is a creature—and what else should it be?—it occurs in that it anticipates its final meaning, which I propose must itself be some anticipation of the universal last End. And unless the members of that culture are to be wholly blind to its final meaning, it must somehow be revealed, that is, anticipated within it, which—I propose—occurs in its interior dramas, enabled by Providence in accord with the possibility of anticipation that is given with the very being of the culture.

One last point on this line. The universal Anticipation that actually occurs, and belongs to the structure of reality, is Jesus the Christ of Israel. Whatever might have been, it is because *he* is that there are dramas and that they mirror in anticipation the cultures within which they occur. We have arrived at another point where a certain—not anonymous but—incognito christology may obtain. It is of course the incognito that is the problem, and gives the opening for so much drama to be demonic parody of the drama Christ is. Why were the Fathers by and large so suspicious of Greco-Roman tragedies and comedies? It was not because they thought them irrelevant; they were all too relevant, just as was pagan religion with its idol-worship.

Finally in this article, this is undoubtedly a place again to say something about the Church's liturgy. Within the culture the Church is, and so indeed within the culture Christ is, liturgies play much the same role as is played within any culture by its dramas. A liturgy, whether long or short, complicated or simple, either hangs together as a dramatic performance or has no coherence at all. Lamentably, the latter is the state of very much of what one experiences in contemporary pews. I do not know if the sheer miscellaneous character of our would-be liturgies is a reason why people decreasingly attend them, but it would be a reason why I did not, were I not driven by fear of divine retribution.

On this matter, I suspect that Catholicism has—or had until recently—more the right sense for the matter than does most Protestantism. I am not here talking about ceremonial styles; the same play can be produced with elaborate costuming and stage setting, and in street clothes behind music stands in a temporary clearing. For my own part, I am a fan of the Metropolitan Opera's style of doing things, but I understand that particular Reforming impetus which simply said "Enough already!" It is even possible to perform the Christian story in the format of sermon with introduction and dismissal, though this puts an enormous burden on the sermon, which then must itself be a bravura performance of the drama.

One cannot but observe a certain desperation in the Churches' liturgical efforts. I will limit myself to observations from my own country. Roman

Catholic congregations silence their organs and recruit a band, maybe to play along with recordings; Reformed congregations, observing that folk seem bored, liven up the service with "liturgical dance" or a nice instrumental solo; Norwegian-Lutheran elderly gentlemen, who only yesterday found even the original rhythmic versions of the chorales unseemly, try to swing with African-American songs, and succeed only in looking ridiculous and rushing the beat. Pastors enthuse over "contemporary" worship and tie themselves in theological knots trying to justify their abandonment of their traditions.

Now indeed desperation is in order. Those who stay away and the congregations who try to attract them agree in one perception: nothing much happens in our churches of a Sunday morning. But what is *supposed* to happen? I suggest that much of our difficulty is that we have forgotten that the Christ-*drama* is supposed to happen, in whatever high, low or intermediate sort of production.

This churchly *Spielvergessenheit* is, I further suggest, part of our captivity to the culture. The Western culture on which we have so long depended is manifestly drawing to its close, in much the fashion of the currently favored version of the end of the universe, by expanding forever into ever-decreasing available energy. Folk do not know the story of Western culture; indeed, the "chattering classes" regard teaching it as a wickedness. In the States, the Pilgrims have become heartless exploiters of the original Americans and the Founding Fathers a conspiracy against blacks. And the little dramas by which a culture knows itself are dying out among us; in the States, the 4th of July has become an opportunity to go shopping, while once-great festivals like Washington's birthday have disappeared altogether. Once every American child knew two texts by heart, or was supposed to: the Gettysburg Address and Longfellow's poem about Paul Revere's ride. Now indeed, our granddaughter in second grade knows Longfellow's poem, but she attends a private school, that is within limits allowed to be eccentric.

There is a painting that has long seemed to me both the effective beginning and the paradigm of high modernism: Manet's *Luncheon on the Grass*. We see a pleasant park, with a picnic group in the foreground. Two nicely dressed gentlemen are discussing something, apparently having finished the provisions. We are invited to imagine a small social story: the decision to have a picnic, discussion about where to have it and what to wear and what to eat, the meal—was it tasty?—an exchange of views after eating, and so on.

But then there is a person occupying a third point in the classical composition of picnickers: a naked lady—not nude, just blatantly naked. Not only is her lack of clothing utterly at odds with the rest of the painting, she pays no attention to the two picnickers nor—impossibly!—do they seem to notice her state. Moreover, every line of her pose detaches her from the group, as their pose detaches them from her. The naked lady has immigrated from another painting altogether.

What is afoot here is the enormously artful destruction of the story the painting would tell if it told one. The painting apart from the lady, and indeed the general compositional placement even of the lady, press us to imagine a story that accounts for the scene. But then the nakedness and pose of the lady prevent us from succeeding. Western late- or postmodern nihilism is the insistence that there are no dramas. It is not merely that we lack a drama in which to live, we are vehement in preventing one.

It may be that the world must live so for some time, or perhaps for its remaining time. The Church, however, need not.

23

Deus est ipsa pulchritudo
(God Is Beauty Itself) *(2007)*

I want to approach my actual topic by a rather lengthy preface. There is a question lurking inside our conference theme: "Why have those workers whom in modernity we lump together as 'artists' turned against beauty?" The milder form of this rejection is to simply regard "beauty" as irrelevant to art; the more virulent is real hostility, often carried into practice. At the moment, a shark pickled in formaldehyde is dominant among Britain's cultural exports to my country.

Often, I think, those who say that beauty is irrelevant to their work assume a popular notion of beauty that is so debased that what the word denotes is in fact irrelevant to their work. Then there is the circumstance that the humanities and "fine arts" departments of Western universities and colleges are the last refuges of Leninism, with its array of "theory" devised only to debunk. But I cannot think that either of these considerations suffices as an explanation. I want to sneak up on my assignment by proposing another explanation.

Artists like everyone else are shaped in what they do and in how they regard what they do by conceptual structures that govern discourse at a time and place. And the more subliminal such a set of rules is, the more powerful is its grip. The promised preface is thus an essay in "the history of ideas."

Once upon a time, artists like everyone else grasped and perhaps talked about beauty within a framework of notions that were called the "transcendentals." I do not suggest that people went about their work thinking of how it related to one or another transcendental—except of course those for whom, who like many in this room, such reflection *was* their work. But that did not diminish the shaping force of those notions, however labelled.

A notion was called "transcendental" if it was thought to display an aspect of being itself, and so to transcend the divisions that otherwise infest finite reality. In a formula, if "F" is a transcendental concept, then if one can say of something that it "is" one can also say of it that it "is F."

When thinkers such as Thomas Aquinas offered lists of the transcendentals, these varied. Indeed Thomas—with whom we are going to spend a good deal of time—offered lists that varied among themselves, and moreover failed to list concepts that he plainly treated as transcendental. But it is, I think, fair to say that through the tradition three transcendentals did most of the philosophical or theological heavy lifting: "the good," "the beautiful," and "the true." Special regard for these three notions has deep roots in our civilization: from the beginning of Western thought we have used "good," "beautiful," and "true" as descriptive terms that—we have hoped—dig deeper into the reality of what we experience than can other descriptive terms.

So when we used to think within the space of the three transcendentals, we thought that if something *is* at all, it must also be somehow good, somehow beautiful, and somehow true. The transcendentals were said to be "convertible" with "being"; that is, "*x* is" and "*x* is beautiful/good/true" can in any discourse be substituted either way without loss of truth. And of course if the transcendentals are convertible with the same thing they must be convertible with one another: so if something is in any way true, it must also be somehow beautiful and somehow good—and so on through the changes.

And here I must make a brief excursus and enter a disclaimer. Someone will surely be thinking that the pickled shark does after all exist and thus must be somehow beautiful—and true and good. Indeed, when Blanche Jenson read a draft of this essay, that is exactly what she said. The observation poses a problem which no one has ever fully mastered. In what sense can evil be said to be—and so in what sense can the ugly and harmful and false be truly said to be ugly and harmful and false? The question has undone thinkers throughout the West's intellectual history. Augustine was surely right, that evil must be construed as the sheer deprivation of being. And Barth was surely right in translating this doctrine protologically and eschatologically, so that evil is construed as what God always leaves behind on his way to the goal of his history with us. And I have no brighter idea to add.

And so back to my point: once upon a time one did not have to choose between making a true thing and making a beautiful thing, or between doing either and making a beneficent thing, or so on through the changes.

Indeed one *could* not make such a choice, and so probably did not think much about the possibility. And to be sure, if the doctrine just rehearsed is *true*, one still cannot make that choice, no matter how vehemently we now may try. It remains true that if we make a morally corrupting thing it will also be ugly and a fake—and again so on through the permutations. No amount of posturing about the "truth" of a blasphemous painting will make it good or beautiful.

It will be seen that the arch of the beauty and beneficence of the true had as its keystone a metaphysical and not merely logical doctrine of being, for it is by way of each transcendental's convertibility with being that it is convertible with the others. If the arch stands, the word "being" must be doing some actual descriptive work, denoting something more than the universally capacious—and just so uninteresting—set.

But what would that *more* be? Any *content* one could propose for the notion of being would just so be something that—to steal from Thomas in a different context—". . . all will understand to be God." For if the notion of Being-itself is not empty, then whatever it denotes must be in one way or another *universally* related to whatever *is*, to all things whatsoever. Being with a capital must be the Creator—or Brahman, or at least the being of the One above being—or whatever.

Absent God and faith in God, the good, the beautiful, and the true become seemingly independent—and thereupon possibly competing notions. Absent God, the artist faces a choice: Does he or she want, to make a painting that is "true to life" *or* one that is beautiful *or* one that is beneficent? Judging from some exhibits over the last two or three decades of the Museum of Modern Art in Manhattan—where Blanche and I used to go to be edified—many recent artists have thought that not only are these alternatives but that the alternatives are exclusive. The choice is, to be sure, illusory: in fact, if the artist does not create a beautiful and beneficent artifact, neither will it be true to anything—and again so on through the changes. That pickled shark does, after all, reveal something: nihilism, the absence of being and so of beauty and truth and goodness. And I am about to entangle myself again in that business about the non-beauty of non-being, etc., and so must stop.

Again back to the point: absent faith in God, the artist must eventually come to think that he or she faces choices between making beauty or making truth or good. In that situation, what would *you* choose?

I will sum up this long preface: the integrity of the beautiful depends upon the convertibility of beauty with being, and so with deity. Since it is the Western problem we are worried about, I will from here on assume that it is the biblical God who is in play. And just here we encounter the first of the substantive problems I have been aiming at. We will let Thomas take us into the problem—since also in this he is the supreme representative of the Western tradition.

Thomas' beginning and concluding proposition about our matter is *Deus est ipsa . . . pulchritudo*, "God is . . . beauty itself."[1] And he can turn this around: *ipsa essentia* [*Dei*] *est decor*, "The very essence [of God] is beautiful."[2] But just that poses the problem. To see why it is a problem, we have to ask what beauty is.

Beauty, according to Thomas—who also here can represent the tradition—is order, considered in a certain aspect. He lists the requirements for—not a definition of—order in this aspect: "For beauty three things are needed: first . . . perfection . . . then . . . consonance. And finally clarity."[3]

First, perfection is needed, in the sense of completeness: if a thing is to be beautiful, it must be a complete instance of its kind, it must be "perfect" in the sense that it has all the parts needed to be the kind of thing it is. A sheep missing one leg will be less beautiful *as a sheep*—though a painting of it may be very beautiful since the parts of the *painting* do not include the missing leg.

Next, "consonance" is needed. Thomas uses this notion instead of simply "order" in contexts where beauty is a theme. He has another as well, "harmony." Plainly, the parts of any real thing must and do *fit together*, in a way that constitutes it as the kind of thing it is; that is, they harmonize, they are mutually consonant. And we should note that when Thomas refers to such order as harmony or consonance he is indeed thinking of music as the paradigm. The parts of the human body, for example, do not in this way of thinking fit together in the way the parts of a machine fit together, in the sense of the vulgar Enlightenment; they make something that is more like a composition.[4]

Finally, precisely as a harmony of parts, that is, as possessed by what the medievals called a "form," a molding coherence of design, a real thing is adapted to be apprehended by the intellect. The ordered plurality of a real

1. *Summa Theologiae* II-II 34,1,1a. [See Aquinas, *Summa Theologiae*, 35:2.—Ed.]

2. Cited from Kovach, *Die Ästhetik des Thomas von Aquin*, 217.

3. "*Nam ad pulchritudinem tria requiruntur. Primo . . . perfectio . . . et . . . conso-nantia; et iterum claritas.*" *Summa Theologiae*, I, 39, 8. [See Aquinas, *Summa Theologiae*, 7:132.—Ed.]

4. And here we may turn aside to consider the possibility, raised in the symposium, that—à la Plotinus—"simples," like sheer red, may be beautiful. Against this, I would argue that the experience of sheer red would be of the entire perceptual field as nothing but redness, which would not be experience at all. What we in fact experience as perhaps some sort of simple, is a patch of red, which of course has boundaries and therefore parts.

thing adapts that thing to intelligence, thus the thing is *clear* to us, it is not muddled, it *manifests* itself, it possesses clarity. Indeed, it *shines itself forth* to intelligence, and does so with the light of the God-given form by which God bestows being and intelligibility on it in the first place. It is this clarity, this shining transparency, that we usually have to the forefront of our minds when we think of the beauty of something we apprehend.

So it seems that God is disqualified at the start from being beautiful, never mind being *ipsa pulchritudo*. For according to Thomas' inherited doc-trine of divine simplicity, God has no parts to be ordered. All his attributes and aspects are plural only for our mode of understanding and not for God himself, they are plural "with respect to us" and not "in the thing in itself."[5] As for those distinctions of essence and existence, or form and matter, or potency and act, that otherwise dominate Thomas' metaphysics, they are the pluralities by the *denial* of which Thomas specifies God's difference from creatures. At best then, God would be beautiful for us, but not for himself and so assuredly not *ipsa pulchritudo*.

I will admit that recent heavy critique of Thomas' doctrine of divine simplicity was sometimes overdone, also by me. But that there is something in that critique is shown by the circumstance that after *asserting* God's beau-ty Thomas simply falls silent on the subject. He has nothing to say about *how it is* that God is beautiful—and for the establishing of that negative I de-pend on the classic study[6] by Francis Kovach, who read everything Thomas wrote, as I have not. To be sure, God's beauty is identical with his essence, and Thomas is surely right that in this life we cannot know God's essence and so not God's beauty itself. But that does not here explain Thomas' si-lence. For though Thomas rightly eschewed asking *what it is* for God to be beautiful he could still very well have asked *how it is* that God is beautiful. This he does not do—and happenstance is an unlikely explanation, given Thomas' otherwise relentless pursuit of every minute line of reflection he can discern with respect to beauty.

So where do we go from here? We might say that there is no place to go from here, and resolve not to say much about God's beauty. Here I will suggest a different move, which I will introduce by turning to another of my theological heroes; perhaps as talented as Thomas but differently located in the tradition and with a different habit of mind.

Jonathan Edwards also saw that for something to be beautiful it must be inwardly plural, and ran the other way from that observation, making it a starting point of his doctrine of God, that is, of his doctrine of Trinity. "One

5. *"in re."*
6. Kovach, *Die Ästhetik des Thomas von Aquin.*

alone cannot be excellent"—"excellent" is Edwards' word for beautiful—he observed, and concluded that since God is in fact beautiful God cannot be only one. For him, the experienced beauty of God trumped our doctrine of his simplicity. It is an obvious train of thought, but one on which Western theology has been reluctant to embark.

I will not go further with Edwards' own development, remarkable though it is, but I will exploit his opening. Thomas has guided us through the tradition and into a dead-end of the tradition. We will try to find a way forward by asking a question Thomas did not: "How does the triunity of God enable his beauty?"

A first proposition on this line; God's triunity precisely *as such* is the perfection, harmony and clarity that Thomas rightly regards as the necessary and sufficient conditions of beauty. *Perfectio, harmonia*, and *claritas* even seem to sort themselves out among the three divine identities. Once made, this observation may seem suspiciously pat, but let me risk it. Clearly, I will have three sub-points—and let me acknowledge in advance that in the following I will be mostly prescinding from the triune *perichoresis*, and so treating my subject crudely.

We begin with the Father. He, sheerly *as such*, sheerly as self-instantiating fatherhood is the *monarchos*, the sole source of the triune God's being, the singular ground that there is God at all—as especially the Eastern tradition has insisted. On the other hand, as much of the tradition has also noted, there is no Father without a Child. Thus the duality of Father and Son is the condition of there being the Father, and there being the Father is the condition of there being God, or anyway of there being the God there is. The mere existence of the triune God demands on the triune plurality in him.

We cannot start by acknowledging the existence of God, and then inquire how there can be plurality in him. Starting that way, God's unity will always occlude his plurality—and thereby the possibility of his beauty. We must start rather with the reality of Father *and* Son in the history drawn on by the Spirit; then we are in position to inquire how the three are together *ipsa pulchritudo*.

In God the plurality requisite for beauty is given with the Father. We move on to the Son. The Son—still continuing in simple agreement with the tradition—is perfectly in harmony with the Father. Indeed, he may said to *be* a harmony with the Father—as in Thomas a "divine person" is in general a "relation subsisting in God"—for there is nothing to the Son except his reflection of the Father, so that he is the Father's perfect Image; so that there is nothing to the Son but his answer to the Father, so that he is the Father's perfect Word—reciprocities that are of course enabled by the Spirit. Thus we do not need to inquire beyond the three to see how there is harmony in God; one of the three *is* the divine harmony.

Plurality and its ordering are given in God. How then about clarity? The Spirit—we continue to mine the tradition—is the "bond of love" between Father and Son. And here a slight amendment of the tradition is needed and has been proposed, by me among others. In traditional trinitarian discourse it can often seem that the Spirit has no relational vantage of his own, but is a sort of impersonal manifestation of the fact that Father and Son love each other. But Scripture—and here one may think first of the Old Testament—gives the Spirit more personal leverage than that. The Spirit, we must say, is the active lover who opens the Father and Son to one another, by involving them in the love that he is. Translating this to the present context, we may say that the Spirit is the active clarity that lets each of the Father and the Son manifest himself to the other, lets each be clear to the other, lets each illumine the another. The Spirit is the clarity of the Father for the Son and of the Son for the Father, the clarity that the ordered plurality of God has. He is this for us, but also and first for God. When we think of the divine beauty, we have, I suggest, the Spirit at the forefront of our sensibility.

A second proposition on the same line: the beauty of God is *ipsa pulchritudo* because it is infinite. We can agree with Thomas: the essence of God is unknowable to us in this life, and therefore God's beauty, insofar as it is convertible with God's essence, is also unknowable. But the divine essence is not, I suggest, unknowable because it is sheer simplicity but rather, à la yet another of my heroes Gregory of Nyssa, because it is sheer infinity, the infinity of God's acts. God is not unknowable because there is a divine essence that as sheer simplicity, as a mere unit, is closed to others; he is *both* fully revealed and unknowable, because we cannot catch up with his revelation, because he is always one step ahead of us.

About *such* infinity we can say something. For whereas absolute simplicity cannot be the simplicity *of* anything, without positing an otherness it intends to deny, infinity must be the infinity *of* something. God's infinity is the infinity of the acts of Father, Son and Spirit. The Father's gift of another than himself, the Son's reciprocity, the Spirit's clarification of this relation, are all infinite in their reach. There is no limit to what can come of them, either in God or among us, either as immanent Trinity or as economic Trinity. The Father puts no limits on the otherness of the Son, even to the Son's being a finite creature and dying on a cross; the Son's return to the Father can extend even to "Nevertheless, not my will but thine be done," where the Father's will is his death. These things we can know.

And in knowing them, we know how God's beauty is beauty itself. For as it is limitless, as it is always going ahead of us, it can and does embrace what it has behind it, which is everything but God

This embrace is itself a final metaphysical fact. But its limitlessness occurs in our history. God's infinite beauty is that Christ died to bring all history to its crisis and was raised for all. The Spirit is indeed the clarity of whatever manifests itself to mind: amoebae, daisies, black holes, whatever. But the clarity of the gospel or of a prayer in Jesus' name is not an instance of this universal clarity; the ontological relations work the other way around.

And so we have come to a second place where theology's attempt to understand God as beauty has been blocked: for until just a few sentences ago we were talking of the Son without regard to the fact that he is the man Jesus of Nazareth. It cannot, I think, be denied: the tradition's trinitarian discourse has often had a certain bloodlessness to it. And assuredly, Thomas' discourse about beauty is, considering the subject, astonishingly bland, even allowing for the character of scholastic writing. We cannot proceed until we find a way to account for the sheer *wonder* of beauty. Let me, moreover, intrude the remark that in my view to contrast infinity and beauty is simply a mistake.

In the incarnational fact, the harmony of God is the perfect obedience of a man to someone he called Father, the obedience of someone with a mother and friends and enemies and a dreadful human conclusion. Saying the same thing another way: the harmony in God that is his beauty and the beauty of all things is a harmony of the shocks and revelations that make the history told in Scripture. Saying it yet again, the harmony in God that is his beauty and the beauty of all things is a *dramatic* harmony; as consonance it is the consonance of a fugue or of a sonata movement.

Thus—precisely to be faithful to everything said so far, to what I have taken from Thomas and Edwards and have devised of my own—we need to think of beauty as more dangerous, more in our face, more narrative in its being, than we have so far. To that end, we may recruit the Old Testament, specifically yet another theological hero of mine, the prophet Ezekiel, and the "priestly" strain of Old Testament theology to which he belonged.

In Ezekiel, God's beauty appears as his *kabod*, his "glory." In the Old Testament generally, a person's *kabod* is his or her personal weight in community, as in English we might say that someone throws his weight around, or carries a lot of weight in some group. *God's* weight in community is then infinite. But in Ezekiel, this sense of *kabod* melds with a sense special to his tradition: when the Lord throws his weight around the weight is his *shining*. His epiphanies are *light*-epiphanies, *manifestations* of his being, of his infinite clarity. The beauty that God has and is and shares with creatures is—if Ezekiel's vision did not deceive him—*overwhelming*.

Moreover, this glory *arrives*. Ezekiel's book opens with the *coming* of the Lord on—and indeed as—his throne, in light and color. an advent whose weight *overcomes* Ezekiel, and will in the course of the book overcome Jerusalem—and then Babylon and Egypt and all the powers of this world. On the throne Ezekiel saw "the appearance" of a gleaming man—whom many of the Fathers said looked like a man because he *was* one; Ezekiel's vision, they understood, is the same vision that chosen disciples would see on the mountain traditionally called Tabor. On Tabor men saw the resurrected Christ, and descended to learn of his coming crucifixion. The glory that *arrives* is the glory of terrible and wonderful drama.

So a third proposition: God's beauty is not the infinite serenity of his being but the infinite drama of his life. And there is no reason why a drama cannot include bit players, in this case, you and me. The Lord's *kabod* tumbled Ezekiel to the ground, and then picked him up to be its servant. Which—finally—is how the brilliantly ordered plurality of God can be *ipsa pulchritudo*, the beauty of whatever is beautiful.

My answer to our theme: the offense of beauty is the offense of God, the triune God.

Bibliography

Aquinas, Thomas. *Summa Theologiæ*. 60 vols. Cambridge: Cambridge University Press, 2006.

Aulén, Gustaf. *Christus Victor: An Historical Study of the Three Main Types of the Idea of Atonement*. Translated by A. G. Hebert. American ed. New York: Macmillan, 1951.

Ayer, Alfred J. *Language, Truth and Logic*. New York: Dover, 1946.

Barth, Karl. *Church Dogmatics*. Edited by G. W. Bromiley and T. F. Torrance. 4 vols. in 14 parts. Edinburgh: T. & T. Clark, 1936–77.

Begbie, Jeremy S. *Theology, Music, and Time*. Cambridge: Cambridge University Press, 2000.

Brunner, Peter. *Erbarmen: Der Christ in der Unordnung dieser Welt*. Stuttgart: Schwabenverlag, 1948.

———. *Leiturgia*. Vol. 1. Kassel: Johannes Stauda, 1954.

———. "Luther and the World of the Twentieth Century." In *Luther in the Twentieth Century*, 52–79. Decorah, IA: Luther College Press, 1961.

Bultmann, Rudolf. *Das Verhältnis der urchristlichen Christusbotschaft zum historischen Jesus*. Heidelberg: Carl Winter, 1961.

Campenhausen, Hans von. "Die Bilderfrage als Theologisches Problem der Alten Kirche." *Zeitschrift für Theologie und Kirche* 49 (1952) 33–60.

Chemnitz, Martin. *De duabus naturis in Christo*. Leipzig: n.p., 1578.

Council of Chalcedon. *Definitio fidei*. In *Decrees of the Ecumenical Councils*, edited by Norman P. Tanner. Washington, DC: Georgetown University Press, 1990.

Crouzel, Henri. *Théologie de l'image de Dieu chez Origène*. Paris: Aubier, 1956.

Elert, Werner. *Morphologie des Luthertums*. Vol. 1. Munich: Beck, 1931.

Eliade, Mircea. *Cosmos and History: The Myth of the Eternal Return*. Translated by Willard R. Trask. New York: Harper, 1959.

Faye, Eugene de. *Origène*. Vol. 2. Paris: E. Leroux, 1927.

Friedländer, Paul. *Plato*. Translated by Hans Meyerhoff. 3 vols. New York: Pantheon, 1958.

Gerhard, John. *Loci Theologici*. Vol. 4. Frankfurt: Hertel, 1657.

Gogarten, Friedrich. *Der Mensch zwischen Gott und Welt*. Stuttgart: Friedrich Vorwerk, 1956.

Harnack, Adolf von. *History of Dogma*. Vol. 4. New York: Dover, 1961.

Hector, Kevin. *Theology without Metaphysics: God, Language, and the Spirit of Recognition*. Cambridge: Cambridge University Press, 2011.

Heidegger, Martin. *Einführung in die Metaphysik.* Tübingen: M. Niemeyer, 1953.

———. *Sein und zeit.* Tübingen: M. Niemeyer, 1953.

Jaeger, Werner Wilhelm. *Nemesios von Emesa.* Berlin: Weidmann, 1914.

Jaspers, Karl. *Nietzsche and Christianity.* Translated by E. B. Ashton. Chicago: Regnery, 1961.

Jenson, Robert W. "About Dialog, and the Church, and Some Bits of Theological Biography of Robert W. Jenson." *Dialog* 11 (1969) 38–42.

———. *Alpha and Omega: A Study in the Theology of Karl Barth.* Nashville: Thomas Nelson, 1963.

———. "The Christological Objectivity of History." In *Story Lines: Chapters on Word, Thought, and Deed: For Gabriel Fackre,* edited by Skye Fackre Gibson, 62–67. Grand Rapids: Eerdmans, 2002.

———. "A Dead Issue Revisited." *Lutheran Quarterly* 14 (1962) 53–56.

———. *Ezekiel.* Grand Rapids: Brazos, 2009.

———. *God after God: The God of the Past and the God of the Future as Seen in the Work of Karl Barth.* Minneapolis: Fortress, 1969.

———. *On Thinking the Human: Resolutions of Difficult Notions.* Grand Rapids: Eerdmans, 2003.

———. *A Religion Against Itself.* Louisville: Westminster John Knox, 1967.

———. "Response to Watson and Hunsinger." *Scottish Journal of Theology* 55 (2002) 225–32.

———. *Story and Promise: A Brief Theology of the Gospel about Jesus.* Philadelphia: Fortress, 1973.

———. *Systematic Theology.* 2 vols. Oxford: Oxford University Press, 1997–99.

———. "A Theological Autobiography, to Date." *Dialog* 46:1 (Spring 2007) 46–54.

Koch, Hal. *Pronoia und Paideusis.* Berlin: de Gruyter, 1932.

Kovach, Francis J. *Die Ästhetik des Thomas von Aquin.* Berlin: de Gruyter, 1961.

Marty, Martin. *The New Shape of American Religion.* New York: Harper, 1958.

McCormack, Bruce. *Karl Barth's Critically Realistic Dialectical Theology: Its Genesis and Development.* Oxford: Clarendon, 1995.

Nissiotis, Nikos. *Die Theologie der Ostkirche im ökumenischen Dialog.* Stuttgart: Evangelisches Verlagswerk, 1968.

Origen. *Homélies sur Ézéchiel.* Translated by Marcel Borret. Paris: Cerf, 1989.

Pabst, Adrian. *Metaphysics: The Creation of Hierarchy.* Grand Rapids: Eerdmans, 2012.

Rad, Gerhard von. *Das erste Buch Mose.* Göttingen: Vandenhoeck & Ruprecht, 1949.

Ratzinger, Joseph Cardinal. *Église, Oecuménisme et Politique.* Translated by P. Jordan, P. E. Gudenus, and B. Müller. Paris: Fayard, 1987.

———. "Luther und die Einheit der Kirchen. Fragen an Joseph Kardinal Ratzinger." *Communio* 12 (1983) 568–82. English translation: "Luther and the Unity of the Churches: An Interview with Joseph Cardinal Ratzinger." *Communio: International Catholic Review* 11 (1984) 210–26.

Rothe, Richard. *Dogmatik.* Heidelberg: J. C. B. Mohr, 1870.

Russell, Bertrand. *A Free Man's Worship.* Portland, ME: T. B. Mosher, 1923.

Schaeder, Hildegard. "Die Christianisierung der Aristotelischen Logik in der Byzantinischen Theologie." *Kerygma und Dogma* 8 (1962) 293–309.

Schleiermacher, Friedrich. *Der Christliche Glaube.* Berlin: de Gruyter, 1960.

Thielicke, Helmut. *Nihilism, Its Origin and Nature—with a Christian Answer.* Translated by John W. Doberstein. New York: Harper, 1961.

Whitehead, Alfred North. *Science in the Modern World.* New York: New American Library, 1946.

Willms, Hans. *EIKON. Eine begriffsgeschichtliche Untersuchung zum Platonismus.* Münster: Aschendorff, 1935.

Yeago, David S. "The Catholic Luther." In *The Catholicity of the Reformation*, edited by Carl E. Braaten and Robert W. Jenson, 13–34. Grand Rapids: Eerdmans, 1996.

Zizioulas, John. *Being as Communion.* Crestwood, NY: St. Vladimir's Seminary Press, 1985.

General Index